Developing Numeracy

in the

Secondary School

Developing Numeracy

in the
Secondary School

A PRACTICAL GUIDE FOR STUDENTS AND TEACHERS

Howard Tanner, Sonia Jones & Alyson Davies

David Fulton Publishers
London

David Fulton Publishers Ltd
2 Park Square, Milton Park, Abingdon, Oxon, OX14 4RN

www. fultonpublishers.co.uk

First published in Great Britain by David Fulton Publishers 2002

Transferred to Digital Printing 2007

British Library Cataloguing in Publication Data
A catalogue record for this book is available from the British Library

ISBN 1–85346–813–4

Typeset by Ann Buchan (Typesetters), Shepperton, Middlesex

Publisher's Note
The publisher has gone to great lengths to ensure the quality of this reprint but points out that some imperfections in the original may be apparent

Contents

Acknowledgements

We are indebted to the many teachers with whom we have worked in researching the effective teaching and learning of mathematics. In particular, we should mention those involved in the Teacher Inquiry Groups and the Raising Standards in Numeracy project.

Our especial thanks, however, go to the pupils and staff at Birchgrove Comprehensive School, Swansea, without whose ideas and help this book would not have been written.

Preface

The results of the major international comparative studies published in the 1990s have contributed to concerns over the standards of mathematics achieved by our pupils. Such concerns are not new. However, they have resulted in a reappraisal of the nature and quality of mathematics teaching and learning in our schools. The National Numeracy Strategy has challenged primary teachers to consider, for example, the adoption of direct interactive teaching and the three-part lesson. Similar challenges have been posed to secondary colleagues by the Framework for Teaching Mathematics.

The advice contained in the Numeracy Strategy and the Framework is based on findings from research. Other research projects, both large and small-scale, have been exploring the effects of implementing such advice. As teachers and researchers we have been involved in trying to analyse and implement the best features of the advice offered in order to improve the quality of our own teaching for the benefit of our students. In this book we attempt to highlight the main findings and to exemplify the implications for classroom practice.

We have structured the book into three sections. In Section 1 we present an overview of the findings from some of the significant studies conducted in the UK and overseas, analyse their recommendations in the light of advice offered by official sources, and consider how these impact on fundamental issues in the teaching of mathematics such as the development of mathematical thinking.

In Section 2 we exemplify this analysis within the classroom context. We describe lessons which we either have taught ourselves or have observed being taught in high value-added schools. The lessons are set in the context of each of the four content areas: number, algebra, data-handling and shape and space. The lessons are chosen to illustrate each of the key strategies recommended in the framework.

The final section is intended as a plenary session, which reflects on the earlier discussions and considers how the advice may be utilised to develop strategies for enhancing numeracy within the mathematics department and across the whole curriculum.

Many of the ideas in this book derive from our own research studies, in particular, the Raising Standards in Numeracy project and our work with Teacher Inquiry Groups. We hope that this book will provide an introduction to the issues in teaching and learning of numeracy for both new and experienced teachers.

Issues in numeracy and mathematics teaching and learning

In this section, after exploring the various definitions of numeracy, we consider the findings of some of the significant studies into the teaching of mathematics conducted in the UK and overseas. Their recommendations are contrasted with advice offered by official sources and we consider how they impact on fundamental issues in the teaching of mathematics such as the development of mathematical thinking.

CHAPTER 1

What is numeracy?

Introduction

The zeitgeist in Britain and much of the Western world at the turn of the century has focused on standards of numeracy and literacy in schools. The standards achieved in such key skills have long been a subject of discussion among the profession, politicians and the public. They were brought to the centre ground of UK politics by the 'great debate' initiated by James Callaghan in his Ruskin College speech of 1976 and have remained there ever since.

Key international studies such as the Third International Mathematics and Science Study (TIMMS: Beaton *et al.* 1996) and its follow up studies (Stigler *et al.* 1999; Mullis *et al.* 2001; OECD 2000) generated league tables and data about teaching approaches. The league tables focused the minds of politicians, who often view such matters in much the same way as football, and motivated a flurry of curriculum development worldwide. We will examine some of the lessons to be learned from international comparisons in Chapter 2.

However, schools in the UK had not been untouched by the spirit of the times and developments in numeracy had already begun. Certainly there had been an increased interest in mental arithmetic in English primary schools during the 1990s (Brown *et al.* 2000) and by the middle of the decade, a number of large and influential projects were investigating the teaching of numeracy (Askew *et al.* 1997; CIMT 1997; Straker 1997; Reynolds 1998a, 1998b). One of the most significant was the National Numeracy Project (NNP) under Anita Straker which was set up in October 1996 with a budget of £2.8 million. It conducted development work in 520 primary schools from 14 LEAs.

Such was the enthusiasm for the early results coming from the Numeracy Project that this formed the basis of the National Numeracy Strategy: Framework for Teaching Mathematics (DfEE 1999a). This framework was highly influential and dramatically changed practices in schools in England within a very short time. A pilot programme to extend the work of the NNS into Year 7 was started in 2000 and, without waiting for the results, the DfEE demanded that all schools use the new framework in KS3 from September 2001.

Prior to the changes set in motion by the NNP and the NNS, Reynolds (1998a: 19) claimed that primary school teachers 'usually deploy only a narrow range of teaching strategies' and that they 'rely too heavily on published schemes, which pupils work through individually' with pupils 'left to teach themselves'. Our own observations lead us to believe that this was probably the case in some of the least successful primary schools.

The RSN Project

Our own research at that time was focused on the most successful schools rather than the least successful. The Raising Standards in Numeracy (RSN) Project was a collaborative project involving five Welsh local education authorities (LEAs) and was funded by the National Assembly for Wales during 1998/9. (For further details see Tanner *et al.* 1999.) The project utilised earlier work by the Vale of Glamorgan LEA involving the development of value-added analyses linking National Curriculum data to prior attainment scores based on pupil-level data.

As part of the project we used value-added analyses to identify schools where pupils obtained significantly higher than expected scores in statutory tests. We then identified two primary and two secondary schools in each LEA whose results were far higher than would have been expected for their intake. On visits to these schools we interviewed head teachers, subject leaders and teachers and asked them to describe the factors to which they attributed their success. Lessons were then observed to examine these classroom processes in practice.

Subject leaders from the schools met as a teacher inquiry group (TIG) during the course of the year to discuss their approaches and our observations in order to identify key features, under the control of the school and the teacher, which represent good practice in the teaching of numeracy.

We were privileged to work with many highly skilled, enthusiastic teachers during the project. Much of the material to be found in this book is based on our observations of their lessons and our discussions with them afterwards when they reflected critically on their own practice.

In the chapters which follow it is not our intention to act as propagandists for the changes demanded by government strategies and frameworks. Rather it is our intention to explore the nature of numeracy and to consider some of the schemes which might be employed by reflective, professional teachers to improve teaching in secondary schools.

Objectives

By the end of this chapter you should be aware of:

- the wide range of abilities associated with numeracy;
- the most influential definitions of numeracy in use today;
- the different knowledge and skills required according to these definitions;
- the extent to which calculators can be used or misused in the development of numeracy;
- some of the implications for teaching and learning, providing a suitable background for the chapters which follow.

What is numeracy?

Numeracy is a theme for our times. However, it is not clearly defined as a concept and seems to have expanded its scope of late to encompass most of the mathematics curriculum at least up to the end of Key Stage 3. Numeracy seems to take on a wide range of meanings according to the aims of the speaker, with politicians enjoying its utilitarian or basic common-sense tone and teachers, such as ourselves, emphasising its further-reaching mathematical characteristics.

Its common usage in Britain began as a mathematical equivalent to literacy – as the 'mathematical literacy' suggested by the Crowther report (1959). Common usage today tends to emphasise the dimension of arithmetical calculation (e.g. Reynolds 1998b). However, just as one would expect a literate person to be able to do much more than read lists of words it is clear that the numerate person must be able to do far more than perform arithmetical calculations to order. This was recognised in the influential Cockcroft report (1982) in which numeracy was defined as an ability to cope with the mathematical demands of everyday life and to develop an 'at homeness' with number.

This is far more than a knowledge of number bonds and multiplication tables, although many would argue that such skills form the basis of numeracy. Although the instantaneous recall of certain simple number facts can be helpful in many circumstances, they do not by themselves ensure that children will feel 'at home' with number or be able to apply their knowledge in real life. In fact the literature is full of evidence of children failing to apply school-taught methods to real-life problems (e.g. Lave 1988; Nunes *et al.* 1993; Schliemann 1994).

During the 1970s some teachers regarded the automatic recall of arithmetical facts as reduced in importance through the common usage of calculators. One of Her Majesty's Inspectorate even went so far as to define numeracy as the 'sensible use of a four-function calculator' (Girling 1977). This view is now well out of kilter with the spirit of the times, but the use of calculators in the development of numeracy remains a contentious issue and we will return to it later.

Task 1.1:   What is numeracy?
Try to write your own definition of numeracy. Numeracy is ...

We hope that your definition of numeracy included far more than swift recall of arithmetical facts. At a recent meeting of a teacher inquiry group we asked a group of primary and secondary teachers to describe what they thought numeracy implied. Some of their answers are listed below and encompass a far wider set of knowledge and processes than simply a facility with a few basic number bonds. Numeracy is:

A   knowing enough mathematical structure to be able to use what you know to be able to work out what you don't know;
B   being fluent with number, being at ease with it, so that you can play around with it to get what you need;
C   knowing the language, grammar and symbolism of mathematics;
D   being able to solve problems with number and language and knowing when your answer is reasonable;
E   coping with the demands of everyday life and knowing how to choose an efficient process in any situation which will lead to a reliable answer;
F   knowing when it is appropriate to use a calculator.

(Tanner and Jones 2000b: 145)

The following definition is offered by the National Strategy for KS3:

> Numeracy is a proficiency which is developed mainly in mathematics but also in other subjects. It is more than an ability to do basic arithmetic. It involves developing confidence and competence with numbers and measures. It requires understanding of the number system, a repertoire of mathematical techniques, and an inclination and ability to solve quantitative or spatial problems in a range of contexts. Numeracy also demands understanding of the ways in which data are gathered by counting and measuring, and presented in graphs, diagrams, charts and tables.
>
> (DfEE 2001a: 1.9)

You may be surprised to find that the definition is so broad, encompassing algebra, shape and space and data handling. You may be wondering what the distinction is between numeracy and mathematics. We like a suggestion we heard Anita Straker make in a presentation to the annual Mathematical Association Conference: 'Numeracy is what you develop when you learn mathematics well.'

We think that numeracy is about using mathematics, both theoretically and practically. We prefer to focus on the ability to use and apply mathematical knowledge in problem solving rather than on specific items of mathematical knowledge. We suggest that, at one level, numerate people have 'the ability to solve simple everyday problems involving number, by using effectively the knowledge and skills that they possess', and that this should include being able to choose and to devise their own appropriate strategies (Mathematical Association 1992: 71). However, on another level, we think that numerate people should be able to use the mathematics they know to solve problems in mathematics itself, in other subjects and in real life. The difficulty of the problems we expect numerate people to be able to solve depends to some extent on the context and the level to which they have been educated mathematically. The extent to which this ability depends on the instantaneous recall of number facts in a mental test or the development of strategic knowledge will be discussed throughout the book.

Mental mathematics

Our teacher inquiry group believed that one aspect of numeracy was a facility with mental mathematics. However, it is worth reflecting on what exactly is meant by mental mathematics. At one level, it is possible to claim that *all* mathematics is of necessity mental mathematics but with varying use of external memory support involving written symbols. However, clearly what is meant here is the ability to operate mathematically without the support of paper, pencil or calculator.

It is important to distinguish here between mathematical facts or results, which have been learned to the point of automaticity, and the ability to process mathematical knowledge in a conscious and strategic manner.

Task 1.2: Automatic or consciously calculated responses
Calculate the answers to each of the following questions in your head (without paper jottings) and make a note of how you performed the calculation.

1. $3 \times 4 = ?$
2. $8 \times 7 = ?$
3. $23 \times 18 = ?$

We suspect that for most readers the answer to question 1 sprang instantly to mind without any calculation occurring. This is because the table fact has been learned in the form of a stimulus and response: the stimulus 3×4 is presented and the response 12 is returned without any conscious processing. The power of such learning is its speed and its automatic linking of significant numbers. A person who has formed such links is likely to be able to cancel the fraction $\frac{8}{12}$ successfully by automatically associating 8 and 12 with the factor 4.

Many children used to learn such table facts by rote (by which we mean stimulus–response training without a demand for understanding). Although such knowledge may lead to some of the power described above, if memory fails, an alternative strategy, such as addition, may not be available.

For question 2, again we suspect that for many readers the answer may have flashed into consciousness through a stimulus–response mechanism. However, we suspect that some of our readers may not have sufficiently secure multiplication tables to be certain of an instantaneous response. For example, we have a friend who is a graduate mathematician, a published author of textbooks and a successful teacher of mathematics who does not know his multiplication tables. His explanation to us is that when presented with a question like '8 × 7 = ?', he is able to calculate in sequence:

$$10 \times 7 = 70, \quad 2 \times 7 = 14, \quad 70 - 14 = 56$$

in less than two seconds. He sees no reason to change. He is able to do this quickly and accurately for most multiplications less than 100, and perhaps more importantly, he knows that he can do this quickly and accurately. You may have performed this or a similar calculation with speed and precision.

We suspect that many of our readers will have found question 3 to be challenging. Those who attempted to perform the traditional long multiplication algorithm mentally, will probably have found it difficult to remember the question and all the intermediate solutions in their short term memory without resorting to side jottings. If such side notes were banned (as they were in early versions of National Curriculum assessments) this would probably be an unsuccessful strategy for most people, although it is the traditional strategy taught in school.

Our mathematician friend who does not know his tables has no such difficulties with '23 × 18 = ?', to which he responds

$$23 \times 20 = 460, \quad 2 \times 23 = 46, \quad 460 - 46 = 414$$

He is using the same strategy as for question 2 in combination with his knowledge of place value. He is combining secure knowledge and strategies together in a way which we think demonstrates an understanding of place value and an 'at-homeness' with number to solve a problem. If you were successful with question 3 we suspect that you will have used a similarly 'home-made' strategy rather than a school taught algorithm.

Task 1.3:   Personal methods

Do you have any quick methods of working or short cuts which you use when performing mental arithmetic?

How did you develop them – by yourself or with the help of a teacher?

What teacher actions could assist the development of such mental methods?

What teacher actions would deter children from developing such approaches?

Our work with the Raising Standards in Numeracy Project (Tanner *et al.* 1999) leads us to the conclusion that even quite young children are able to play with number, and develop their own mental strategies if encouraged to so do, by appropriate teaching approaches. As you will see in Chapter 3, such approaches are based on the children articulating their own developing ideas for discussion in a supportive classroom environment. Such classrooms emphasise multiple methods, experimentation and reflection rather than 'correct methods' and repetition (Tanner *et al.* 1999). Some of this experimentation involved the use of calculators.

Calculators

The indiscriminate use of calculators has been blamed for a decline in students' arithmetic skills and their failure to develop elementary mathematical thinking (Bierhoff 1996; Gardiner 1995). However, research evidence suggests that the situation is more complex than this.

Two large-scale longitudinal projects have explored the potential of calculator use at primary level. The Calculator-Aware Number (CAN) project (Shuard *et al.* 1991) explored the impact of calculator use on primary school pupils' understanding of number in 24 LEAs in England and Wales. The Calculators in Primary Mathematics (CPM) project (Groves 1994) used calculators to enrich the teaching and learning of mathematics. Over 1,000 pupils and 60 teachers from six Australian schools were involved from 1990 to 1993.

CAN investigated the effect of allowing primary school pupils unrestricted access to calculators. The traditional vertical paper and pencil methods for the four rules of number were not taught. The project required the children to explore 'how numbers work', emphasising mental methods and demanding that children discuss their strategies and approaches.

Although the use of calculators was encouraged, the evaluators found that the CAN children developed a wide range of non-calculator, mental strategies. These often demonstrated an intuitive understanding of mathematical principles and structure. Discussion was the crucial mechanism through which children shared, extended and elaborated their ideas.

Although no overall statistical evaluation of the effects of the project was conducted one local education authority was able to use standardised tests to compare the performance of the CAN pupils with their non-CAN peers. The results of a group of 116 CAN pupils were compared with a random group of non-CAN pupils. The CAN pupils outperformed the others on 28 of the 36 test questions. The results also suggested that the CAN pupils were more willing to attempt questions and to work independently (Shuard *et al.* 1991).

The CPM project (Groves 1994) involved over 1,000 pupils and 60 teachers from six Australian schools from 1990 to 1993. Each pupil was given a calculator to use when they chose. Professional support was provided for the teachers, who also met regularly in school and project meetings to plan and to share their teaching activities.

As in the CAN project, the teachers modified their teaching practices to make more extensive use of discussion and the sharing of children's ideas. The project children did not become reliant on calculators, rather they outperformed their comparison groups of pupils without long-term experience of calculators on a range of estimation and computation tasks, and displayed a better knowledge of number, especially place value, decimals and negative numbers (Groves 1994: 12).

In research studies of primary-age pupils, when the use of calculators was accompanied by an emphasis on mental strategies there was a positive impact on pupils' mathematical development. This was confirmed in a meta-review of research into the effects of calculator use (Hembree and Dessart 1992). Nearly 90 research studies were analysed, each of which had compared the progress of pupils who were allowed use of calculators in mathematics lessons to matched control groups who were not. Generally the calculator children matched or outperformed their peers on measures of computational skill and problem solving.

It should be noted that the successful teachers in the RSN project rejected the blanket bans on the use of calculators beloved of politicians. Rather the successful teachers in the RSN schools were able to articulate when they considered it appropriate to use calculators to support the learning of mathematics.

We classify calculator use into four categories:

- as a crutch to avoid learning;
- as scaffolding to assist learning;
- as a window into mathematics;
- as a tool for thinking.

(Tanner and Jones 2000b: 168)

When a calculator is being used to perform calculations and the process contributes nothing to the pupils' mathematical development, we suggest it is being misused. Fluency with basic arithmetical processes develops with practice. But how much practice is necessary? If Year 7 pupils always reach for a calculator when a question like $0.5 \times 23 \times 4$ arises in a problem, then they will not practise key mental techniques in context. Using a calculator as *a crutch to avoid learning* like this is unhelpful. We would usually expect pupils to calculate such results mentally. However, fluency with such techniques develops slowly and not all our pupils will be fluent when they require such techniques in problem situations.

The trouble is, there is a limit to the number of new ideas and difficult processes a person can deal with at one time. Calculations such as $0.5 \times 2.4 \times 3$ might arise in a lesson whose main aims were associated with calculating areas of triangles. Pupils who are fairly fluent with such mental processes would probably be able to deal with both the area concepts and the mental calculations. However, for other pupils, who are less fluent, it might be a matter of dealing with either the area concepts or the calculations but not both. In this context, the calculator can act as *scaffolding to assist learning* by enabling pupils to progress through the curriculum before full fluency has been achieved. However, scaffolding should be temporary. Once the concept has been established, then the scaffolding provided by the calculator should be removed, and pupils asked to utilise their arithmetical knowledge in conjunction with the new concept, forging links between areas of knowledge. Exactly when it is appropriate to allow calculator support should always be a judgement call for the teacher on the spot, depending on the pupil and the context.

The calculator is a tool, which works according to mathematical principles. When children are encouraged to explore its workings, it becomes *a window into the world of mathematics*. Calculators are attractive devices, which can be explored by pupils behaving as autonomous learners. They operate according to mathematical rules and by exploring the rules to which they work pupils learn deep mathematical rules and processes. When calculators are freely available, as they were in the CAN project, children often discover unexpected results about number. For example, it was quite common for CAN children to 'discover' negative numbers on their calculators.

Whether this then results in a deepening mathematical understanding depends on the classroom culture and the attitude of the teacher to such discoveries. If the classroom culture supports conjecturing by pupils, then the new fact may be reported to the teacher with excitement. The teacher then has the opportunity to help the pupil or the class to explore further in a more structured manner, linking the new fact to prior knowledge.

There are many calculator tasks which can be set whose main objective is to place pupils in a situation where specific discoveries are likely to be made. Discussions arising from such discoveries, whether arising through serendipity or planning, can often form the basis of very effective whole class discussions. When the calculator acts as a window into the world of mathematics it can afford pupils opportunities to gain insights into mathematical structure and encourage the play and exploration of number necessary for numeracy.

Examining mathematical structure with a calculator: a short investigation with Year 7

The teacher distributed 15 scientific calculators and 15 simple 'left to right' calculators around the room so that each double desk had one of each. She then wrote on the board:

$$4 + 2 \times 3 = ?$$
$$2 \times 3 + 4 = ?$$
$$18 - 3 \times 3 = ?$$
$$8 + 8 \div 8 = ?$$

and asked the class to work out the answers on their calculators, checking the results carefully.

Working noise in the classroom quickly increased as pupils noticed that they were sometimes getting different answers from their partners. After waiting for two or three minutes she called the class to order.

A pupil was called to the board to give an answer to $4 + 2 \times 3 = ?$. The teacher then asked him to explain how his calculator had produced the result 18. She then asked 'Who had a different answer?' and invited a pupil out to demonstrate how the answer 10 might be calculated.

After explaining that the scientific calculators were based on the agreed rules for order of operations, she then invited the class to experiment with similar simple calculations to investigate when different answers resulted on the two types of calculator, writing down any rules they could spot.

As an extension, the quicker pupils in the class were asked to investigate what happened when brackets were used. The class worked animatedly on the task for the next 20 minutes.

The final 15 minutes of the lesson consisted of a plenary session in which groups of pupils were called to the board to report their findings. The plenary ended with the class helping the teacher to list a simple set of rules to describe the order of operations.

When working in an exploratory mode, calculators can act as *a tool for thinking* to enable pupils to extend their understanding of mathematics through:

- abstraction and generalisation;
- graphical representation;
- programming.

(Tanner and Jones 2000b: 171)

Many mathematical investigations in secondary schools involve the collection of data, searching for patterns, and abstracting and generalising from the pattern. In such situations, the calculator can sometimes perform the relatively mundane tasks associated with calculation while the pupil focuses on the structure of the problem. The calculator can act as a test-bed on which ideas and hypotheses are tested out. For example, here is a question which would be very difficult to explore without a calculator:

Task 1.4: Means and standard deviations
Find a set of ten marks which has a mean of 5 and a standard deviation of 1. Are
there any other marks which would have the same mean and standard deviation?
Find sets of marks with means of 5 and standard deviations of 0, 1, 2, 3, 4, and 5.

When graphical calculators are used, exploration of relationships may be extended, and links made between algebraic and graphical representations, for example exploring the relationship between straight lines and the constants in the equation $y = mx + c$. When a graphical calculator is attached to an OHP display unit, it becomes possible to develop effective whole-class interactive discussion and teaching based on children's explorative hypotheses.

With the development of technology, the distinction between calculators and computers has become blurred. There are many cheap calculators on the market which are capable of being programmed by teachers or pupils to support the learning of mathematics.

The teacher can program a calculator, or a set of calculators, to act as a number machine with which the pupils can play 'Guess the function'. Of course this game may also be played very effectively as a whole-class activity without a calculator with teachers and/or pupils acting as the number machine. However, a set of programmed calculators can act as a very effective follow up for individual or small group work. In this context calculators have the advantage of being non-judgemental when you guess incorrectly while exploring.

When pupils program calculators for themselves they are placed in the position of teaching the machine how to perform a process. This demands a higher level of understanding and helps children to formalise their knowledge of processes and techniques. Many old text books from the 1980s on contain helpful examples of tasks which were originally intended to generate short programs in BASIC, before mathematical contexts went out of fashion in computer studies. For example:

Task 1.5: Programming a calculator
Write short programs on your calculator to generate prime numbers between
a) 1 and 100
b) 100 and 1000.

We conclude that, when used appropriately, that is as a window into mathematics or as a tool for mathematical thinking rather than as a crutch to avoid thinking, in combination with an emphasis on the discussion of mental strategies, calculators enhance the teaching and learning of mathematics and the development of numeracy.

In the two projects described above, the calculator often replaced the role of the traditional written algorithm in the development of mathematical thinking. Several researchers have commented critically on the early stage at which such formal algorithms have been introduced into UK schools (Bierhoff 1996).

Algorithms

Task 1.6:   Explaining algorithms
Use the written algorithm which you were taught in school to explain how to calculate 365 – 197.
Does your explanation stand up to questions like 'Why do we put that one there?'
*Does your explanation deal with **why** the procedure works or just on how to follow the procedure?*

There are two commonly taught algorithms in the UK today which we show below. They are commonly known as *decomposition* and *equal addition*. We comment on both below. You should compare your commentary with ours, and try to understand the algorithm that is not the one you were taught in school.

Decomposition

Written form   **Oral commentary**

$$3 \overset{5}{\cancel{6}} \overset{1}{5}$$
$$-\ 1\ 9\ 7$$
$$\overline{\qquad 8}$$

5 take away 7, we can't do.
So we use one of these 6 tens, turning it into 10 units.
That gives us 5 tens and 15 units altogether.
15 take away 7 makes 8.

$$\overset{2}{\cancel{3}} \overset{1_5}{\cancel{6}} \overset{1}{5}$$
$$-\ 1\ 9\ 7$$
$$\overline{\quad 6\ 8}$$

Now the tens. 5 take away 9, we can't do.
So we use one of these 3 hundreds and turn it into 10 tens.
That gives us 2 hundreds left and 15 tens altogether.
15 take away 9 makes 6.

$$\overset{2}{\cancel{3}} \overset{1_5}{\cancel{6}} \overset{1}{5}$$
$$-\ 1\ 9\ 7$$
$$\overline{\ 1\ 6\ 8}$$

Now the hundreds.
2 hundred take away 1 hundred makes 1 hundred, so the final answer is 168.

The decomposition algorithm is probably the most commonly taught in primary schools today due to the ease with which it can be explained in depth, requiring only a knowledge of place value. Our commentary was based on a mathematical justification of the procedure rather than just a description of the procedure.

However, we think that our 'oral commentary' is a clear exposition or lecture rather than a good explanation (see Love and Mason 1992; 1995). Explanation requires *interaction* between the teacher and the pupil. During exposition pupils listen to the words of the teacher. During explanation, teachers listen to the words of pupils and build on them. Teachers ask questions during explanations in order to find out what their pupils are currently thinking so that they can base their next utterance on the pupils' responses (Tanner and Jones 2000b: 29).

Task 1.7: Questioning pupils
Try to list appropriate questions which you could ask as a teacher leading a pupil to understand the algorithm.

Equal addition

Written form	**Oral commentary**
$3\,6\,\overset{1}{5}$ $-1\,9\,7$ ___ 8	5 take away 7, we can't do. So we borrow 1 from the tens making 15 units. 15 take away 7 makes 8.
$3\,\overset{1}{6}\,\overset{1}{5}$ $-1\,9^{1}\,7$ ___ 6 8	Because we borrowed 1 earlier we have to pay 1 back. 9 + 1 makes 10. 6 take away 10 we can't do so we have to borrow 1 making 16. 16 take away 10 makes 6.
$3\,\overset{1}{6}\,\overset{1}{5}$ $-1^{1}\,9^{1}\,7$ ___ 1 6 8	Because we borrowed 1 earlier we have to pay 1 back. 1 + 1 makes 2. 3 take away 2 makes 1. So the answer is 168.

The equal addition algorithm is still used in a significant minority of primary schools. It is certainly neater in the children's books requiring fewer crossed out figures. The oral commentary we have offered is the usual version that supporters of this algorithm offer. It is certainly the one we were taught in school and is easy to follow and reproduce.

Unfortunately, our oral commentary offers simply a routine procedure to follow rather than a mathematical justification. Close examination reveals that the 'borrowing' does not really seem to happen, and that the 'paying back' occurs to an unexpected digit. It certainly works, but why? The oral commentary which we were taught as children serves to disguise the mathematical processes at work rather than illuminate them.

Task 1.8: justifying the algorithm or process used
Examine the equal addition algorithm with a fresh eye. Ignore the traditional commentary. Try to justify why the process works.

Here is an alternative commentary on the equal addition algorithm, which justifies the process and explains the name.

Written form   **Oral commentary**

$$\begin{array}{r} 3\ 6\ \overset{1}{5} \\ -\ 1\ 9^1\ 7 \\ \hline 8 \\ \hline \end{array}$$

5 take away 7, we can't do, so we add 10 units to the top number making 15 units.
To maintain the difference we also add 10 to the bottom number, adding 1 to the tens column. 9 + 1 makes 10. 15 take away 7 makes 8.

$$\begin{array}{r} 3\ \overset{1}{6}\ \overset{1}{5} \\ -\ 1^1\ 9^1\ 7 \\ \hline 6\ 8 \\ \hline \end{array}$$

6 take away 10, we can't do, so we add 10 tens to the top number making 16 tens.
To maintain the difference we also add 10 to the bottom number, adding 1 to the hundreds column. 1 + 1 makes 2. 16 take away 10 makes 6.

$$\begin{array}{r} 3\ \overset{1}{6}\ \overset{1}{5} \\ -\ 1^1\ 9^1\ 7 \\ \hline 1\ 6\ 8 \\ \hline \end{array}$$

3 take away 2 makes 1
So the answer is 168.

Although this alternative commentary appears more complex, it justifies the algorithm mathematically rather than merely describing the procedure to be followed. Of course, there is no guarantee that pupils will attempt to learn the process with understanding. Some children persist, in spite of their teachers' best endeavours, in focusing on the learning of a routine and ignoring the mathematics. Such 'instrumental learning' (Skemp 1976) is brittle and difficult to apply out of context. As such it contributes little to the development of numeracy.

Surprisingly, some teachers encourage children to develop algorithms at the expense of understanding. We consider that the first oral commentary on equal addition is an example of such an approach and consider it to be an example of poor teaching. Such techniques persist because the limited objectives they seek are easier to achieve than proper mathematical understanding and true numeracy.

In order to develop true numeracy, teachers try to focus the attention of their pupils on the underlying mathematics which justifies the routine. One way of doing this is to encourage pupils to compare and contrast different ways of performing simple calculations. This has the advantage of creating opportunities for mathematical discussion and encouraging a conjecturing atmosphere in your classroom. In our experience it is also interesting and motivating for pupils, giving them 'ownership' of the mathematical processes which are eventually developed. We believe that this distinction lies at the heart of the effective teaching of numeracy.

Learning to subtract: which method is best?

A short lesson extract from the RSN project with a middle ability Year 7 class
The teacher began the lesson with the class in silence and wrote 365 −197 on the board. She paused for a few moments and then said, 'OK, silent working, no conferring. Use any method you like to calculate the answer – in your heads, on paper, I don't mind which. When you have finished, sit up straight, looking at the board and try to think of a different way you could have done the question.'

She then gave them two minutes in which to get an answer, insisting on silence throughout. Some pupils sat up straight immediately, looking pleased with themselves, others busied themselves with jottings on paper.

When everyone was sitting up straight, she said 'Now turn to your neighbour, quietly compare answers and take turns explaining your methods to each other – two minutes.'

The class compared answers and methods enthusiastically while the teacher circulated, listening in to the conversations. She then called the class to order and said 'Who is going to be the first to volunteer to come out to the board to explain their method to the rest of the class? The first one out has the easiest job.'

A sea of hands went up. The class was confident of their answers and approaches having tried them out on their neighbours. They wanted to explain their method before someone else did.

When a pupil came out to explain their method the teacher demanded silence and close attention from the class, allowing the pupil a good chance to explain their ideas. When the pupil's explanation was over the teacher summarised the pupil's ideas to the class and asked them if it would always work. After a short discussion other pupils offered their own methods s using the same approach. When there was doubt about the validity of a method the class experimented to test it.

A short class discussion followed about when it might be most appropriate to use particular methods. The teacher then set a question for the class to attempt using someone else's method.

The teaching of algorithms has traditionally been considered to be a highly significant aspect of mathematics teaching in Key Stages 2 and 3. We suggest that unless such algorithms are understood by the pupils who learn them, they contribute little to the development of numeracy.

We have traditionally taught such algorithms earlier than many other European nations and it is to international comparisons that we turn next.

Conclusion

Numeracy is a complex and ill-defined concept, in spite of being a major focus of attention in the UK at present. We hope that you share our view that it is far more than a rote knowledge of number bonds and tables which can be recited in swift response to a question. Although numeracy is based on knowledge of a few key facts and processes, we think that there are other issues, which are far more important. Numeracy is associated with beliefs and attitudes towards mathematics, an understanding of how mathematical processes work and an ability to apply such knowledge in problem solving and the learning of new mathematics.

In conclusion we would like to define numeracy by examining the characteristics of the numerate person.

Task 1.9:   What are the characteristics of the numerate person?
Think of a child or adult you know who is numerate.
List the characteristics of attitude and behaviour which make you think they are numerate.

Numerate people:

- are willing to have a go at questions involving number;
- have confident knowledge of some basic number facts and are willing to use them to derive new facts, about which they are then equally confident;
- have a sense of the size of the numbers they know and how they fit together;
- often know how to perform calculations or solve problems in more than one way, perhaps having a range of different written, mental or calculator strategies to choose from;
- sometimes check answers by performing a calculation by another valid method;
- are able to estimate the answers to simple calculations;

- sometimes check through the use of inverse operations;
- often have their own personal ways of working things out mentally or in writing;
- sometimes have their own ways of recording their mathematics;
- are able to explain and justify the methods they have used orally;
- make effective use of a calculator when it is appropriate, but;
- prefer to use mental calculations as their first resort;
- enjoy doing and talking about mathematics

(Tanner and Jones 2000b: 126).

CHAPTER 2

Comparing mathematical performance – what can we learn from overseas?

Introduction

Interest in standards of numeracy is widespread. 'Application of number' is one of the key skills which are considered to provide a foundation for all other school learning (DfEE/QCA 1999). Basic numeracy is also perceived to be a significant contributory factor in economic prosperity (Jaworski and Phillips 1999). Concern over standards of mathematics and numeracy in our schools is not new.

> It has been said, for instance, that accuracy in the manipulation of figures does not reach the same standard which was reached 20 years ago. Some employers express surprise and concern about the inability of young persons to perform simple numerical operations involved in business.
>
> (Board of Education Report 1925, from Cockcroft 1982: xii)

Such concerns have been fuelled recently by media reporting of the results of international studies that appear to show poor performance by pupils from England and Scotland:

> International tests show English pupils 'lagging'.
>
> (*The Times*, 14 January 2000)

In fact, data from the most recent surveys show Year 9 pupils in England to be performing in line with the international average on tasks closely related to common school curricula (Beaton *et al.* 1996; Mullis *et al.* 2001) and well above average on problem solving tasks (OECD 2000). Although such studies require careful interpretation they can raise interesting questions about standards and provide data on educational practices elsewhere. In this chapter we shall explore the findings of several major international studies and consider whether they indicate ways by which our standards of numeracy might be improved.

Objectives

By the end of this chapter you should:

- have an overview of the performance of English pupils in recent international comparative studies;
- understand some of the factors which influence pupil performance in such studies and hence the conclusions which can be drawn from them;
- know the findings of the studies on key issues such as setting and home-work;
- understand the extent to which different classroom practices have been shown to be effective;
- be able to adapt these effective strategies for use with your own classes.

We shall start by considering the findings of two recent large-scale studies: the Third International Mathematics and Science Study which was conducted in 1995 (Beaton *et al.* 1996), and its follow-up, the repeat study TIMSS 1999 (Mullis *et al.* 2001). These findings will then be contrasted with those from the most recent study PISA: the Programme for International Student Assessment (OECD 2000).

TIMSS 1995 and TIMSS 1999

These studies were the latest in a series of evaluations of international perform-ance conducted by the International Association for the Evaluation of Educational Achievement (IEA) (see Brown 1996, for an overview). Over 40 countries, in-cluding England and Scotland, participated in TIMSS 1995. Wales and Northern Ireland did not take part. TIMSS 1995 compared the mathematical attainment of representative samples of pupils aged mainly nine and 13 years and those in their final year of secondary schooling. The study also gathered data from pupil and teacher questionnaires, videotaping of lessons, and 'performance assessments' of pupils' abilities to solve practical, problem-solving tasks. (Further details may be found on: http://nces.ed.gov/timss.) TIMSS 1999 replicated parts of the 1995 study with grade eight pupils (Year 9 in England) in order to identify trends in performance. This was the same cohort of pupils who had been tested in 1995 when they were aged nine. The degree of progress of the cohorts could, therefore, be compared across countries.

Overall, there was no significant increase in performance between 1995 and 1999 (Mullis *et al.* 2001: 34), nor was there any significant change in the relative performance of English pupils, whose overall scores remained similar to the inter-national average. Their performance was still equivalent to pupils from the USA and New Zealand, and still significantly worse than those from Singapore, Korea, Japan and Hungary. As there had been no major curriculum initiatives in England for this cohort of pupils (they would have started secondary school before the introduction of the National Numeracy Strategy), this relative lack of change might be unsurprising. However, the difficulties of changing the educational system of a country is illustrated by the results for the USA. Since the early 1990s, far-reaching reforms had been advocated for the teaching of mathematics, yet their relative position remained unchanged (Mullis *et al.* 2001: 1.35).

Five content areas were covered by the tests: fractions and number sense; measurement; data representation, analysis, and probability; geometry; and algebra. Most of the questions were in multiple-choice format. Although the performance of boys and girls was similar in most countries, in England the boys performed significantly better than the girls (Ruddock 2000). This contrasts with their performance on the National Curriculum statutory tests taken in the same year, in which the girls did better than the boys on average. One difference between the two assessments is in the style of question used. The TIMSS papers asked mainly short, decontextualised, questions which required little reading. Boys also tend to perform better when a multiple-choice format is used (Gipps 1990; Keys *et al.* 1996: 58).

Task 2.1: **Sample questions from TIMSS**
Here is a selection of questions from the TIMSS 1999 papers. Try to estimate what percentage of your Year 9 pupils would be able to answer them correctly. Would you expect boys to do better than girls?

Fractions and number sense

1. Subtract:

    $$7003$$
    $$-4078$$
    $$\overline{}$$

    A   2035   B   2925   C   3005   D   3925

2. The sum 691 + 208 is closest to the sum:

    A   600 + 200   B   700 + 200   C   700 + 300   D   900 + 200

Algebra

3. Find the value of x if $12x - 10 = 6x + 32$.

Geometry

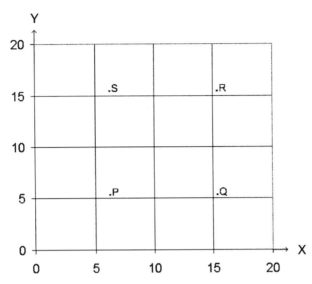

Figure 2.1 Geometry question from TIMSS 1999

4. Which point on the graph could have coordinates (7, 16)?

    A Point P **B** Point Q **C** Point R **D** Point S

Data handling

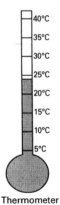

Temperature					
	6 a.m.	9 a.m.	Noon	3 p.m.	6 p.m.
Monday	15°	17°	24°	21°	16°
Tuesday	20°	16°	15°	10°	9°
Wednesday	8°	14°	16°	19°	15°
Thursday	8°	11°	19°	26°	20°

Thermometer

Figure 2.2 Data representation question from TIMSS 1999 (Mullis *et al.* 2000: 2.89)

5. On which day and at what time was the temperature shown in the table the
same as that shown on the thermometer?

    A Monday, noon **B** Tuesday, 6 a.m. **C** Wednesday, 3 p.m.
    D Thursday, 3 p.m.

Measurement

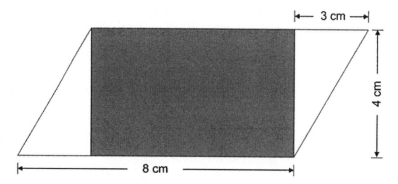

Figure 2.3 Measurement question from TIMSS 1999 (Mullis *et al.* 2000: 2.74)

6. The figure shows a shaded rectangle inside a parallelogram. Find the area of the shaded rectangle.

(Mullis *et al.* 2001)

Table 2.1 gives the results for England, the USA, Japan and Hungary, and the international average. English pupils performed comparatively poorly on questions 1 and 3. However, we suspect that some of the features of question 1 might have contributed to underperformance. Its layout implies the need for a formal written algorithm. However, the decomposition method (which is more widely taught in the UK than on the continent) is difficult to apply here because of the need to decompose over the two zeros. Erroneous solutions arising from other common errors, such as always subtracting the smaller digit from the larger, or forgetting to 'pay back' when using the 'equal additions' method, are not offered, thereby possibly artificially inflating the success rate for other approaches.

The other questions require a degree of interpretation and choice of strategy. English pupils performed better than the international average on such questions although still below the level achieved by the top-scoring Pacific Rim countries.

Table 2.1 Sample test question results for England, USA, Hungary, and Japan: TIMSS 1999

Question	International Average %	England %	USA %	Hungary %	Japan %
1. 7003 – 4078	74	51	81	87	86
2. 691 + 208	80	92	93	93	95
3. Equation	44	26	34	74	85
4. Graph	58	75	67	71	84
5. Temperature	79	92	89	87	96
6. Area	43	48	34	45	80

(Source: Mullis *et al.* 2001)

The types of questions in which English pupils performed less well than their international counterparts were those which could be solved merely by following standard algorithms. However, decontextualised questions, such as question 1, have been de-emphasised in both the National Curriculum and the National Numeracy Strategy in favour of tasks set in real-life contexts, and those which require pupils to apply their mathematical knowledge to problems (Brown 1999a). Other countries, however, place a greater emphasis on the memorisation of routines each designed to solve a standard type of problem. Simultaneous equations, for example, have been classified by Taiwanese teachers into twenty distinct categories and a solution procedure taught for each type (see Hoyles *et al.* 1999). If the questions set on tests conform to these standard types then all a pupil needs in order to be successful in mathematics is a good memory! However, such pupils would not meet the criteria for being described as numerate, which we discussed in Chapter 1.

Performance on problem-solving tasks

English pupils performed significantly better than the international average on the few questions which required problem solving and mathematical thinking. Students' practical, investigative, problem-solving and analytical abilities were assessed, in TIMSS 1995 only, through the Performance Assessments. In these assessments, Year 9 pupils from England were ranked seventh out of the nineteen countries which participated and the results were better than the same students' results in the written tests (Harris *et al.* 1998).

This superior performance was confirmed in the PISA study (OECD 2000). PISA surveyed 265,000 students from 32 countries and assessed 15-year-old students' 'mathematical literacy': their capacity to use their knowledge and skills to meet real-life challenges. Japan and Korea came top of the table. The students from the United Kingdom were ranked eighth, well above the international average. Interestingly, the United States, Germany and Hungary were all ranked below average. We shall examine further the factors which lead to problem-solving success in Chapter 5. However, the comparative performance of the English pupils on international surveys would appear to vary according to the particular curriculum aspects examined.

Comparing performance across countries

The comparison of the performance of countries on the tests is not easy. For example, although the content of the tests was agreed by all participating countries to reflect their mathematics curriculum for that grade, the extent to which a particular topic was emphasised within the curriculum varied. Some countries reported placing a much greater emphasis than others on, for example, number work.

There were also variations in the ages of the pupils tested. TIMSS intended to assess 13-year-old pupils, i.e. those in the eighth grade (Year 9 in England). In England and much of the Pacific Rim, pupils are allocated to a grade strictly by age but in other European countries more than 25% of pupils can be in classes below their expected grade because of examination failure (Brown 1999a). Several countries, therefore, had a significant percentage of their pupil cohort missing from the test sample, for example in TIMSS 1995, Switzerland excluded 8% of the pupil cohort, Hungary and Hong Kong excluded about 10%, and Germany 25% (Beaton *et al.* 1996). In contrast only 1% of the cohort were excluded in England. Of course, testing only the upper end of the cohort enables such countries to appear to have a shorter tail of low achievers than if all pupils had been included (Brown 1999a).

It has been suggested that England has a wider range of performance with a longer tail of low-achievers than in many other countries (see, for example, Reynolds and Farrell 1996). This is not supported by either of the TIMSS studies, which in fact indicate that the range of performance for England is smaller than that for many other countries (Mullis *et al.* 2001: 32).

In summary then, although there are aspects of the TIMSS studies in which English students performed well, they could be described as under-performing in comparison with other apparently similar countries. Some of the caveats associated with interpreting the results have been discussed above. What other factors might have influenced pupils' performance?

Task 2.2:   International factors
Consider what features might have contributed to the success or otherwise of the pupils from the various countries reported above. Which of these features are under the control of the school or the educational system?

There are large numbers of factors which might have contributed to the success of the high-performing countries. Indeed, cultural and social differences are, of themselves, likely to have a significant influence. We shall now look at the information gathered on the different educational and social cultures by the studies.

Influences on performance

The TIMSS studies used questionnaires to collect information from pupils and teachers on a range of variables, e.g. home background, class size, teaching approaches employed, use of computers and calculators, frequency and duration of homework, and pupils' attitudes to mathematics. Two strong, positive correlations were found.

The first, perhaps not surprisingly, was that mathematical achievement correlated strongly with the level of educational support found in the home. This included the availability of a dictionary, a study desk, a computer, the number of books, and the level of parental education (Beaton et al., 1996; Mullis et al. 2001).

The second factor was that of 'opportunity to learn': the extent to which the whole curriculum is taught to all the pupils. This relates to the degree of differentiation by setting or ability-grouping within the school system. Countries with less tracking by ability were found to perform better (see Brown 1999a: 199 for details). Such a finding conflicts with current advice encouraging the adoption of setting as a strategy for English schools. It also emphasises the importance of cultural factors which influence beliefs about education. Rather than attributing educational success to innate ability, Pacific Rim countries, such as Japan, emphasise the importance of effort and hard work. Pupils tend to be taught in mixed-ability classes where the classroom ethos implies that individual difficulty is a signal for the pupil to work harder. The prevalent view in Pacific Rim societies is that all pupils are capable of attaining core skills in core subjects (Reynolds and Farrell 1996). It is possible that by resorting to differentiation we foster unnecessarily low expectations of some pupils. It will be interesting to see if the targets set by the National Numeracy Strategies will be attained partly through increased expectations of pupils. We will discuss this issue further in Chapter 3.

The relationship between attainment and most other factors was unclear. For example, no clear relationship was found with class size, the amount of time spent in mathematics lessons, or the time spent on mathematics homework (Mullis et al. 2001: 194). Part of the explanation offered for this is a variation in practice. Some low-attaining pupils receive extra tuition in small groups with additional homework to help them keep up. Other low attainers report doing little homework, either because they simply do not do it or because it is not set. The National Strategy for KS3 requires that homework is set regularly (DfEE 2001a: 1.30) yet TIMSS found wide variation in teachers' use of homework. For example, in one-quarter of the USA lessons observed, students worked on their homework in class. This happened in only 2% of the German lessons and never in the Japanese classrooms (Stigler et al. 1999: 83). Allowing homework to be done in class appears to us to be a waste of teacher time. If homework is to improve standards then it needs to complement classwork not replace it.

Despite the impression given by some reports in the media, no clear results emerged as to the most effective way to teach mathematics. Indeed, variables related to teaching style, such as classroom organisation, or the amount of whole-class teaching, were found to have little correlation with attainment. This echoes the findings of similar studies conducted in the UK, and elsewhere (Brown 1999b). There are diverse routes to educational success; no single solution seems to lead infallibly to educational achievement (Beaton *et al.* 1996; Brown 1999a; Keys *et al.* 1997). It is the quality of the whole teaching and learning process, rather than its more obvious but superficial features, which matters.

The comparison of performance, using average scores or data on national policies, cannot provide information on what actually happens within the school or classroom. Detailed classroom-based observations are needed to elicit how strategies such as whole-class teaching are implemented in practice.

Studies of classroom practices

Lessons were videotaped in three different countries, Japan, Germany and the USA, in order to identify and compare their characteristic mathematics teaching practices (see Stigler *et al.* 1999 for details). The countries represent an interesting range of mathematical performance: Japan was ranked third overall, performing significantly better than Germany or the USA, both of whom were close to the international average with scores similar to those of England. Over 200 lessons were videotaped, 100 in Germany, 50 in Japan, and 81 in the USA. In each country the classes contained a representative sample of pupils and the teachers were asked to teach a 'typical' lesson. The videos were transcribed and analysed by native speakers.

> *Task 2.3:   Contrasting classroom practices*
> *As you read on through the lesson descriptions you may like to consider which country's practices are most similar to your own classroom experiences.*

In all three countries approaches which could be described as whole-class teaching were commonly used and pupils were frequently required to come to the board to present their work. Unsurprisingly, this suggests that merely changing to this type of teaching approach will not of itself raise standards. This contrasts with superficial interpretations of the National Numeracy Strategy as a return to traditional teaching approaches. Differences in practice were found, however, in the type of mathematics taught, the level of mathematical thinking required of the students, and in the ways lessons were structured and presented.

The standard of the mathematics taught was judged to be higher in the Japanese lessons (equivalent to ninth-grade standard) than in the German (eighth-grade) or the USA lessons (seventh-grade). Japanese teachers were significantly more likely to focus on new work, with only 3% of their lessons spent reviewing previously taught work in comparison with a quarter of lessons in Germany and the USA (Stigler *et al.* 1999: 44).

When the teachers were asked what the main thing they wanted the students to learn from the lesson was there was a significant difference between Japanese teachers and those from the two other countries. 73% of Japanese teachers identified mathematical thinking as their main aim: for pupils to understand mathematical concepts or to discover multiple solutions to a problem. Over half of the USA and German teachers identified mathematical skills as their priorities: for the pupils to learn how to solve specific problems or to use standard formulae (Stigler *et al.* 1999: 45). The aims for the lesson will, of course, influence the types of activities and emphases which occur within it. When the types of tasks given to the students during the 'seatwork' or exercise phase of the lessons were analysed, Japan differed significantly from Germany and the USA by spending far less time on the practice of routine procedures and more time inventing new solutions or thinking about mathematical problems (Stigler *et al.* 1999: 103).

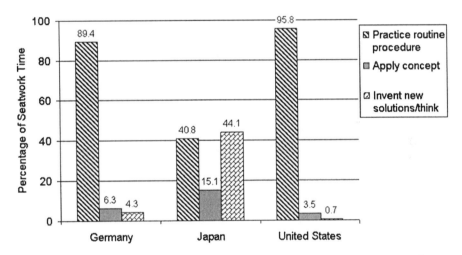

Figure 2.4   Percentage of seatwork time spent on different types of task (after Stigler *et al.* 1999:102)

Japanese students were expected to think for themselves. In 40% of lessons the students had to decide for themselves how best to approach a problem. In the majority of the USA lessons, however, students were directed to apply the exact procedure demonstrated by the teacher (see Figure 2.5).

Mathematical concepts can be introduced by being developed through examples, experimentation and discussion, or pupils can simply be told what the result is, e.g. the area of a triangle is half base times height. More than three-quarters of teachers in Germany and Japan (77% and 83%) usually developed the

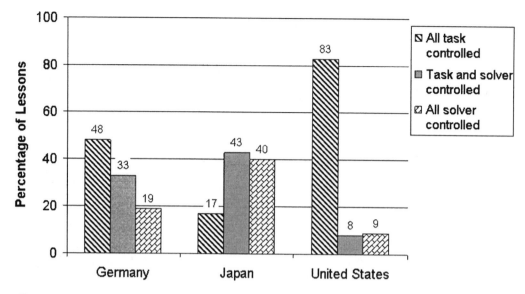

Figure 2.5 Percentage of lessons containing teacher/student-controlled tests (adapted from Stigler *et al* 1999: 69)

mathematical concepts needed for the lesson in comparison with just 22% of USA teachers. The implicit assumption here, that it is important for pupils to understand the mathematics, was evident again when the lessons were examined for the emphasis placed on mathematical proof. Over half (53%) of the Japanese lessons included an emphasis on proof compared to 10% in Germany and none of the USA lessons (Stigler *et al.* 1999: 52). Stigler concluded that Japanese teachers emphasised mathematical understanding whereas in Germany and the USA the focus was on students being able to 'do' the mathematics (Stigler *et al.* 1999: 46).

Despite the superficial similarities across the three countries in their use of whole-class teaching and pupil involvement it was concluded that typical lessons in the three countries actually followed different 'scripts' from each other. To help explain what these different scripts are, we summarise below two of the lessons shown on the TIMSS videotape study.* Each lesson focuses on an algebraic topic: simplifying algebraic fractions by finding the lowest common denominator, and solving word problems which involve the solution of inequalities (Stigler *et al.* 1999).

Task 2.4:   Comparing teaching approaches
Before reading the descriptions of the lessons consider how you would approach the teaching of these two topics to a Year 9 class.

---

*Copies of the video may be obtained from http://nces.ed.gov/timss

A lesson from the USA: simplifying algebraic fractions

The lesson begins with warm-up questions which are unrelated to algebraic fractions. The teacher circulates helping individuals and then invites students to call out the answers. Brief explanations are given by the teacher in response to queries. This phase takes over 15 minutes. The teacher then reminds the class of the ongoing work:

Teacher: Yesterday we worked on [finding] the lowest common denominator. Try this problem:

$$\frac{1}{(x-7)} + \frac{1}{(x^2-49)} =$$

What is the lowest common denominator?

After one minute when the students discuss and/or start working on the problem the teacher asks for solutions.

Teacher: OK, let's have the common denominator ... Molly?
Molly: $x^2 - 49$
Teacher: And the numerator [for the first fraction]?
Molly: $7x$
Teacher: How did you get $7x$?
Molly: I squared the 7 and the x.
Teacher: Not quite ... you have to do some factorising.

Another student is called on to continue.

Student 2: $x - 7$ is a factor of $x^2 - 49$ so we find the other factor, $x + 7$, and then add 1 [for the numerator of the second fraction].

The teacher writes this up on the OHP and finishes the simplification describing the steps as she does them. At the end she asks if there are any queries. Molly asks why her method was wrong. The teacher explains:

Teacher: You have to find the lowest common denominator that includes both of these as factors (points to the denominators). I want to turn this denominator $(x-7)$ into x^2-49, so I multiply by the identity element $\frac{(x+7)}{(x+7)}$ (writes this next to the first fraction) and then I do 1 times $(x+7)$ which gives $x + 7$ and then I have 1 here (pointing to working). Now then, this one looks easier ...

And she moves on to the next example, writing on the OHP:

$$\frac{5}{(x+6)} - \frac{(2-x)}{(x+6)} =$$

Again the students have just over a minute to consider it. The teacher then uses short-answer questions, e.g: 'Subtracting is the same as what?' to lead the students through the steps in the solution algorithm. The time taken to discuss both examples is about six minutes.

The class is then set a number of different tasks to complete by the end of the lesson including finishing off previous work and correcting previous homework. When they have finished these they may start the worksheet on algebraic fractions which is to be completed for homework. The students work on these tasks for about 11 minutes until the end of the lesson.

A lesson from Japan: solving word problems involving inequalities

Six inequality questions of the type:

Solve $4(x-2) \leq 5(2x-3)$

had been set for homework. Six students are called to write up their answers to one of the questions on the board. The rest of the class check their solutions and identify any errors. This takes about six minutes. The teacher then introduces the main theme of the lesson:

Teacher: Today will be the last lesson on this topic and, today, everyone will have to think a little. Until now we've just been doing calculation practice but now I will be asking you to think of methods to solve the problem. So it will be more difficult than just calculating ... This is your problem.

The question is displayed on a poster stuck on the board and a student is asked to read it aloud to the class.

Student: There are two different types of cakes. One type costs 230 yen and the other, 200 yen. You have to buy 10 cakes altogether but you only have 2,100 yen. You want to buy as many of the 230-yen cakes as possible, what is the maximum number that you can buy?

[A few moments for thought as the teacher rereads and rephrases the question.]

Teacher: Think about what you need to do to find out how many you can buy and find the answer.

Five minutes pass as pupils work individually on the problem. The teacher then calls on pupils to describe their methods which he writes up on the board.

Student 1:   I started by working out how much it would cost if I bought 10 of the 230-yen cakes but that came to … too much so I tried 9. That was too much as well. I would have got to the answer but I ran out of time.

Another student who has used the same arithmetical approach supplies the answer. The teacher summarises this method on the board as:

230 cake	× 3	… × 8	× 9	× 10
	690		2070	2300
200 cake	× 7		× 1	
	1400		200	
	2090		2270	

He explains this in a more analytical form:

Teacher: I thought of doing it by starting by buying 10 × 230-yen cakes. This would cost 2300 yen which is 200 yen too much. So I have to substitute some 200-yen cakes. Each 200-yen cake I substitute saves me 30 yen. How many do you have to substitute …? If you substitute seven cakes then you save 210 yen which takes care of the shortage of money. So you buy three 230-yen cakes.

He then asks another pupil who has used an algebraic method to explain her approach. Again, he summarises this onto the board.

Student 2:   Make the number of 230-yen cakes be x.
Then the number of 200-yen cakes becomes $10 - x$.

230	200
x	$10 - x$

and so the cost of the cakes is

$$230x + 200(10 - x) \leq 2100$$

Another student is asked to re-explain this method 'so that even more students will understand'. The discussion takes about ten minutes in total. The teacher then moves on to formalise this method.

Teacher: To tell you the truth, what I want to do in today's lesson is this method that Rika (Student 2) has just described but I wanted you all to come up with a number of ways to solve it. So now we are going to try to do the problem using the inequality equation.

The next seven minutes are spent leading the students step by step through the inequality method. At the end of this discussion, he points out the advantages of using this method over the trial-and-error methods presented earlier in the lesson: 'The answer will come out quickly... you don't need to figure out each number one by one.' Worksheets with questions of a similar type are then handed out and the pupils work on these while the teacher circulates, helping individuals. After about ten minutes, two students are asked to write their answers on the board and the teacher leads a class discussion of their methods.

The lesson ends with the teacher summarising the main point:

> 'What we talked about today was the solution (of word problems) using inequality equations. That is, when you work out problems, instead of counting things one by one and finding the number, it's usually easier if you set up an inequality equation.'

Discussion

The lessons were selected to typify the teaching approaches seen in the two countries. The extracts, summarised above, illustrate an underlying difference in mathematical purpose as well as in the structuring of the lessons.

In the USA lesson, the main teaching episode began with the teacher telling the pupils how to do the examples. The emphasis was very much on what steps to carry out next in the procedure. Molly's query about why she couldn't just square individual terms was answered by a reiteration of the algorithm. The students' task was to learn to use the method provided by the teacher.

The main underlying aim for the USA teacher was for the students to be able to 'do' the types of problems set. The Japanese teacher, however, made his aim clear at the start of the lesson, 'Today, you have to think, not just calculate.' His lesson started differently by asking the students to attempt to find approaches for solving the problem. Their methods were then compared in a whole-class discussion during which students were expected to consider a variety of strategies. The teacher intervened to argue for the importance of mathematical elegance and general applicability.

The TIMSS study considered Japanese lessons to be qualitatively different to those in the other two countries. The USA and German lessons were analysed as following an 'acquisition/application script'. In this script, the teacher leads the pupils through an example and shows them how to do it. Having acquired this skill the pupils then practise it by applying it to a similar exercise. In contrast, the Japanese lessons follow a 'problematising script'. The solution to a problem is not the purpose of the lesson, rather problem solving is the means through which pupils come to understand the underlying mathematical principles. Instead of the lesson starting with the teacher instructing the class, a problem is posed which the pupils struggle to solve. The teacher then uses a discussion of the students' ideas to develop the mathematical principles (Stigler *et al.* 1999: 135).

Table 2.2   How Japanese approaches compare with those from the USA and Germany

Japan	USA and Germany
• teacher poses a complex thought-provoking problem;	• teacher instructs students with a concept or skill;
• students struggle with the problem individually or in groups;	• teacher solves example problems with the class;
• a range of students present their ideas or solutions to the class;	• (in Germany, some pupils work through problems at the board);
• the teacher summarises the class's conclusions;	
• students practise similar problems.	• students practise individually while teacher helps.

(adapted from Stigler *et al.* 1999: 135–6)

> *Task 2.5:   Analysing and adapting your approaches*
> *Choose a topic which you are about to teach and consider which approach it is most like.*
> *How could you adapt your usual approach to mirror those used by Japanese teachers?*

The video study has been replicated as part of TIMSS 1999 although, at the time of writing, its findings are not yet published. Other results of the 1999 study, however, report that students in classes where teachers emphasised mathematical reasoning and problem solving had higher achievement than those in classes with less emphasis on such activities. In Japan, nearly half the students (49%) were in classes where mathematical reasoning and problem-solving activities were emphasised in most or all lessons. This compares with 18% in the USA, 16% in Hungary, and 3% in England (Mullis *et al.* 2001: 208).

Conclusion

The precise implications drawn from international studies vary from country to country. In the USA, the TIMSS results have been used to support the implementation of progressive reforms to mathematics teaching. In Korea, the second-highest scoring country in TIMSS 1995 and 1999, recent reforms to its mathematics curriculum aim to move away from a focus on memorisation of skills and facts to a greater emphasis on creativity and problem solving (Lew 1999). In the UK, however, the results of TIMSS have largely been used to support calls for 'a return to the basics'. While we might wish to improve the performance of English pupils on the written papers, this should not be at the expense of damaging their higher-order problem-solving and mathematical-thinking skills.

The results of the video study comparing classroom approaches indicate subtle but critical differences in emphasis on an 'acquisition' script versus an approach which uses problem solving to develop mathematical principles. These classroom-based findings are supported by the link between problem solving and achievement found in TIMSS 1999 and the results of the PISA study.

There has been no significant improvement in overall performance between the two studies. Trying to alter the educational practices of a country, however, must be rather like trying to change the course of a super-tanker: you have to start early and even small changes take time to become noticeable! Individual teachers, though, can have a marked influence on the attitude and progress of the pupils in their classes. Several initiatives have tried to incorporate some of the key features identified in higher-scoring countries into mathematics teaching and learning practices in the UK. We shall examine some of these in the next chapter.

CHAPTER 3

Numeracy initiatives

Introduction

In the last chapter we discussed international studies which identified countries where pupils are outperforming their English counterparts in mathematics. Such findings have led to initiatives designed to improve standards in mathematics in England and Wales through the identification of more effective teaching approaches. In this chapter we shall examine some of these studies and compare their recommendations with current practice and with the guidance provided by the National Strategy for Mathematics in Key Stage 3.

Objectives

By the end of Chapter 3 you should:

- be aware of the recommendations to improve standards in numeracy made by some of the key projects;
- recognise how some of these recommendations compare with practices overseas;
- understand the principles underpinning the recommendations of the National Strategy for KS3;
- be aware of the suggested structure of a typical numeracy lesson;
- understand the nature and purposes of mental and oral sessions;
- understand what is meant by 'direct teaching' and the forms that this may take;
- appreciate the value of effective plenary activities, in particular those involving collective reflection.

The National Numeracy Strategies

Based on the work of the National Numeracy Project (Straker 1997) and the Numeracy Task Force (Reynolds 1998a, b) the National Numeracy Strategy was introduced into English primary schools in 1998. It aimed to improve standards in mathematics teaching and learning so that at least 75% of 11-year-olds would achieve a Level 4 or above in National Curriculum Tests by 2002. At the time of writing (autumn 2001), although results have improved this target has not yet been achieved. Attention has now moved, however, to ensuring that pupils continue this improvement after they transfer to secondary schools.

From September 2001, all English secondary schools must have regard to the National Strategy for Key Stage 3 (DfEE 2001a). The strategy is similar to that for the primary phase with schools expected to raise their expectations of pupils, to set ambitious targets for National Tests, to provide prompt support to enable those pupils who have not achieved the target Level 4 at the end of KS2 to 'catch-up', and to utilise effective teaching approaches.

Task 3.1:   Ambitious targets?

Choose a topic that you are currently teaching in KS3. Compare the learning objectives detailed in your lesson plans/scheme of work with those given in the KS3 Framework. Are your expectations in line with those of the framework?

Many of our secondary partnership schools have commented favourably on the improvement in standards exhibited by their Year 7 intakes over the last few years. Although some of the expectations set out in the KS3 Framework might currently be above those previously anticipated for the majority of pupils, we consider them to be ambitious but generally achievable, especially if the improvement at KS2 is sustained.

As well as listing the content to be taught, the framework also offers guidance on the frequency and duration of lessons, the lesson structure, and effective teaching approaches. We shall summarise the main recommendations of the Framework here and then consider how they compare with those of other key projects.

As in the NNS for primary schools, the Framework places great emphasis on a three-part structure for a typical lesson:

- whole class oral and mental work (about 5–10 minutes)
- the main teaching activity (about 25–40 minutes)
- a final plenary to round off the lesson (about 5–15 minutes).

(DfEE 2001a: 1.28)

The use of an oral/mental activity as a lesson starter has received much attention, possibly to avoid its misinterpretation as a return to the mechanical rote learning previously associated with mental arithmetic lessons. The framework claims that a lively interactive start to lessons engages pupils' attention and produces a more lasting effect than periodic numeracy lessons. However, it continues with the warning that, in order to achieve this, the starter activities must be much more than mere testing of pupils' recall of facts or the marking of homework. Activities must be carefully planned to ensure coherence and progression (DfEE 2001a: 1.29).

The framework advises the adoption of teaching strategies which include a high proportion of 'direct, interactive teaching' often to the whole class (DfEE 2001a: 1.26). At the primary level, direct teaching of the whole class now seems to have been adopted almost uncritically although the research evidence in its support is controversial. National and international studies show, on average, little or no advantage for whole-class teaching over individualised approaches, while exceptions to the average indicate whole-class teaching producing poor results and excellent standards being achieved through individualised approaches (Askew *et al.* 1997; Brown 1999b). Whole-class teaching, for example, when done well may inspire otherwise unexceptional pupils. Conversely, if whole-class teaching is done poorly, then the whole class is adversely affected. Merely incorporating more whole-class teaching is, of itself, unlikely to produce better outcomes, rather it is the quality of the interaction between teacher and pupils which is important (Brown 1999b).

The meaning of direct, interactive teaching could be interpreted in a variety of ways. It is clear, however, that the framework intends more than a monologue of telling to occur:

> High-quality direct teaching is oral, interactive and lively, and will not be achieved by lecturing the class, or by always expecting pupils to teach themselves indirectly from books. It is a two-way process in which pupils are expected to play an active part by answering questions, contributing points to discussions, and explaining and demonstrating their methods and solutions to others in the class.
>
> (DfEE 2001a: 1.26)

Pupils are seen not as sponges, uncritically soaking up the wisdom transmitted by the teacher, but as active participants in the learning process. They are expected to consider the information being presented, to relate it to their existing understanding and to check their interpretations by presenting their strategies to others. For this to occur requires a balance of teaching and learning approaches, for example:

directing and telling	sharing your teaching objectives with the class, ensuring that pupils know how to set out work;
demonstrating	giving clear, well-structured demonstrations of mathematical methods, or modelling a technique, e.g. using a graphical calculator to find the solution to an equation;
explaining and illustrating	providing accurate, well-paced explanations and **discussing why methods work**;

questioning and discussing	using open and closed questions to involve all pupils, **asking for their explanations, challenging their assumptions and making them think;**
exploring and investigating	**asking pupils to pose problems or to suggest possible approaches;**
consolidating	providing opportunities for pupils to practise new skills, to apply these across the curriculum, **to reflect on and talk through their work, and to compare and refine methods;**
reflecting and evaluating	identifying and **discussing pupils' errors** and any underpinning misconceptions, **discussing pupils' justification of methods,** evaluating pupils' presentations of their work to the class;
summarising	reviewing what has been learned, identifying and correcting misunderstandings, **inviting pupils to present their work** and picking out key ideas, linking work to other topics, other subjects and to the next stage of the pupils' learning.

(summarised from DfEE 2001a: 1.26–27, our emphasis)

In many ways the framework is telling us nothing new here: similar advice has been offered to teachers for decades (see, for example, the Cockcroft report, DES 1982). There are two aspects which are worthy of comment, however. First, the teaching strategies highlighted in the above list illustrate the emphasis given to pupils articulating their thinking and comparing their ideas with others. Second, the emphasis placed on the plenary activities – reflecting, evaluating and summarising – is much stronger than hitherto. Up to one-third of lesson time is allocated to plenary activities by the framework. This represents a marked increase on current practice and indicates its perceived importance in the learning process. In addition to the approaches identified above, the plenary may also be used to:

- summarise what has been learned, and stress what needs to be remembered;
- generalise some mathematics from examples generated earlier in the lesson;
- use questioning to assess pupils informally;
- highlight progress made and remind pupils about their personal targets;
- set homework to extend or consolidate class work and prepare for future lessons.

(after DfEE 2001a: 1.30)

We shall discuss later the benefits of introducing such activities into classroom practice.

The framework offers wide-ranging guidance on all aspects of mathematics teaching. Some of this advice will be familiar to many teachers and will represent their current good practice. Other aspects of the guidance will be less familiar or even controversial.

Task 3.2: *Appraising the framework*
Identify three aspects of the KS3 Framework which you consider mirror your current practices.
Identify three aspects which might lead to an improvement in mathematics standards in your classroom. Why should these improve your pupils' learning?

The recommendations for KS3 are based on the experiences of the NNS in the primary phase and a limited trial in secondary schools. Much of the guidance, however, is also supported by the findings from other projects and research into how children learn. We shall now move on to consider these aspects in more detail.

The Mathematics Enhancement Project (MEP)

One of the more influential projects in recent years has been the Mathematics Enhancement Project (CIMT 1997). The project analysed the ways in which mathematics was taught in countries which performed well in international comparisons, and drew, in particular, on observations of mathematics lessons in Hungary. From this MEP has made strong recommendations on the nature of the mathematics curriculum, its assessment, and the need for particular teaching strategies.

MEP suggests that Hungarian teachers are all trained to manage and teach their classes in a standard, consistent fashion with an emphasis on whole-class interaction (Graham *et al.* 1999). Similar training has been required for schools wishing to follow the MEP scheme. Textbooks and other resources, such as outline lesson plans, are supplied to support a consistent and controlled approach to teaching and learning (see www.ex.ac.uk/cimt/mep/index.htm for examples and availability). This contrasts with the framework, which outlines a three-part lesson format but cautions that:

> This outline structure is not a mechanistic recipe to be followed. Use your professional judgement to determine the activities, timing and organisation of the beginning, middle and end of the lesson to suit its objectives.
>
> (DfEE 2001a: 1.28)

MEP lessons are based on the structure of a typical Hungarian lesson. This can be summarised as:

- lessons begin with the teacher summarising the homework, which is then self-marked by the pupils;
- the whole class is taught together;
- the teacher only moves on to the next phase when everyone has understood: the class moves at the pace of the slowest pupil;
- oral and mental work is emphasised;
- there is a balance between whole-class teaching and individual work;
- pupils work individually for short, intermittent periods;
- pupils' mistakes are used as teaching points;
- pupils come to the board to demonstrate their work;
- there is an emphasis on precision in mathematical expression;
- pupils' progress is monitored continuously and every mistake is checked by the teacher before the class moves on;
- summarising is a key feature throughout the lesson with the main points reviewed at the end;
- homework is set each lesson to help to prepare for the next.

(after Graham *et al.* 1999: 55–6)

How does this list compare with what you would consider to be a typical mathematics lesson in your school?

Task 3.3:   Analysing MEP lessons
Which of the features listed above are novel to you?
Are there any which you consider to be problematic?
Are there any which you would consider incorporating into your own practice?

In many ways this list describes what we would consider to be standard features of mathematics lessons in Britain. For example, the use of homework to reinforce classwork and to link lessons together is a common example of good practice, its value being echoed by the KS3 Framework (see page 1.30). However, we reject the suggestion that all homework should be marked by the pupils at the start of the lesson. The way in which homework is marked should depend on its nature and the purpose for which it was set.

More extended pieces of work, especially tasks that involve justification or proof, need to be marked thoroughly by the teacher. Marking also provides diagnostic information for us as teachers about the common problems encountered by pupils and those pupils who need additional support etc.; and for this to inform our planning it must be known in advance of the subsequent lesson. Such information cannot be gathered from a mere show of hands or the calling out of marks. There also are implications for class management if homework is only ever marked by the pupils themselves. The marking of pupils' work sends strong signals about its importance to the pupils. If such checking does not occur regularly then they are unlikely to maintain their work at a satisfactory standard.

Although particular emphasis is placed by MEP on lessons being led by the teacher, in our experience this approach is the norm. Few departments now seem to rely on pupils working individually through a published scheme with the risk that they work at a slow pace. One advantage of teaching the class as a whole, MEP suggests, is that the teacher can drive the lesson forwards. To facilitate this, periods of individual work are kept short. This certainly helps to maintain pace and focus the pupils' attention, at least in the short term. However, a false picture of mathematics is created if pupils only ever encounter problems that can always be solved within a few moments. Learning mathematics should involve learning how to persevere with challenging, multi-stage problems. We shall discuss this further in Chapter 5.

Another feature which concerns us is the requirement that all pupils should move on only when all have understood. This seems to imply that the brighter pupils would not be adequately challenged. Indeed, in the small sample of MEP schools that we know well, the teachers have adapted this recommended approach by including more taxing problems for the faster workers. Even when pupils are set by ability, a degree of differentiation is necessary to ensure that adequate support and challenge is offered to all pupils.

Despite some of MEP's recommendations, we do not believe that teaching can be reduced to a standard format. Recommendations may provide useful guidance and advice but a variety of teaching and learning approaches is necessary if only to prevent predictability leading to boredom.

Other MEP recommendations are reflected in the guidance offered by the framework; for example, the need to emphasise mental and oral work, and the importance of lesson summaries. Exactly how these features are translated into classroom practice may well vary, however. As we saw in the last chapter, lessons may apparently be structured in a similar fashion and yet differ significantly in the quality of the interactions which occur. In the next section we shall consider how such strategies have been implemented effectively in practice.

The Raising Standards in Numeracy Project (RSN)

The teachers studied here were working in schools where pupils were outperforming in value-added terms on national tests and external examinations (see Chapter 1 for details). Although the schools differed in character and location it was possible to identify several common features of the teaching and learning process which were considered to underpin their pupils' success. Some, but not all, of these features are echoed in the recommendations of the National Strategy and MEP. In this section we shall explore the practices of the RSN teachers and illustrate our discussions with excerpts drawn from lessons and teaching plans.

Preparation and planning

Both MEP and the NS consider that teachers would benefit from having a structure to guide their planning. Lesson plans are provided by MEP, and the KS3 Framework is intended to be 'a valuable tool for reviewing and adjusting [teachers'] practice, and ... for planning their lessons' (DfEE 2001a: 1.2). From 2001, all English secondary schools are expected to use the framework or to be able to justify not doing so. The criteria suggested for use in reviewing the extent to which a department's practice should be modified include:

- the pupils' level of attainment;
- the achievement of departmental targets;
- quality of departmental self-evaluation and developmental planning;
- quality of teaching and assessment;
- the degree of match of expectations with the level and rigour of those in the framework;
- ongoing involvement in comparable, developmental projects.

(adapted from DfEE 2001a: 1.3)

To what extent have you already modified your practice to incorporate key features of the Framework? By what process did you arrive at these decisions?

Task 3.4: Developing and refining schemes of work
What are the procedures in your department for considering the recommendations of major reports such as the KS3 Framework? Is it left to the head of department? Discussed at departmental meetings? Referred to smaller working groups? Left up to individual teachers?

One of the features of the RSN schools was the extent to which staff had worked collaboratively to develop their schemes of work and to share teaching ideas. Sometimes the need for the selection of a new set of textbooks or other teaching resources had been used as a stimulus to provoke reconsideration of existing schemes of work and current approaches. Teachers would often work in small groups to develop sections of the scheme of work and then present their suggestions at a departmental meeting. In the ensuing discussions, good practice was shared across the department and a common understanding was reached on acceptable approaches and standards. (See Chapter 12 for a fuller discussion.) Discussion of the KS3 Framework could be used as a stimulus for a similar process.

Expectations

One of the concerns of the MEP project was the rate of working associated with individualised learning schemes. When a class of pupils are all working individually it can be very difficult to judge the level of effort being made: had the pupil really needed all that time to understand the worksheet or was it due to a lack of motivation and teacher pressure? When the activity is being led by the teacher, however, it is more difficult for pupils to hide or to drift along at a slow pace. It was notable that the RSN teachers had very high expectations of both the standard and the pace of work in their classes.

Whole-class teaching sequences were usually pitched at the upper quartile of the class with the teachers stating that 'they believed that the less-able pupils benefited from listening to the explanations of the others' and that for all pupils 'a good way to develop your understanding was to try to explain your work to others'. Many teachers commented that they were continually surprised by how much pupils gained from listening to each other, even when the teachers would have considered that part of the topic to be too hard for them. During whole-class sessions teachers often used a mix of carefully targeted and more open questions to ensure that all pupils could participate and remained focused on the task. Such lessons were often reminiscent of the Japanese approaches (described in the last chapter) which were underpinned by the expectation that all pupils in the class were able to succeed.

Teaching strategies

The lessons we observed as part of the RSN project were well planned with clear learning objectives, an obvious structure and a variety of learning activities. In contrast to the advice given by MEP their lessons did not follow a standard format but interaction was a key teaching and learning strategy. Their approaches varied depending, for example, on the age and ability of the pupils, the topic being taught, the pedagogical preferences of the teacher, and the constraints of the teaching environment. However, many characteristic strategies and approaches were apparent across the teachers and schools and we shall now consider these in more detail. You might find it interesting to note the similarities with some of the recommendations of the NNS (DfEE1999a) while remembering that the practices being described had been developed over the period 1995–98, that is, prior to the publication of the Strategy.

Mental and oral work

At the same time as the National Numeracy Project commenced, we conducted a survey of mathematical practices in Welsh secondary schools (Jones and Tanner

1997). Only half of the heads of department reported mental arithmetic practice to be a regular feature in their Year 7 classes with the frequency of such practice declining sharply after Year 8. In contrast, mental and oral work formed a significant part of the mathematics curriculum in the RSN schools. Opportunities for mental and oral work had been identified in the schemes of work together with suggestions for suitable activities and resources.

We sometimes observed lessons beginning with mental/oral activities although they often formed an integral part of the main teaching activity. It was clear that both teachers and the pupils themselves expected to be able to approach simple problems mentally and that there were occasions when it was considered inappropriate to resort to paper and pencil methods or to a calculator. Mental and oral work was rarely set in a mental-test format but rather was based on activities which emphasised pupil participation and developed quick responses. A popular warm-up in some schools was a variation on the '24-game'. As the class entered the room the teacher would write four numbers on the board. The task was to use those four numbers with any arithmetic operations to create a given total, say 24, in as many ways as possible. For example:

2, 3, 5, 7

TARGET: 24

Possible solutions:

$3 \times 7 + (5–2) = 24$

$3 \times 5 + 7 + 2 = 24$

Pupils were expected to start work on the problem immediately. This helped to settle the class and get them into a mathematical mindset. As soon as a few pupils had found at least one solution the teacher might allow a further minute for thought before brainstorming the solutions on the board and asking the pupils to explain the strategies used to obtain the solution. The task was adapted by changing the target total and by making the generator numbers easier or harder. The pupils enjoyed this activity and became quite competitive at it. Some teachers capitalised on this by splitting the class into teams and, after an initial period for individual thought, used a team discussion to generate as many solutions as possible.

The 24-game can be used to revise and extend the pupils' mental arithmetic skills irrespective of the main teaching topic. Many of the warm-up activities used by the RSN teachers however were directly linked to the main theme of the lesson. At the start of a lesson reinforcing the equivalence of fractions, decimals and percentages a Year 8 class were asked to consider the claim that:

My friend says that because 8 > 4 > 2 then $\frac{1}{8} > \frac{1}{4} > \frac{1}{2}$.
Do you agree? Why?

Similar 'mathematical rumours' can be generated for other areas of mathematics besides number work:

A square has four equal sides.
So does a rhombus.
Therefore a rhombus is a square.

Or, as a warm-up before a lesson on rules of indices:

Does $p^2 = 2p$?
Can it ever? Never?
What about p^3 and $3p$? p^4 and $4p$?

The RSN teachers identified several aims for such activities:

- to help pupils adopt a mathematical mindset – warming them up for the lesson;
- to re-establish a culture of collaborative oral participation by all pupils which would continue throughout the lesson;
- to revise and practise mathematical facts, conventions, and techniques which had been learned in previous lessons;
- to establish new mathematical facts, conventions, and techniques from previously known material;
- to improve speed of mental calculation.

(after Tanner and Jones 2000: 131)

We suspect that you would agree with the first four aims but the demand for speed of calculation might provoke some debate. The NNS requires that pupils in Year 6 know by heart multiplication facts to 10 × 10 and that they can derive quickly the corresponding division facts (DfEE 2001a: 2.2). Pupils in Year 7 are required to know or derive quickly:

- prime numbers less than 30;
- squares of numbers 0.1 to 0.9, and of multiples of 10 to 100, and the corresponding roots;

while pupils in Year 8 are required to know or derive quickly:

- cubes of numbers from 1 to 5, and 10, and the corresponding roots;
- the prime factorisation of numbers to 30.

(from DfEE 2001a: 4.90–91)

Task 3.5:   Recall of mathematical facts
What priority do you place on your pupils knowing the above facts?
What facts do you expect your Year 7 pupils to know or be able to derive quickly?
And your Year 8 pupils?
Are these expectations listed in the scheme of work and agreed across the department?
What priority do you place on speed of recall?

The identification of the key facts and strategies which pupils should know at the end of each year is necessary to ensure progression. Some of the RSN teachers had such expectations written in pupil-friendly language displayed on the classroom walls and pupils were encouraged to set themselves personal targets against these.

We would not dispute that the learning of key mathematical facts can facilitate progress but we are concerned that an over-emphasis on rapid recall and speed of calculation may alienate pupils from mathematics. Sensitivity is needed when rehearsing such skills in a whole-class situation. The RSN teachers had planned differentiated questions to ask the pupils so as to avoid public humiliation and yet offer an appropriate challenge. Games such as 'follow-me' cards can provide practice of recall of required facts in a fun situation. If the cards are coded, perhaps with a dot or cross in a corner, then it is possible to ensure that suitable questions are allocated to the faster or less able pupils. Some teachers used the same set of follow-me cards repeatedly with their classes and timed how long it took to complete the round. Pupils enjoyed trying to beat their time and deliberately tried to memorise the answers to speed up the game. Some teachers extended this further and ran an inter-class challenge with the times for each game listed in a league table. Care has to be taken in such a situation not to let the competitive spirit get out of hand, however. One school reported a pupil being severely teased at break-time for letting the class down by failing to respond quickly enough!

'Show-me' cards were used to ensure privacy of response during whole-class sessions while providing instant feedback to the teacher on the extent of success within the class. Rather than the digit cards used in primary classrooms, several schools have adopted the use of blank laminated cards on which the pupils write their answers in erasable felt pen. This allows a wider range of questions with non-numeric answers to be asked, for example:

Sketch the line $y = 2x - 3$
Sketch a bearing of 217°
Expand $2x(x - 3)$

Their use has even been extended to sixth-form classes:

Sketch the function $y = 2\cos 2x$
Integrate $2x^{-3}$

Attention to the development of numeracy and mental agility should not stop at the end of Key Stage 3.

Main teaching input: questioning and interaction

Many of the RSN teachers claimed to be very traditional in their approaches, although the meaning of this term clearly needed further explanation when it was used to describe a Year 10 lesson involving the use of computer graph plotters to investigate the effect of varying a in curves such as sin ax, $a$cos x, etc! The RSN teachers often started their lessons by posing a problem. For example, after asking pupils out to the board to sketch sin x, cos x and tan x, curves representing related functions, such as 2sin x or cos 2x, would be displayed (without the equations) on the OHP and the class asked to investigate how they might generate these. Starting with a problem engaged the interest of the pupils and gave them an overview of how the particular techniques being taught could be used. Such approaches are reminiscent of the Japanese lesson described in Chapter 2.

Another characteristic feature was the frequency with which pupils were called on to explain and justify their work to the class. One teacher termed this 'the pen of doom' as he gave out the board pen and required pupils to explain their methods as they wrote their solutions on the board. Of course it is not the physical act of pupils coming out to the board that is important here but the quality of the support that the teacher provides to the interaction.

There are two qualitatively different forms of questioning which a teacher may use to support learning: funnelling and focusing (Bauersfeld 1988; Wood 1994). In funnelling it is the teacher, as the expert, who selects the mathematical strategies and controls the decision process to lead the class discourse to a predetermined solution. Funnelling questions often require short answers demonstrating a recall of factual knowledge, for example:

> So, we'll use Pythagoras here. What is 9 squared?
>
> Now, we have to convert our answer. How many metres in a kilometre?

While such questions are useful as part of a warm-up or to ensure all pupils are involved in the task, the decision about what mathematics to use has been taken by the teacher. The pupils' role is to try to follow and fill in the gaps. With this style of questioning the teacher's mathematical thinking is often implicit and the underpinning mathematical structures and connections remain hidden from the pupils unless they choose to analyse the recurring patterns. Pupils in such classrooms tend to concentrate on the superficial features of the problems or algorithm, as this is what appears to be emphasised. Funnelling questions do not help to probe or to develop pupils' thinking.

In focusing, the teacher's questions draw attention to critical features of the problem, which might not yet be understood. The questions are intended to expose areas of potential confusion or uncertainty. The pupil is then expected to resolve perturbations which have thus been created (Wood 1994: 160). Focusing questions require longer, more reasoned responses and provide opportunities for the pupils to rehearse mathematical thinking processes as well as their factual knowledge. To a much greater extent than in funnelling the pupils are responsible for trying to suggest the strategies to be used to solve the problem. Examples of focusing questions include:

> So, we need to find the length of this side of the triangle. What might we try first?
> Can you explain what we should do next?
> When would you solve by substitution rather than elimination?
> Will that method always work?

Such questions are similar in character to those suggested by the KS3 Framework which recommends that pupils should be asked 'to suggest lines of enquiry ... to investigate whether particular cases can be generalised, to seek counter examples ... to expand on their ideas and reasoning ... to compare and then refine their methods' (DfEE 2001a: 1.27).

The RSN teachers viewed mathematics as essentially a problem-solving activity. Problems would be set that could be approached in a variety of ways but not be solved instantly. Pupils were asked to think individually about the problem, then discuss their plans in small groups before reporting back to the whole class. As pupils explained their potential approaches the teacher provided just enough support through focusing questions to ensure progression towards a solution without 'stealing the problem' by dictating how it should be solved. Such support required the teachers to think quickly 'on their feet' as they listened to the pupils' tentative ideas and added just sufficient help to enable them to move on. As one teacher described it:

> You bounce off the kids. You have to be a good listener and a quick thinker. The trick is that no matter how much help you end up giving to make it work, they must still think that they would have done that by themselves. It has to be their plan and not just yours.

If you think back to the lesson extracts discussed in Chapter 2, we consider that one lesson clearly illustrates the use of focusing questions while the second could be characterised as funnelling the pupils. Which lessons would you classify as demonstrating which approach?

We think that the above description of the use of focusing questions could be applied to the Japanese lesson. The USA teacher, however, seems to be funnelling the pupils down a pre-determined path.

A variety of styles of questioning was used by the RSN teachers to scaffold the pupils during their explanations but their emphasis was on focusing. A pupil might be asked to justify a particular strategy or others in the class might be called upon to suggest what step should be taken next. While this might sound quite threatening in the abstract, the teachers had carefully developed a classroom atmosphere which was supportive and the pupils appreciated the value of such interactions for their learning. As one of the pupils expressed it: 'If you can explain it then you know you understand it.'

From our observations and discussions with the RSN teachers we would describe their 'traditional' approaches as signifying teachers actively leading lessons with clear objectives, good pace, a balance between periods of individual work, small group work, and whole-class interaction, and with a high level of pupil involvement. Many of these features are echoed in the recommendations of MEP and the KS3 Framework.

Encouraging reflection

The majority of RSN lessons ended with some type of plenary activity, which offered pupils an opportunity to report back on their findings and to reflect on what they had learned. The plenaries were usually driven by focusing questions from the teacher and many of the classes had obviously learned to anticipate such a session. For example, one class was not surprised when their teacher asked 'Well, how was it for you?'. She accepted comments relating to the difficulty of the work, personal concerns about success and failure, and mathematical patterns which had been identified. However, she used supplementary focusing questions such as:

> Which bits were the hardest? Why?
> What mistakes did you make that you won't do again?
> What warnings would you give to my next class who are going to do the same lesson?
> What was important about today's lesson that you need to remember?

In addition to helping the pupils to reflect on their progress, the answers to such questions provide valuable diagnostic information for the teacher regarding the progress made by pupils and which aspects of the task remained problematic. We will return to the formative aspect of the plenary in Chapter 6.

The RSN pupils expected to have to explain and justify their approaches and findings to the rest of the class. This meant that the explanation itself became the focus of their thinking as they considered it for coherence and rigour. Many psychologists argue that such objectification of thought through speech is associated with the development of reflective awareness and conscious control of mental strategies (e.g. Vygotsky 1978; Prawat 1989a). Our own research indicates that those teachers who were most successful in creating whole-class reflection in plenary activities were the most effective in developing their pupils' mathematical thinking skills (Tanner and Jones 1999a, b). This will be discussed further in later chapters.

Conclusion

Teachers are now being offered a wealth of advice on how to improve standards, some of it contradictory. In this chapter we have attempted to identify the common features and to contrast these with practices exhibited by some other more successful countries. The findings from international and national studies into mathematics teaching indicate that there is no simple recipe for success and that it is the quality of classroom interaction which is the determining feature, not the superficial structure of lessons. The projects described here suggest that effective teaching strategies emphasise the development of pupils' mathematical thinking skills, not just a knowledge of facts. The use of questioning to provoke pupils to think for themselves, and the value of requiring pupils to articulate and reflect on their learning through discussion and plenary activities, are strategies recommended by the framework and by evidence from other projects. In the next two chapters we shall examine how such strategies can be implemented within your classroom.

CHAPTER 4

Making connections and developing concepts

Introduction

The National Numeracy Strategy is founded on four important principles:

Expectations: establishing high expectations for all pupils and setting challenging targets for them to achieve;
Progression: strengthening the transition from Key Stage 2 to Key Stage 3 and ensuring progression in teaching and learning across Key Stage 3;
Engagement: promoting approaches to teaching and learning that engage and motivate pupils and demand their active participation;
Transformation: strengthening teaching and learning through a programme of professional development and practical support.

(DfEE 2001a: 1.2)

At first sight, these principles undeniably represent *a good thing* and few would argue with them. However, for teachers in England the KS3 Framework is far more problematic, representing a reworking of the National Curriculum which reintroduces the excessive level of detail found in older versions but with far greater prescription in both planning and pedagogy. Even so, it is worth pointing out at this stage that the framework is not statutory; its status is clearly defined as 'recommended' on the front of the folder. In fact the framework specifically states that there is:

no point in teachers re-inventing solutions to problems and challenges that are common to all. However, schools should make a professional judgement about this, once they have studied the framework, reflected on their training and reviewed their current practice.

(DfEE 2001a: 1.2).

We are happy to be based in Wales, where the National Assembly emphasises the freedom of teachers to make their own professional judgements about the

Framework. In England, on the other hand, although teachers are not obliged to implement the framework, the rhetoric which has surrounded its introduction has created a social situation which severely constrains their options in reality. In fact teachers in both countries feel pressured to adopt the framework to varying degrees according to their context and the attainment of their pupils.

If your school has GCSE results which are above national norms and a good A level uptake you may feel relaxed about the extent to which you need to adapt your current practices to meet the recommendations in the framework. On the other hand, if your school is in a socially deprived area and a large proportion of the cohort is performing below national expectations, you may feel obliged to implement the framework to protect yourself from criticism when you are called to account for pupils' progression and attainment.

In either case you are likely to be concerned about the extent to which you can use the ideas and strategies in the framework to engage and motivate your pupils, to raise expectations and ensure progression. We hope that this chapter will help you to focus on those aspects of the framework which are most likely to assist you in that aim.

Objectives

By the end of this chapter you should:

- be aware of the structure of the teaching programmes and the extent to which you can plan to ensure that expectations are high in your own school;
- appreciate the importance of planning to make connections between mathematical topics and concepts to deepen understanding;
- understand that children often bring misconceptions to lessons, and that some of these misconceptions are deep-rooted and difficult to modify;
- be aware of strategies to reveal and modify misconceptions;
- understand how aids such as number lines can be used along with interactive teaching approaches, open questions and mathematical language to develop sound mathematical concepts.

The teaching programmes

The framework intends to ensure effective transition from KS2 to KS3, avoiding the drop in standards and expectations that inspectors have often claimed to have found at the start of secondary school. Furthermore, there is an overt intention to establish high expectations for all pupils and to set challenging targets. Thus the yearly teaching programmes demand that although work in Year 7 may include revision of Level 4, it should mainly be pitched at Level 5 or above.

Although many schools will find such demands represent their usual expectations for the average or above-average child, many schools view such expectations as too challenging. Even high-achieving schools in the leafy suburbs may regard the expectation that the vast majority of pupils will be taught at this level as challenging.

Traditionally, the culture of the British education system has been to accept low attainment from a proportion of pupils as inevitable, perhaps due to their low intelligence or poor backgrounds. The framework intends to move us towards a culture more typical of that claimed to be found in high-achieving, Pacific Rim countries, in which low attainment is seen as a need for extra effort to be made to help pupils to catch up (see Chapter 3).

The yearly teaching programmes provide a set of key objectives for each year which represent suggested expectations for the majority of pupils. The aim is that nearly all pupils should experience teaching in certain key areas of mathematics, ensuring that lower-attaining pupils do not fall even further behind. In many ways we would like to regard these key objectives as describing an *entitlement curriculum* for the majority of pupils in mathematics.

Task 4.1: Auditing your current curriculum against the entitlement curriculum

Compare the objectives in the yearly teaching programme for Years 7, 8 and 9 with your current scheme of work. Do you teach the key objectives? Which strand of the curriculum is most in need of revision?

Catching up?

Alongside the ambitious set of key objectives is a *catch-up* programme of 'Springboard' materials targeted at pupils whose attainment is below Level 4 at entry to Year 7. Even if the ambitious targets for KS2 are met in 2002, 25 per cent of pupils will fall into this category.

Perks and Prestage (2001) claim that the concept of 'catch-up' is offensive and denies dignity to low-attaining pupils. We disagree. 'Catch-up' has the potential to offer inclusion and access for more pupils to an entitlement core curriculum.

Springboard is not intended to represent an alternative mathematics curriculum for the less able. The catch-up programme is intended to be additional to the standard curriculum which low-attaining pupils are following alongside their more able peers.

It is crucial that pupils in catch-up groups are not withdrawn from mathematics lessons for their year group since they need to maintain the development of their

> mathematical skills along with their peers. More than most, they need to consolidate new learning as well as catching up on unlearned skills
>
> (DfEE 2001a: 1.34).

The framework suggests that catch-up might occur in tutorials, lunchtime clinics or after school, but also admits the possibility of extra timetabled sessions. To accept the principle of teaching a largely undifferentiated curriculum supported by catch-up sessions for the less able would represent a major culture shift for most secondary schools. Although it is not being trailed as such by politicians, it could be interpreted as a return to comprehensive ideals which have been unfashionable since the 1970s. Furthermore we consider that the principle runs counter to the current pressure to organise teaching in ability sets, in spite of research evidence in favour of mixed groups (e.g. Brown *et al.*1998). Although the framework considers the possibility of sometimes creating 'express' sets for the very able, it suggests that the more able

> ... can be stretched by being given extra challenges and harder problems to do when other pupils are consolidating by offering occasional differentiated group work.
>
> (DfEE 2001a: 1.33)

The Springboard and catch-up materials are designed for use with pupils who are working at Level 3 at the start of Year 7 and can be used in a variety of ways, for example:

- as a complete course of about three hours per week;
- as a supplement to the Year 7 curriculum at various points;
- as an intensive course of 60 minutes per week in one lesson or three 20-minute slots.

> (DfEE 2001b: 22).

The framework is not prescriptive with regard to the organisation of catch-up programmes. Suggestions from the pilot schools are given for both setted and mixed-ability classes. However, we consider that the principles underpinning the framework stance on expectations would be best served through organising teaching around mixed-ability groups, at least in Year 7. In a mixed-ability class, it is easier to ensure that all pupils receive teaching related to the key objectives.

The advice offered for mixed-ability classes includes the suggestion that catch-up materials might be used by a teaching assistant during a 20-minute period of differentiated group work. Alternatively, extra-curricular, supplementary tutorials are suggested with the implication either that children are to be withdrawn from non-core areas of the curriculum, or that imaginative solutions involving classes outside of normal school hours, for example, breakfast or lunchtime classes, are considered (DfEE 2001b). In either case, expectations for lower-attaining pupils would be challenging and the principle of an entitlement curriculum honoured.

The advice offered for schools organised on ability sets includes the suggestion that work for lower sets is based on the catch-up materials 'followed or enhanced by work from the main teaching programme for Year 7'. This sounds like little more than the usual reduced curriculum for low attainers even though the interesting exhortation 'focussing ruthlessly on making progress against the key objectives' is included (DfEE 2001b: 23).

Expectations

There is an unreconciled conflict at the heart of the NNS, with the framework demanding high expectations and expecting the majority of pupils in Year 7 to work at Level 5 while recognising that a large minority of pupils will need to work at consolidating or even attaining targets at Level 4 or below. It is even suggested that lower-attaining pupils in Year 7 'leave higher-level work, particularly algebra, until later in Key Stage 3' (DfEE 2001a: 47).

> And hereby lies the challenge, be it one of accountability or intent. It is blatant nonsense to expect a pupil to learn Level 5 content, as well as learning Level 4 and perhaps consolidating Level 3.
>
> (Perks and Prestage 2001: 31).

While there is an element of truth in this assertion, it is not as straightforward or obvious as it first appears and we beg to differ. Although it is important for children to understand equivalent fractions, to be able to order decimals to three places and to be able to recall multiplication table facts to ten, they do not need to have a full understanding of such basic knowledge in order to begin learning about algebra.

Teachers implementing the NNS in Key Stage 2 often use whole-class teaching strategies with mixed-ability classes. In the RSN project we found many primary school teachers who had been pleasantly surprised at the extent to which low-attaining pupils were often able to develop meaningful knowledge when dealing with concepts which should have been beyond them according to their prior attainment. Although mathematics is often described as a hierarchical subject, in which the development of knowledge must follow a strictly predetermined order, experience suggests that learning (as opposed to teaching) rarely follows such a logical path.

Of course, just because a government department sets ambitious targets for attainment and produces a set of challenging objectives for teachers to use in their planning, it does not follow that pupils' learning will improve. The connection between teaching and learning has never been as simple as curriculum documents often seem to imply (Brown *et al.* 1998). As always, the hardest part is to transform teaching objectives into pupils' learning. The framework focuses on teaching strategies and objectives. To some extent this is to be expected as its aim is to offer guidance about teaching, but the absence of the learner from the document is a cause for concern.

> The learner is not mentioned ... at some stage you will have to stand up for the learner ... This approach through detailed objectives can lead to the reinforcement of the race through the curriculum and the model of progression as a netting-in as many topics as possible.
>
> (Perks and Prestage 2001: 12–13)

We are sympathetic to such criticisms, believing that the learning process and the needs of the individual learner must be our main concerns if teaching is to be effective. However, there is always a tension between the individual learner's development of mathematical concepts and the externally imposed targets provided by a curriculum and its assessment structure. This tension can often be productive, motivating the learner and driving progression. Unfortunately, it can also be counter-productive, leading to teaching for instrumental understanding, purely for the purpose of passing a test, rather than aiming for the relational understanding demanded for numeracy (Skemp 1976).

The distinction between the two possible forms of mathematical understanding is a significant one. Teachers aiming for limited instrumental knowledge focus on teaching mechanical processes or algorithms by rote, without considering the mathematical reasoning behind them. Teachers aiming for relational understanding want children to understand the underlying concepts so that they can use their knowledge out of context, adapting it to new situations and inventing their own processes and strategies based on their mathematical understanding. It seems obvious to us that the forms of numeracy we discussed in Chapter 1 demand relational understanding.

Although instrumental teaching appears to give quick success when assessment is through standard text-book questions, it does not help in the development of numeracy. Furthermore, GCSE and National Curriculum examiners are very skilled at asking questions which demand relational understanding. For example, consider

$$53*4 - 1*8* = 4097$$

Pupils who have learned a standard algorithm for subtraction, without considering *why* it works or developing any sense of place value, would be lost with such a question.

In the end, although learning in school is a social experience occurring in classes and groups, children are individuals and develop their own personal understandings of mathematical constructs as they interpret shared experiences in the light of their own backgrounds. If teaching is to be effective, children must be able to relate its content to their prior knowledge in a meaningful way. The 'principle of engagement' is significant in ensuring that pupils are actively involved in their learning and that teachers are adapting their teaching strategies to connect with the knowledge which individual children actually have rather than that which is 'expected' of them.

Making connections

A research study into effective teachers of numeracy classified primary school teachers into three broad groupings according to their beliefs: connectionist, transmission and discovery (Askew *et al.* 1997). Although these categories may be criticised for being caricatures of the beliefs underpinning both discovery and transmission models of learning, few would argue with the characteristic features of good teaching which they ascribe to the most successful teachers, who they described as 'connectionist'. Similar features were observed in the lessons of the most successful teachers in the RSN project (Tanner *et al.* 1999). Based on the results of these studies, we claim that successful teachers of numeracy:

- use interactive approaches based on dialogue and discussion to explore under-standing;
- recognise pupils' misconceptions as issues to be worked on explicitly and as opportunities for learning;
- discuss different methods of calculation, refining pupils' methods to encour-age efficiency and effectiveness;
- emphasise the connections between mathematical ideas and between differ-ent aspects of the mathematics curriculum;
- integrate problem solving and using and applying mathematics with their teaching of mathematical concepts;
- challenge pupils to reason, justify and, where possible, prove results in math-ematics.

(Askew *et al.* 1997: 31–2; Tanner and Jones 2000b: 160–3)

Planning

The Key Stage 3 Framework suggests a structure for the year based on long-term, medium-term and short-term plans. Long-term planning should be based on what the framework describes as the 'yearly teaching programmes', which are in fact a list of ambitious objectives for each year. The objectives are supported by a 'supplement of examples', which exemplify specific outcomes which pupils should achieve. Although the framework acknowledges that 'some existing schemes of work will be easily adapted', the 'new emphases to planning and teaching mathematics' imply that departments will have to do more than simply check their current scheme of work for coverage (DfEE 2001a: 1.51).

Examples of medium-term planning charts are provided to indicate how units of work might be constructed and timed for each year. The charts are helpful in demonstrating how such a large set of objectives might be met within a year, while maintaining balance between the strands. However, they also serve to emphasise how crowded the curriculum has become and how quickly teachers are expected to cover it. The danger is that this might encourage a race through a syllabus which is based on only instrumental understanding. Furthermore, the use of behavioural objectives tends to present a view of mathematics as a series of isolated items of knowledge. This is not the intention of the authors.

> Mathematics is not a group of isolated topics or learning objectives but an interconnected web of ideas, and the connections may not be at all obvious to pupils. Providing different examples and activities and expecting pupils to make the links is not enough; pupils need to be shown them and reminded about work in earlier lessons.
>
> (DfEE 2001a: 1.46)

The planning charts indicate some of the links between the strands and each chart demands that the use and application of mathematics is integrated into each unit. However, good planning is required if mathematical concepts are to be learned in a way which demonstrates the links which exist between the different strands of the subject. Furthermore, there is a danger that too close a focus on the specific objectives associated with the teaching of mathematical content knowledge will lead to the more difficult-to-describe process skills of mathematics being either missed out or addressed only as an afterthought.

The framework offers advice on how to ensure that connections are made.

- As far as possible, present each topic as a whole, rather than as a fragmented progression of small steps ...
- Bring together related ideas across strands...
- Help pupils to appreciate that important mathematical ideas permeate different aspects of the subject ...

- Use opportunities for generalisation, proof and problem solving to help pupils to appreciate mathematics as a unified subject ...

(DfEE 2001a: 1.46)

Task 4.2:   Reviewing a topic

Choose a topic from within your scheme of work which might be in need of review.
To what extent does your approach follow the advice above?
Consider the examples provided for your topic in the supplement of examples. To what extent do you meet the expectations of the framework?

If you have determined that a topic or unit within your scheme of work is in need of review, we suggest that you should begin by forming an overview of the topic. You need to be clear about the way the objectives for the year build on earlier work and lead on to higher levels. You also need to be aware of the extent to which the knowledge and skills developed in this unit can support or practise material from other programmes of study or strands within the curriculum. You should be alert to the possibility of supporting or developing some of the big ideas in mathematics such as inverse operation, generalisation or proof.

Some help is provided by the medium-term planning charts, which indicate where some backward links can be made, reminding pupils of earlier work and using prior knowledge when teaching a new unit of work. The charts deliberately make the link between some key concepts which should be taught together, such as fractions, decimals, percentages, ratio and proportion.

Examining the key objectives for the year in question and then tracking your topic backwards and forwards through the years may help you to gain a sense of its progression. The teaching programme for each year shows the objectives for all the strands on one double page and provides page references to the supplement of examples. You may be able to use this summary of the curriculum to help you to identify which objectives you hope to teach within the unit and the most significant links which you hope to make.

The teaching which occurs within mathematics should contribute to learning across the curriculum. In particular, mathematics has a special role to play in the teaching of key skills and thinking skills, which we list below:

Key Skills

Application of number
Communication
Improving own learning and performance
Information technology
Problem solving
Working with others

Thinking Skills

Information processing
Reasoning
Enquiry
Creativity
Evaluation

(From DfEE: http://www.nc.uk.net/learn.html)

Many of these skills are closely associated with the targets in Using and Applying Mathematics and should be integrated into your teaching in every unit. The framework reports that:

> Some schools have devoted one lesson in each six-hour unit to 'using and applying mathematics' and 'thinking skills'. These schools have reported spin-offs in other lessons when pupils apply the problem-solving skills that have been drawn to their attention in the focused teaching.
>
> (DfEE 2001a: 1.53)

In the Practical Applications of Mathematics Project (Tanner and Jones 1995b; 2000b) we also found that the deliberate, interactive teaching of mathematical thinking skills accelerates mathematical development. We will discuss the teaching of mathematical thinking in more detail in Chapter 5.

The Framework suggests that you note the objectives, which will be the main focus for the unit, making sure that you include some 'using and applying' or 'thinking skills' objectives in your list. You should begin with those that are appropriate for the middle attainers, that is the ones from the teaching programme for that year. Appropriate objectives for the more- and less-able pupils are then selected from the years above and below, creating a unit description expressed as core, extensions and simplifications. The supplement of examples is especially useful at this point as it includes examples for each objective. The examples for Years 7, 8 and 9 are provided next to each other on a double page, making it easy to analyse the intended progression over the key stage and the levels of differentiation which might be appropriate.

Although teaching is sometimes seen as a process of breaking down a complex task into a series of simpler tasks which can gradually build on each other before being reconstituted into the full task, this is not always the best way to proceed. If taken to an extreme it can lead to a topic losing coherence as it becomes a 'fragmented progression of small steps ...' (DfEE 2001a: 1.46) which seem pointless in isolation from the rest of the subject. The teaching of algebra has often been criticised for this fault with, for example, lessons being focused on isolated skills such as the collection of like terms (Cockcroft 1982).

Task 4.3:   The simplification of linear expressions by the collection of like terms

If you were to focus on this objective from Year 7, how would you teach it to form links with other areas of mathematics?

We suggest that you should begin by examining the relevant pages from the Supplement of Examples (DfEE 2001a: 4.116–17). We like to focus on the reasoning behind the rules which are taught, and the power which results from the simplification of expressions, by starting with numerical examples such as:

Calculate mentally: $3 \times 27 + 7 \times 27$

$$\frac{6 \times 15}{8 \times 15}$$

Such examples can be used very effectively in a mental warm-up. In the resulting discussions of pupils' own methods, links can be made to earlier work on order of operations, mental strategies and simplification of fractions. This has the advantage of keeping some key skills and techniques 'simmering' as well as giving access to children's thinking processes.

It is important to recognise that as well as teaching about the content knowledge of mathematics, all pupils should have:

- frequent opportunities to explain, reason and justify their mathematical thinking;
- opportunities to solve problems, some of which may have extended solutions or lead to other problems, and where the focus is on the problem rather than on a particular range of techniques.

(DfEE 2001a: 1.52)

Opportunities for pupils to explain and justify their mathematical thinking should arise in every lesson. Making connections means more than just linking the different branches of mathematical knowledge which we teach. It is also about making connections between the concepts which are being taught and the prior knowledge and concepts which the child brings to the lesson. Some of the knowledge which the child brings to the lesson will be real-world knowledge, which all too often fails to make contact with the official school knowledge which is being taught.

Many pupils (and adults) seem able to hold two parallel sets of knowledge: one which applies to school mathematics and the other to real life. Numeracy is about being able to apply mathematics in problem situations. The research evidence is clear that many people are unable to apply their school-taught mathematics in real-life situations, relying instead on naive, intuitive methods which are often based on misconceptions (Lave 1988; Berry and Graham 1991; Nunes *et al.* 1993).

Knowledge which fails to connect with children's prior or real-world knowledge is built on sand, easily forgotten and rarely applied. Even worse, because they often remain disconnected from school and undisturbed by teaching, misconceptions are extremely resilient and are recalled long after school-taught methods have been forgotten.

Misconceptions

Large-scale studies conducted in the 1970s (Hart 1981) and 1980s (Foxman 1985) revealed that identical incorrect responses were given by many of the pupils. For example, 51 per cent of twelve-year-old pupils thought that dividing 16 by 20 was impossible (Hart 1988: 20). Such responses are more likely to be the result of common misconceptions than coincidental carelessness. More recent surveys, both national and international (see, for example, Jones and Tanner 1997; Keys *et al.* 1996; Williams and Ryan 2000) indicate that pupils continue to exhibit similar errors and difficulties.

Misconceptions may arise in a number of ways, for example:

- through developing a conceptual structure which is flawed, e.g. reading 2.75 as two point seventy five through misunderstanding place value;
- by the over-generalisation of a rule, principle or concept, e.g. $\frac{2}{3} + \frac{3}{4} = \frac{5}{7}$ through extending the rules learned for whole numbers to fractions;
- through the systematic application of a flawed procedure, e.g. always subtracting the smaller digit from the larger within the subtraction algorithm;
- by misinterpreting notation, e.g. thinking that '=' means 'makes' or 'work out the answer';
- by misreading diagrams or tables, e.g. by assuming that angles which look equal in a sketch diagram are equal;
- by using prototypes of concepts, e.g. thinking that a rectangle cannot be a square;
- by using colloquial as opposed to mathematical language, e.g. confusing 'divide into halves' and 'divide by a half';
- over-generalising additive strategies to multiplicative structures, e.g. in ratio and proportion problems such as enlarging a 4 by 6 rectangle to a 6 by x, where pupils calculate x to equal 8 by addition rather than $x = 9$ by multiplication.
  (see Hart 1980; Greer and Mulhern 1989; Bell 1993a, b; DfEE 1998; Ryan and Williams 2000)

Dealing with misconceptions

We mentioned above that effective teachers view pupils' misconceptions as something to be worked on directly and as offering opportunities for learning. But how should a teacher deal with misconceptions like those listed above? You might imagine that careful re-teaching with a clearer explanation would remedy the situation. However, a clear, logical exposition is not usually enough to remedy a misconception.

Pupils try to make sense of teaching, accepting those aspects of the lesson which fit into their existing ways of thinking and often ignoring knowledge which does not seem to fit. Only occasionally do they modify their existing mental structures to accommodate new knowledge. Such restructuring is hard work requiring deliberate mental effort and a recognition by the pupils that their existing concepts are inadequate in some way.

We have often met children who listen patiently to a teacher's explanation of how to follow a particular algorithm, only to revert to their old, imperfect approach as soon as the teacher leaves them. On being asked why the reply is often: 'I don't do it that way.'

This presents teachers with a difficult task. Pupils will not spontaneously volunteer that they have a misconception; if you have a misconception, you don't usually know you are wrong!

One of the many advantages to be found in interactive teaching approaches is that if children are expected to articulate their thinking, you might gain some insight into their thinking processes and begin to understand what the misconceptions are that you have to overcome.

Courses in initial teacher education in England and Wales are now required to teach about some of the most common errors which children make, and as teachers gain experience they usually develop a deeper understanding of the misconceptions which underpin such errors. There is now a wealth of research evidence into misconceptions which you can consult (e.g. Hart 1980; Keys *et al.* 1996; Williams and Ryan 2000). However, how should you use such knowledge to develop effective teaching strategies?

Task 4.4: Dealing with misconceptions arising in the addition of decimal fractions
What misconceptions have you encountered when teaching addition of decimals?
How should teachers plan to deal with such misconceptions?

Some teachers use their knowledge of the likely misconceptions to help them to set questions which help children to avoid the possible pitfalls. Children often make the mistake of lining up the right-hand column when adding decimals, instead of placing the numerals in their appropriate columns. You might try to avoid the problem by ensuring that most of your examples had identical numbers of decimal places, or even writing the questions with the numbers already in columns. For example:

27.25 + 48.54 =   5.6 + 3.9 + 4.2 =   23.45
                                                    14.56 +
                                                    ———

We have seen far too many text books which use precisely this strategy! It often results in a quiet lesson with apparently successful results in that children often answer most of the questions correctly. Unfortunately if a pupil had the misconception listed above, at best that misconception will remain undisturbed at the end of the lesson. Even if the teacher talked about place value during the exposition, the pupils can safely ignore that and gain success by using a limited strategy based on a misconception. The misconception is then reinforced.

We think that rather than steer pupils safely around the pitfalls, good teachers should deliberately design their examples to place pifalls directly in pupils' paths. For example:

> 5.07 + 1.6 + 43
> 12.5 – 4.93
> Jo says that 5.23 – 3.7 = 5.14. What should the answer be? What mistakes did Jo make?
> Add one-tenth to 6.9.
> Write down the most difficult question you can think of which has an answer of 3.6.

Of course, the second set of questions is harder than the first, and if your class are used to being taught in an instrumental way they may have difficulties dealing with them. However, that is what teachers are there for! We do not suggest that pupils attempt such exercises unaided in the first instance. The questions could provide a good introduction to a discussion on place value in which children offered alternative strategies for their solution and were encouraged to justify their approaches.

We suggest that there are six steps to follow when teaching a lesson to address misconceptions:

1. Identify the most common misconceptions in the topic to be taught by reflecting on your past experience and reading research on the topic.
2. Devise a short set of questions which expose that misconception directly. Try to write questions which are sufficiently open to allow an element of discussion.
3. Ask pupils out to the board to explain their answers to the class and justify their reasoning.
4. Intervene to support pupils' explanations, stimulate discussion and focus the attention of the class on key points.
5. Provide an opportunity to attempt problems involving the most likely misconceptions individually.
6. Demand reflection in a plenary, discussing answers, asking pupils to summarise the key points, identifying likely errors and possible applications.

Of course not every lesson is targeted at suspected misconceptions. Effective teaching should help children to form robust concepts from the start.

Developing mathematical concepts

Much of the work which pupils do in mathematics lessons involves following algorithms or procedures which teachers have demonstrated. Procedural knowledge is the 'know-how' of mathematics and is clearly a significant aspect of the subject. Conceptual knowledge, on the other hand, involves 'knowing that' (Ryan and Williams 2000) and perhaps we might add, 'knowing why'.

If procedural knowledge is to make an effective contribution to numeracy it must be underpinned by sound conceptual knowledge. To be numerate requires the application of procedures out of context, the modification of procedures to fit new situations and the justification and communication of results. All of these demand a sound conceptual basis from which procedures can be adapted, applied and discussed.

Discussion-based interactive teaching approaches can contribute significantly to the development of conceptual knowledge. This is particularly so if pupils are asked to use mathematical language to talk about their own ideas, listen carefully to the ideas of others, and engage in mathematical argumentation and collective reflection.

Although children form their own versions of mathematical concepts, they usually construct them around the metaphors and analogies which are used by teachers to introduce them to the abstract ideas of mathematics. It is important to realise that these are not all equally effective in developing children's conceptual structures. For example we think that it is important to avoid the use of metaphors or analogies which may lead to the pupils forming restricted concepts which are not generalisable to more advanced mathematics and have to be unlearned later. Restricted concepts may sometimes represent prototypes of the true concept and can be further developed later, but others are dead-ends which can lead to misconceptions in the future.

Consider our earlier discussion (Task 4.3). Many text books approach this topic by using the analogy which we refer to as 'fruit salad' algebra, interpreting

$$3a + 5b + 2a - 3b =$$

as three apples add five bananas add two apples take away three bananas 'makes' five apples and two bananas.

We think that the 'fruit salad' analogy is a dead end, representing 'quick and dirty' teaching which keeps the class quiet and gives a set of correct answers but fails to make mathematical sense or develop algebraic understanding. Letters in algebra represent *variables*; they can take a range of values, and represent numbers not objects or pieces of fruit. We still find the original analysis of this area by Küchemann (in Hart 1981) extremely helpful in understanding the misconceptions children have in this area. Consider this question taken from that research:

Task 4.5:   *Why you should avoid fruit salad algebra*
Pens cost 12p each and rubbers cost 10p each.
Write an expression which shows how many of each I can buy for £1.
One boy wrote 5p + 4r = 100p
What do you think he means by p*?*

We think he means that one solution is that you can buy 5 pens and 4 rubbers, so the first *p* means pens rather than the number of pens (or even pence). We think that you should avoid using 'fruit salad' analogies, to avoid this 'letter = object' misconception. It also helps during the early stages if you avoid using the initial letter of an object as the variable.

Even analogies which are mathematically sound can cause problems when extended beyond their usefulness. For example, one of the most common analogies used for the concept of fraction is shading out a pie.

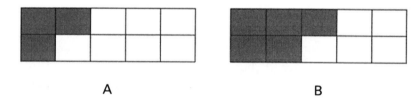

A   B

Figure 4.1   The use of shading to represent fractions

Clearly rectangle A represents the fraction ³⁄₁₀. Rectangle B represents the fraction ⁵⁄₁₀. So far so good, the analogy seems to help. Unfortunately, if we try to move on and add the two fractions the analogy raises some difficulties. Clearly we have 8 shaded pieces and 20 pieces in total, so the sum should be ⁸⁄₂₀. Thus the concept we have encouraged children to construct leads naturally to the common fractions misconception 'add tops and add bottoms'. Representations of mixed numbers are also difficult using this analogy.

Shaded areas are not incorrect mathematically, and the apparent failure of the analogy in this case can be argued through. In fact we observed a teacher from the RSN project using this example as the basis of very interesting discussion with able Year 8 pupils, effectively challenging some of their misconceptions. However, we would not wish to begin an *initial* discussion of addition of fractions from here! We think that would be pushing the analogy beyond its usefulness.

The NNS encourages work on fractions, decimals and percentages using the number line. There are obvious advantages to this representation through its analogy to the concrete, everyday processes of measuring with rulers. (In fact we often find old-fashioned rulers which have scales in quarters, eighths and sixteenths of an inch in addition to fifths and tenths very useful as teaching aids for fractions!)

The advantage of the number line/measurement analogy is that fractions, decimals and percentage representations of number can all be seen easily as alternative representations of number, and addition and subtraction of these forms as a natural extension to the analogy. As you will see in Chapter 7, the number line can be used very effectively as a basis for whole-class interaction and discussion, making connections and developing concepts.

Conclusion

The Framework sets challenging expectations for the majority of pupils. In many ways it represents an attempt to change the culture of English education away from one in which the failure of a proportion of pupils is expected to one in which success is expected for the majority. We welcome this as a return to comprehensive and inclusive principles although we do not underestimate the challenge involved.

We regard the objectives in the framework as an *entitlement curriculum* for the majority of pupils. We also consider that the concept of catch-up, which necessarily underpins the *entitlement curriculum*, should be a positive feature of education for low-attaining pupils. Catch-up has the potential to offer inclusion and access for more pupils to an entitlement core curriculum.

However, we share the concerns which have been expressed about the objectives and yearly teaching programmes leading to a race through the curriculum, emphasising the instrumental learning of procedural knowledge rather than the development of relational understanding.

We have emphasised the need for pupils to make connections between different aspects of the mathematics which they learn including learning to use and apply their knowledge in problem-solving situations. This includes making connections with their prior learning and their real-world knowledge in order to develop conceptual understanding.

Misconceptions are common and very resilient. We suggest that you address common misconceptions directly rather than attempt to avoid them. For learning to occur:

- pupils need to realise something is not quite right, that their current approach is not working;

- the failure of their own approach must be significant and the issue important enough to the pupils for them to make the effort to change;
- just telling them is not enough; you need to help them to develop new concepts for themselves.

In order to meet these conditions, we suggest that it is necessary to select problems which are sufficiently complex to allow pupils to engage in mathematical discussion and argumentation. Some of the best lessons that we saw in the RSN project began with a problem for discussion. There can be no genuine discussion or argument without an issue to debate. Problem solving should be at the heart of most lessons.

CHAPTER 5

Numeracy, mathematical thinking skills and problem solving

Introduction

In Chapter 1 we discussed the nature of numeracy and how it relates to mathematics. Your first thoughts on this might have been that numeracy referred to those parts of the mathematics curriculum which involve number. However, the definition given in the framework indicates that numeracy is associated with positive beliefs and attitudes towards mathematics, a deep understanding of how mathematical processes work and an ability to apply such knowledge to the solution of problems and the learning of new mathematics.

It is of little use merely to be able to reproduce mathematical facts or techniques. Knowledge, of Pythagoras' theorem for example, is not an end in itself. Similarly, it is not sufficient for students only to be able to complete successfully the exercise at the end of the chapter. Knowledge is of value only if you can apply it to the solution of other tasks.

To be described as numerate, pupils need to be able to apply the mathematics which they have learned, to solve unfamiliar problems set in a range of contexts. The problems might lie in another area of mathematics, in the learning of a new mathematical topic, or arise in contexts from outside school. One reason that mathematics is a core subject in the curriculum is because it is needed to solve practical problems in other subjects, in everyday life and in the workplace. Knowledge of mathematical facts and techniques are, however, only some of the tools which pupils need to acquire as part of the process of learning to think mathematically. They must also be confident and willing to apply their existing knowledge to solve novel problems.

The best mathematics lessons have a problem at their centre which is sufficiently difficult or complex to prevent the pupil from immediately applying an obvious and well-known routine that leads directly to its solution. The best problems demand that pupils pause to think and consider a range of possible alternative strategies before selecting which mathematical techniques might be worth exploring or developing. All too often, however, mathematics is taught in a closed and directive fashion with interesting, challenging problems left until the end of the exercise. Yet research suggests that posing a problem at the start of the lesson provides a context for learning and enhances pupils' numeracy (Stigler *et al.* 1999).

Our pupils need to leave school with knowledge and skills that they are able to apply to real-life situations not just schoolroom exercises. They must be interested, engaged and motivated, ready to continue learning for the rest of their lives, able to take responsibility for their own learning and not always dependent on spoon-feeding by teachers.

In this chapter we focus on the thinking skills which are necessary for the use and application of mathematics. Such thinking skills do not develop spontaneously and we examine teaching approaches which build pupils' confidence, increase motivation, and lead them to becoming effective problem solvers and lifelong learners.

Objectives

By the end of this chapter you should:

- understand the importance of incorporating a range of challenging problems into your teaching;
- know which teaching strategies have been shown to be effective in teaching children to solve problems;
- understand the importance of metacognition for problem solving;
- appreciate the value of activities which encourage collective and individual reflection by pupils.

What do pupils need to become good problem solvers?

The use and application of mathematics is intended to permeate the teaching of mathematics across the four content areas of the curriculum. Pupils have to be taught, for example, how to select the mathematics to use in a task, to monitor their approaches, to explain and justify their reasoning and to communicate their findings clearly (DfEE/QCA 1999; ACCAC 2000). Such abilities are examples of mathematical-thinking skills.

> *Task 5.1:   Characteristics of good problem solvers*
> *Before reading on, think of a pupil or a colleague who is good at solving mathematical problems. Try to list the main features which contribute to their problem-solving success.*

In order to solve problems pupils need some mathematical knowledge, including a repertoire of techniques. This much is uncontentious. For such knowledge to be of use in solving problems, however, it must be *accessible* to the pupils. That is, they must be aware that they have that knowledge and also realise that it would be of use for this problem. To facilitate this, the *connections* between mathematical topics must be known explicitly by the pupils. We have all met pupils who can successfully complete pages of exercises demonstrating mastery of a technique, converting percentages to fractions for example, yet who fail to realise that the application of that technique in a different context would enable them to solve a task. It is one thing to solve word problems at the end of an exercise where the task is to work out how to translate the question into the mathematical technique you have just been studying. It is quite another to be faced with a task where no such clues are given and you have to select how to approach it from all the mathematics you know.

As we discussed in the last chapter, pupils often have naive, intuitive approaches which are quite different from those taught in school. Some of these methods are very effective within the context in which they are used, but fail to be useful when pupils are faced with more formal school methods. This may be because their methods are flawed, being built on misconceptions and misunderstandings. Alternatively, it might be that they fail to make connections and to generalise their strategies within the school context. For example, studies of young Brazilian street children who make their living selling produce in street markets show that they have very well-developed strategies for mental arithmetic calculations, yet when faced with equivalent tasks in school they fail to utilise this knowledge to complete them successfully (Nunes *et al.* 1993). School practices do not always capitalise fully on pupils' prior knowledge.

The accessibility of knowledge and pupils' awareness of the connections between topics can be enhanced by requiring pupils to talk about their ideas and tasks. A number of studies have shown that articulation of pupils' thoughts increases their awareness of what they know and helps them to make connections between the new knowledge and their existing concepts and techniques (see, for example, Prawat 1989a, 1989b; Cobb and Bauersfeld 1995; Glaser 1995). During the pupils' explanations the teacher can gain insight into their thinking. Pupils' attention can be focused on important mathematical points and any misconceptions may be challenged and corrected. The need for pupils to explain and discuss their thinking is emphasised throughout the National Frameworks (DfEE 1999; DfEE 2001a). Unfortunately however, even if pupils possess accessible, connected, mathematical knowledge, this is not sufficient. Pupils must also be able to choose to use that knowledge and to apply it efficiently.

We wonder if you recognise any of the following scenarios? We have sometimes struggled with a task and failed, only to exclaim when we saw the solution, 'Oh, I never thought to do it that way!' We knew the necessary mathematics but we didn't *think to use it* for this problem. Or, on other occasions, having thought of an approach we persist with it doggedly, page after page, even though it is leading us nowhere? Or those times when on being presented with a problem you look at it in resignation as a little voice in your head says 'There's no way you're going to be able do this; you know you can't do statistics.' and you resort to talking about last night's TV instead! Good problem solvers do not necessarily know more mathematics than novice problem solvers but *they use their knowledge in different ways and have greater confidence in themselves as mathematicians* (Schoenfeld, 1985).

These two characteristics help to determine whether pupils are to be successful problem solvers. First, they must have skills relating to the problem-solving process. They must be able to analyse their own knowledge, to determine a range of possible approaches to the problem and then to select the most likely to pursue. They must monitor the process, rejecting their initial strategy if it seems to be failing. They must evaluate any solution they reach, comparing it with the initial problem, reflecting back on the process and learning from the experience. Second, and equally important, is the affective side of problem solving. They must have the confidence to use and apply their mathematics without direct instruction from the teacher, i.e. an inclination to tackle novel problems. Both these aspects have been described as higher-order because they involve pupils knowing about their own knowledge and controlling the way they think. You will also see them referred to as metacognitive knowledge and skills (meta = higher, cognitive = thinking).

The role of metacognition in problem solving

Metacognition refers to the knowledge and control which you have of your own thinking (Flavell 1976; Brown 1987). There are two elements to metacognition:

- metacognitive knowledge: knowing what you know
- metacognitive skill: your ability to monitor and control your own thinking processes.

(after Flavell 1976: 232)

Metacognitive knowledge involves not only your awareness of what mathematics you know but also your beliefs about how likely you are to perform well in a given situation. This self-knowledge, whether accurate or not, is heavily influenced by your previous experiences in similar situations; it underpins your mathematical self-confidence and thus strongly influences your mathematical behaviour. For example, if a problem appears to need the use of fractions but all your previous attempts at fractions have met with failure, then you are unlikely to wish to attempt the problem nor to persevere when you encounter difficulties.

Your self-knowledge is also influenced by your beliefs about the nature of mathematics. If your normal mathematical diet consists of single-stage problems where the answer is always obtained within a few moments after following an approach provided by the teacher then you will be ill-equipped to cope with the demands of novel problems.

Metacognitive skill describes how well you employ your knowledge: how you choose to explore the problem, plan your strategies, monitor progress during the task and evaluate the outcomes. It helps to avoid the selection of ineffective strategies or the pursuit of dead ends and helps you to cope when you get stuck.

Research has shown that good problem solvers have high levels of metacognitive knowledge and skill (Schoenfeld 1985; Gray 1991; Tanner and Jones 1994). They are aware of their mathematical strengths and weaknesses and try to select techniques with which they are confident. They consider a variety of possible strategies before deciding on their approach. As they work on the problem they monitor their progress against their plan. They are able to recognise when they are following a dead-end and to re-start with an alternative approach. Finally, they are able to evaluate their performance and compare their strategies with those of others.

The Programme for International Student Assessment (PISA), which was discussed in Chapter 2, assessed the capacity of 15-year-old pupils to use their knowledge and skills to meet real-life challenges rather than just regurgitate facts or follow algorithms. PISA reports that the aspect of learning most closely associated with performance is 'controlling the learning process' (OECD 2001). Successful students:

- figure out exactly what they need to learn;
- work out as they go what concepts they still have not really understood;
- look for additional information when they do not understand;
- force themselves to check whether they remember what they have learned;
- make sure they have remembered the most important things.

(OECD 2001)

These strategies are processes which are metacognitive in character and underpin successful problem solving and the learning of new mathematical knowledge. As you will see later in this chapter and in Chapter 6, they are developed most effectively through techniques which are based on collective reflection and formative assessment.

The processes and strategies underpinning problem solving have been categorised by the framework into five 'thinking skills':

- *Information processing*, e.g. identifying what information is needed to solve the problem, analysing relationships, interpreting results, drawing conclusions.

- *Enquiry*, e.g. defining the problem, making predictions, making connections across different aspects of mathematics, explaining and justifying conclusions.
- *Creative*, e.g. generating alternative approaches, using differing representations, making conjectures and hypotheses, generalising findings.
- *Reasoning*, e.g. breaking the problem down into simpler steps, working systematically, constructing logical arguments, seeking counter examples.
- *Evaluation*, e.g. selecting efficient strategies, reviewing progress, checking solutions, evaluating effectiveness of approaches.
  (adapted from DfEE 2001a: 20–2)

Although such strategies form an essential part of a pupil's mathematical repertoire for effective problem solving, we do not think they describe the full picture. If you think back to the pupils you identified at the start of this chapter as being good at problem solving, we suggest that while they would be likely to have skills in these areas, they would also possess other knowledge and skills in addition to those on the DfEE list. In particular we think they would be aware of their mathematical strengths and weaknesses and be able to monitor and control their thought processes. You might consider such metacognitive knowledge and skills to be implied within the 'evaluation' thinking skill, but they are not stated overtly.

Reflection is a key feature in the development of such thinking skills. Every problem solution ought to be an opportunity for learning. The learning might relate to the particular result achieved, or to the strategy which led to the solution, but it might also be about the way the individual monitored and controlled the problem solving process itself.

Some pupils appear to be naturally 'mindful'; they need little prompting or teaching to develop such knowledge and skills. Other pupils need far more help. Research suggests that lower-ability pupils tend to lack metacognitive awareness and skills (Cardelle-Elawar 1992; 1995). However, the studies show that all pupils can acquire such knowledge and skills when appropriately taught. The next question we need to consider is how can we best teach pupils to be mindful?

Task 5.2:   Teaching pupils to be good problem solvers
In what ways does your department teach pupils to develop the metacognitive knowledge and thinking skills described above?
How does your department teach the knowledge and skills demanded in Attainment Target One: 'Using and Applying Mathematics'?

Thinking skills are certainly not developed if the only problems pupils encounter are based on the repetition of an algorithm which has just been demonstrated! Pupils need a 'good diet' of challenges, problems and investigations to resolve which includes:

- problems and applications that extend content beyond what has just been taught;
- problems in a range of contexts, from both the real world and the world of pure mathematics, some with a unique solution and others with several possible solutions;
- activities that develop deductive reasoning and concepts of proof;
- occasional opportunities to sustain thinking by tackling more complex problems.
(adapted from DfEE 2001a: 1.20)

However, this advice should not be novel for most teachers. It echoes that which was given in the Cockcroft report (1982), *Mathematics from 5 to 16* (DES 1985), and the non-statutory guidance to the National Curriculum (NCC 1989). If your department has an effective strategy for teaching the knowledge, skills and processes of Ma1, you should be well-positioned for teaching the key objectives and thinking skills described in the framework. In most areas, the framework attempts to simplify and clarify the principles and aims which had underpinned earlier guidance, rather than to initiate a new direction. However, the search for simplicity and an over-emphasis on behavioural objectives has resulted in a lack of subtlety in what is a complex domain.

Although many teachers had found the language of Ma1 difficult to interpret at first (Tanner 1992) we think that by the Millennium most had come to terms with the complexity of the issues involved and were providing a high-quality experience for their pupils as a result. As you may recall from Chapter 2, the PISA study reported children from the UK to be attaining a standard significantly higher than the OECD average on tasks which demanded the application of mathematics to authentic problem situations (OECD 2001).

Task 5.3:   Comparing the key objectives with the strands in Ma1
The three strands in Ma1 are Application/Strategies, Communication, and Reasoning/Logic/Proof.
Examine the key objectives for 'Using and applying mathematics to solve problems' from the teaching programmes in Years 7, 8 and 9 and compare these with the old strands of Ma1.
Examine the examples offered for this strand in Section 4 of the framework. Do they redefine the nature and purpose of Ma1?

The match between the strands of Ma1 and the objectives in the teaching programmes is not a perfect one, although many of the main features remain. We offer our analysis in Table 5.1 below. For simplicity we have only listed the key objectives and in the case of overlap we have repeated the objective.

Table 5.1   Comparing the strands of Ma1 with the key objectives of 'Using and applying mathematics to solve problems'

	Year 7	Year 8	Year 9
Applications and strategies	Solve word problems and investigate in a variety of contexts Break a complex calculation into simpler steps, choosing and using appropriate operations and methods	Identify the necessary information to solve a problem	Solve substantial problems by breaking them into simpler tasks using a range of efficient techniques methods and resources, including ICT
Communication	Explain and justify methods and conclusions	Represent problems and interpret solutions in algebraic, geometric or graphical form	Present a concise reasoned argument using symbols, diagrams, graphs and related explanatory text; give solutions to problems to an appropriate degree of accuracy
Reasoning, logic, proof	Explain and justify methods and conclusions	Use logical argument to establish the truth of a statement	Present a concise reasoned argument using symbols, diagrams, graphs and related explanatory text

Our analysis suggests that while some of the spirit of Ma1 is maintained, much has been lost in the translation to behavioural teaching objectives. Although the section entitled 'Using and applying mathematics and thinking skills' (DfEE 2001a, 1.20–2) provides a helpful elaboration of the critical thinking skills discussed above, the aspects identified in the key objectives are less extensive and more limited in their scope.

For example, although the strategy of breaking a problem into smaller steps is very useful, it is only one strategy among many and it is difficult to justify its position as a key objective while other strategies are ignored. A famous analysis of traditional school mathematics problems listed 80 useful strategies (Polya 1948) not just the one listed in the key objectives!

Perhaps of greater concern to the mathematics community is the lack of emphasis on proof in the key objectives. Although the guide to the framework mentions 'deductive reasoning and proof' as a part of a 'good diet' in mathematics and the discussion of 'reasoning skills' mentions the distinction between practical demonstration and proof, such laudable aims are not mentioned in the key objectives or the yearly teaching programmes. Given the focus on key objectives we suspect that this omission will mean that many teachers will ignore this key aspect of mathematical thinking.

The key objectives are modified slightly in the supplement of examples in Section 4 of the framework. The examples listed under 'Using and applying mathematics to solve problems' are grouped under five teaching objectives:

1.   Solve word problems and investigate in a range of contexts.
2.   Identify the information necessary to solve a problem; represent problems mathematically in a variety of forms.
3.   Break problems into smaller steps or tasks; choose and use efficient operations, methods and resources.
4.   Present and interpret solutions, explaining and justifying methods, inferences and reasoning.
5.   Suggest extensions to problems, conjecture and generalise; identify exceptional cases or counter examples.

(DfEE 2001a: 4.2–35)

These objectives represent only a very limited subset of the thinking skills which underpin Ma1 yet the authors of the framework seem to have used these as a basis for their thinking about using and applying mathematics.

Unfortunately much of their thinking seems to have been driven by the limited aim of improving pupil performance in the end of Key Stage Tests. National assessment in England and Wales focuses on learning outcomes which can be easily measured in short examinations at the expense of those which require more complex assessment during extended investigation or problem solving. The use of national tests for accountability purposes raises the stakes further, and leads teachers to demand predictability from the questions and to focus on the test content at the expense of other activities.

However, such teaching to the test is a false goal. Although test scores may improve initially, underlying abilities may be untouched or even deteriorate, due to impoverished teaching aimed at passing the test rather than developing useful, applicable knowledge. This results in a lower standard of numeracy, which in the long term leads to deteriorating performance in the very examinations which were the target. The end point in this spiral of decline is when governments treat such tests as if they were significant for their own sake, rather than being crude indicators of more complex underlying knowledge and skills, and therefore use them to drive the curriculum. An over-emphasis on summative assessment for accountability at the expense of formative assessment for learning is counter-productive (see Wiliam (2000b) for a more detailed discussion of this issue). We will discuss the positive impact which *formative* assessment can have on learning in the next chapter.

The impact of this impoverished strategy on the framework is that there is an excessive emphasis on word problems in the supplement of examples. There are 33 pages of examples relating to Ma1, of which 23 focus on 'Solve word problems and investigate in a variety of contexts'. Most of the examples are unexciting and harmless, but have little to do with the development of either problem-solving ability or thinking skills. Many are more closely associated with English comprehension exercises than the use and application of mathematics. Many are set in apparently real-world contexts, but scratch the surface and you will discover that it is only a thin veneer and woe betide the pupil who brings real-world knowledge into play. For example:

> £1 is worth 3 Australian dollars (A$). A girl changed £50 into Australian dollars, went on holiday to Australia and spent A$96. At the end of the holiday she changed the Australian dollars back into pounds. How much did she get?
>
> (DfEE 2001a: 4.5).

Apparently this is a real application of mathematics. However, it ignores commission charges or the difference between buying and selling rates. Furthermore, although £1 = A$3 might be a good approximation to use in mental calculations, a real rate of exchange will almost certainly be more complex. Finally, will she be able to exchange all A$54 or only the notes? In order to solve such a problem successfully, you have to forget all your real-world knowledge, suspend disbelief, and play by the rules of the unreal world of the mathematics classroom. It is no wonder that children find it difficult to apply their mathematics in the real world when this is what we offer them as an example.

Instead of focusing on the kind of interesting and challenging problem which can be a rich context for learning the mathematical thinking skills associated with Ma1, the supplement of examples is focused on the form of problem which is often found at the end of Key Stage Tests. You might be happy to have such a resource when coaching children to pass the tests, but you should bear in mind that this is a very limited objective, which has little to do with the development of numeracy or mathematical thinking skills.

Of necessity the tests are based around short tasks which can be completed quickly. Real-world problems are often too complex to include within a timed written test, although they may provide an excellent basis for a lesson. You should be careful to ensure that your teaching is not driven by the form of question demanded by the problems at the end of the Key Stage Test. We appreciate that teachers are inevitably concerned about their pupils' performance in external examinations but, as you will see later in this chapter, time spent developing mathematical thinking skills is not wasted, but results in improved examination performance.

The supplement of examples includes a number of questions which are apparently aimed at developing mathematical thinking skills; a very small number even include a demand for reasoning or proof. Unfortunately however, most are presented in a closed form which restricts the potential for strategy choice and pupil control of the problem-solving process. To be useful as contexts for developing mathematical thinking skills, you would have to modify the tasks to make them far more open in character and useful for teaching purposes rather than summative assessment.

Many teachers are afraid of using open-ended problem-solving activities and investigations in their classrooms, fearing that if their pupils are presented with tasks in which the strategy to choose, or algorithm to select, was not immediately obvious, or even told to them, then discipline problems will follow. Unfortunately such an attitude leads to a vicious circle in which children expect spoon-feeding and lose the ability to think for themselves. If our children are to become numerate in the sense of being able to apply their knowledge in the real world then they must develop the metacognitive knowledge and thinking skills we described above. The issue is how to teach those skills.

Effective approaches to the teaching of problem solving

The Use and Practical Applications of Mathematics Project (PAMP)

Between 1991 and 1994, we led a school-based project, funded by the Welsh Office, to research the use of practical, problem-solving activities in Key Stages 3 and 4. In the initial phase of the project, we worked with a team of teacher-researchers to develop teaching approaches and materials to teach problem-solving skills in practical contexts (Tanner and Jones 1993, 1994). In phase two, these materials and approaches were used to develop a mathematical thinking-skills course. The effectiveness of the course was then evaluated by our systematic observations of around 200 lessons, and through a quasi-experiment with over 600 pupils. Pre-tests, post-tests and delayed tests were used to compare the results of pupils who had followed the course with those of control classes (Tanner and Jones 1995a, 1995b, 2000a; Tanner 1997). The findings led us to make strong recommendations about the most effective teaching approaches.

Two types of approach were unsuccessful. In the first, pupils were just given problem-solving tasks and left to think for themselves. Teachers did not offer help when pupils were struggling; they were left to sink or swim. Many sank. Inadequate support was provided for them to succeed with the task and they learned to fail. In the second, the teachers adopted a cookbook approach and provided pupils with a mathematical recipe to follow. All the mathematical thinking was done by the teacher. The pupils merely responded to the instructions, collected the required data, and filled in the table of values. Although lessons were quiet and purposeful, when faced with similar tasks the pupils were unable to proceed without help, thus indicating that learning had not occurred. The scaffolding provided here was reminiscent of the 'funnelling' described in Chapter 3. The test results of these groups of pupils were no better than their control classes.

A third approach resulted in the pupils significantly outperforming their control classes on tests of problem-solving ability. This approach was referred to as 'start-stop-go, named by the teacher who used it most. It included a variety of activities which are described below. As you read on, you may like to consider how this start-stop-go approach could contribute to the development of the mathematical thinking skills identified by the framework.

Start-stop-go

The problem-solving tasks begin with the pupils thinking in silence about the problem and starting to plan how they might tackle it. They then discuss their ideas in small groups and formulate a group plan. These ideas are brainstormed on the board for discussion and evaluation before the groups are asked to decide on their preferred approach and to start work. This strategy ensures that every pupil has thought about the problem and has started to consider what knowledge might be applicable. The group discussion and whole-class brainstorm enable a range of potential strategies to be shared and to help pupils to consider which features are necessary for plans to be viable.

Organisational prompts: Throughout these phases, the teacher would scaffold mathematical thinking through a range of questions that aimed to focus pupils' attention on the structural features of the problem and help to organise their thoughts. Such questions were termed *organisational prompts* and included, for example:

> What are you trying to find out?
> What variables are there? Which ones can you change easily here today?
> Can you explain your plan to me?
> When you have found that, how will it help you?
> What are you going to do next?
> Can you make any predictions?
> Do your results make sense? Can you use them to test your predictions?
> Will that always happen? How do you know?

These questions could be applied to a wide range of problems and were asked on a regular basis. Some teachers had them listed on a poster on the wall; others had their pupils list them for reference on the inside cover of their books. The pupils came to expect that such questions would be asked and used them as a basis for their planning.

Scientific argument: After working on the problem for a short time the class would be stopped and selected groups asked to report back on their interim findings and results. Reports were followed by questioning and constructive comment. Initially, this was led by the teacher but gradually pupils began to contribute, often echoing questions previously used by the teacher. Questions were based on the organisational prompts and probed for logical reasoning and justification. It became evident that pupils expected to be asked similar questions during their presentations and had tried to incorporate suitable responses into their reports. As pupils realised that reporting back would occur they began to monitor their progress in anticipation. The pupils were learning to participate in a 'scientific argument' (Wheatley 1991).

Peer and self-assessment: Pupils were usually required to write up their work individually but some groups also presented their draft reports to the class. Questions and discussion provided constructive criticism to inform the final write-ups. A key question which had to be answered was: 'If you were to do this task again, what would you do differently?' This peer-assessment led pupils to reflect back on their own work and to self-assess it against similar standards.

Outcomes of the project

When the results of the project were analysed, the pupils who were taught using start-stop-go outperformed their control classes on tests of problem-solving ability. This is, perhaps, unsurprising as the start-stop-go approach leads pupils to mimic the behaviours of expert problem solvers. For example, novice problem solvers often jump in too soon and use the first strategy which comes to mind, persisting with it even when it fails to progress. Expert problem solvers usually think of a number of approaches and then select the most promising, monitoring its progress and abandoning it if necessary. The start-stop-go approach forced children to consider more than one strategy at the start and then later on to stop and reflect on progress.

Conscious control of thought processes is usually achieved only after such control has been practised unconsciously and spontaneously (Vygotsky 1962: 90). The start-stop-go approach helps to develop pupils' metacognitive skills implicitly by teaching them to behave as experts, before directing their attention explicitly to the thinking processes employed.

This implicit knowledge is formalised into metacognitive knowledge through articulation and reflection in plenary sessions, when the thinking processes which were used were explicitly discussed. Some of the project teachers placed particular emphasis on the need for articulation of thoughts, for self-evaluation, and for reflection on what had been learned from the tasks. They deliberately generated a 'reflective discourse' in their classrooms (Cobb *et al.* 1997) which provided the teacher with opportunities to focus attention on key points and the strategic learning which should have occurred during the lesson. Pupils in these classes performed significantly better than their control groups not only in problem solving but also on tests of mathematical content.

Mathematical thinking skills are not only useful when solving problems. They also help when you are learning new mathematics. The pupils who were in the intervention classes had developed their metacognitive knowledge and skills and had become more effective learners of mathematics. They performed better than the control groups in tests of their mathematical content knowledge in spite of having given up some lesson time to activities focused on problem solving (for further details see Tanner 1997; Tanner and Jones 1999a).

Other research findings

The findings of the PAMP project are supported by other studies; for example, low-attaining pupils improved on tests of problem solving after explicit teaching to improve their metacognitive skills (Cardelle-Elawar 1992; 1995). Similarly, the Cognitive Acceleration in Mathematics Project (CAME) reports improved mathematical performance following a course designed to improve pupils' thinking skills (Adhami *et al.* 1998).

As you may recall from Chapter 2, Japan is consistently among the highest-performing countries in international comparisons. Japanese teaching strategies appear to be very similar to the start-stop-go approach. Start-stop-go also describes the approach used in many of the lessons seen in the RSN project. Many of the RSN teachers described themselves as teaching in an investigative fashion whereby problem-solving activities were used to prompt pupils to think for themselves. The RSN teachers used problems in a variety of ways:

- to provoke interest at the start of a topic;
- to challenge pupils to apply mathematics they already knew (and, at the same time, allow teachers to assess pupils' prior knowledge);
- to motivate the learning of a new mathematical topic by setting it in a practical context;
- to support the learning of new mathematics by investigating within mathematics itself;
- to provide an opportunity to develop particular problem-solving strategies.

You might like to compare this list with the advice given in the National Strategy (DfEE 2001a: 1.20). Depending on the aim of the lesson, some problem activities were short, perhaps merely a lesson starter. On other occasions, the problem would extend over several lessons.

The strategies included in the start-stop-go approach fully support the development of the thinking skills identified by the framework. For example, the information-processing and enquiry skills of defining the problem and planning potential approaches are encouraged during the individual preparation period and the group discussions. The creative skills of generating alternative strategies and the use of differing representations are discussed during the class brainstorm. Reasoning skills are strengthened as pupils present their ideas to others and debate their findings. Evaluation skills are required as pupils review their progress in preparation for reporting back and as they compare their progress with that of others.

While these thinking skills clearly contribute to the development of pupils' metacognitive skills they should also contribute to metacognitive knowledge. Just as the framework suggests that plenary sessions could be used to draw pupils' attention to links between current work and past or future learning (DfEE 2001a: 1.46), the skill of evaluation should include the ability to identify what they have learned and how they could improve. Research suggests that the use of peer- and self-assessment is crucial here; we shall discuss this in more detail in Chapter 6.

Research shows that teaching strategies which encourage the development of metacognition also contribute to improvements in pupils' general mathematical performance. In the next section we shall illustrate how such strategies can be applied in practice.

Developing mathematical thinking through problem solving

Figure 5.1 shows the 'Snakes and Ladders' worksheet, which was used by some of the teachers on the PAMP project. The pupils worked in small groups of two or three to complete the task. Each group was given: squared paper, a die or a spinner, and some counters.

Task 5.4:   Snakes and Ladders
What mathematical thinking skills could this task develop?
The task could also contribute to 'content' knowledge. Make a list of the mathematical knowledge and skills which might be taught during this task. Probability has a large number of common misconceptions associated with it. Which are the main ones you would expect this task to expose?

Teachers' aims for the task often included developing pupils' abilities to identify and control variables, and to practise the strategies of working systematically and

Snakes and Ladders

Howard and Sonia have decided to make a
game of snakes and ladders to play.

Here is the board they made:

FINISH	14	13	12
8	9	10	11
7	6	5	4
START	1	2	3

They have cut out some snakes and ladders to stick on the board – but where?

Their friend Alyson wants the game to last a long time.

Alyson wants most players to land on a snake after two goes. Where should she put it?

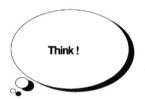

Think !

Which is the most likely number to come up on one throw of a dice?
Which is the least likely?

How could you find out where you are most likely to be after two
throws of the dice?

Would you do any experiments? What would you write?

Decide on a plan for your group to follow and write it down.
Decide how you will record your group's results.
Try to predict your results before you start.

Discuss !

Extension:
Put as many snakes and ladders on the board as you like and try to make predictions.
Try to make: a fast game, or a slow game, or a good game.
Don't forget to explain WHY you think your game will be fast/slow/good.
Try out your game and test your predictions.

Figure 5.1   Snakes and Ladders worksheet

exhaustively. In terms of misconceptions, pupils may assume that a six is the
hardest number to throw, or that the relative frequency obtained from a small
number of trials will equal the theoretical probability, e.g. they expect to get
exactly one double six in 36 throws.

The mathematical content knowledge which was developed depended on the
mathematical background of the class and the approach chosen by the teacher.
Different teachers used slightly different approaches to each other, but the most
successful tried to use the start-stop-go approach along the lines described
below.

Introduction and scene setting

The teacher asked the class if they had ever played Snakes and Ladders and reviewed the basic rules of the game. She said that they were going to investigate the mathematics of snakes and ladders and divided them into groups of two or three, emphasising the need for cooperative working.

Making the class behave like experts

She then gave out the worksheet and asked the class to read it in silence for two minutes, thinking about the questions next to the 'think' bubble. No one spoke during the period of silent reading and no questions or comments were allowed. She later commented that this ensured that all pupils had engaged with the task as individuals and had begun to form their own ideas before any discussion or teaching began.

After the period of silent reading the class were invited to discuss their ideas with the other members of their group and to begin to form a plan as suggested next to the 'discuss' bubble. The groups were allowed to talk animatedly for the next few minutes. The teacher then said 'I'm going to ask you to tell me about your plans in one minute, so make your minds up quickly.' She later explained that working in small groups allowed them to discuss a number of different approaches and to gain confidence in their ideas prior to the brainstorming session.

Scaffolding thinking during brainstorming

In the brainstorming session, she invited representatives from several groups to explain their ideas for possible approaches to the task. Ideas were repeated back for clarification and key aspects of plans jotted on the board. Plans were accepted non-judgementally at this stage to encourage participation. The brainstorming session revealed some pupils who thought that a six was the least likely outcome. When several ideas had been summarised the teacher began to discuss the main points, focusing the attention of the class on key issues, inviting constructive comments and questions from the class and effectively validating some ideas above others. At this stage the issue of the six was addressed directly and one group was encouraged to devise a plan to investigate it.

Most other groups worked on the main problem. The task may be approached theoretically or experimentally. The teacher allowed either approach from the pupils; the brainstorming session did not push them one way or the other, but she ensured that viable plans had been developed for either approach.

Some pupils wanted to list all the possible combinations from two dice in order to make predictions. Others planned to list all the possible ways of getting the numbers from 1 to 12. As these plans progressed she encouraged them to make predictions which could then be tested experimentally and to try to explain their experimental results. Most pupils taking this approach expected to find the exact theoretical values, e.g. exactly one double six in 36 throws. Their failure to do so caused much debate.

Other pupils planned to start with a more practical approach, calculating experimental probabilities. As the task progressed she encouraged these pupils to explore possible combinations to explain their results.

During the brainstorm, the teacher's role was crucial in drawing the attention of the class to several possible approaches before allowing them to select their preferred option. In this way the teacher coached the class to act as expert problem solvers by ensuring that they evaluated a range of options before starting work.

Monitoring

After the class had been working for about 15 minutes, they were stopped and the teacher selected a few key groups to report back on their progress so far. She explained that this was an opportunity for groups to compare the progress of their plans with those of others and to change their plan if need be. Pupils who were making slow progress were given strong encouragement to modify their plans at this stage. At the end of the first lesson, the teacher spent a further ten minutes getting selected groups to report back, validating key ideas and encouraging reflection.

The teacher acted as a metacognitive coach each time the class was stopped for reporting back. The sharing of findings provoked pupils to consider their findings from alternative viewpoints. Throughout the reports, the teacher probed for justification and generalisation of findings. The class were asked to continue working on the task at home and to come to the next lesson prepared to finish the task by the end of that lesson. As many pupils as possible were encouraged to attempt the extension task. She discussed the need for simplifying assumptions with the class. They were encouraged to simplify the situation according to their own rules and to test their predictions through experimentation (one ladder and one snake is a suitable restriction).

The plenary

The second lesson began with a short reporting back session on progress so far and encouraging comments from the teacher on how to proceed. At the end of the lesson, selected groups were invited to make formal presentations of their findings to the rest of the class. The problem-solving process itself became the subject of discussion and she focused the attention of the class on key features of certain approaches, suggesting which features might be worth remembering for other occasions. This helped to formalise the knowledge gained about problem-solving strategies.

During formal reports the teacher invited the class to question groups about their findings, encouraging debate about results and demanding reasoned arguments to justify claims. The class were asked to identify features which were worthy of merit in particular approaches and to suggest ways in which reports could have been improved. She explained that this was a form of peer assessment and that it taught pupils both what was important in their own work and also how to improve.

At the end of the second lesson the class were set homework which was to write individual reports on the task in the light of the comments made during the plenary. We found that reports written following peer assessment were of a far higher quality than those written without such support.

Conclusion

Numerate pupils are good problem solvers and teaching pupils to solve problems enhances their numeracy. Good problem solvers possess accessible, connected mathematical knowledge, but this in itself is not sufficient. They must also develop problem-solving skills and positive attitudes. Two key aspects of problem-solving ability are metacognitive knowledge and metacognitive skill: knowing what you know and the skill of monitoring and controlling your own thought processes. The thinking skills listed in the framework are metacognitive in character.

The time invested in the development of such mathematical thinking skills pays off, not only when using and applying mathematics, but also when learning new mathematics. Focusing on the development of thinking skills leads to improved attainment in examinations whereas teaching to the test does not.

The most effective teaching approaches for the development of mathematical thinking skills are based on the modelling of expert behaviour and collective reflection. The approach which we entitled start-stop-go has been demonstrated to be particularly effective. This approach involves making pupils behave as experts, considering several strategies before selecting one, monitoring progress, engaging in scientific argument, evaluating solutions and reflecting on the problem-solving process, and peer assessment.

An emphasis on the formative as opposed to the summative aspects of assessment is clearly indicated, and it is to a discussion of assessment for learning that we should now turn.

CHAPTER 6

Assessment for learning

Introduction

In previous chapters we emphasised the importance of using interactive teaching approaches and encouraging children to join in reflective discussions which are closely supported by the teacher. The evidence from research supports what we consider to be a self-evident proposition: that the effectiveness of learning depends most of all on the quality of the interactions between teachers and pupils (Brown 1999b). The structural and managerial issues which exercise the attention of politicians and the press such as whether or not schools are organised as comprehensives or whether or not pupils are in mixed-ability groups are of much less significance (Beaton *et al.* 1996).

Interactive teaching approaches are essentially founded on a two-way communication process between children and teachers. Effective assessment is at the heart of that communication process. It is through assessment that pupils gain feedback on their learning and teachers gain feedback on their teaching.

There are, of course, many purposes for assessment and different forms of assessment should be used according to your aims. We make a distinction between those aims of assessment which are essentially managerial in character and those which are professional, being aimed at supporting the teaching and learning process directly. Managerial aims, such as demonstrating or testing the effectiveness of government policies; holding schools and LEAs accountable for pupils' progress; producing league tables to inform parental choice; or motivating teachers through payment by results schemes, are not our interest here. This chapter focuses on the use of assessment to support learning. This is broadly referred to as *formative assessment*.

Objectives

By the end of this chapter you should:

- understand the nature and importance of formative assessment;

- understand the role which effective questioning can play in assessment for learning;
- understand how children can be involved actively in their own assessment;
- be able to devise effective feedback and marking strategies;
- be able to devise effective strategies for recording and reporting.

Formative assessment

Formative assessment is professional in its character and is assessment *for* learning as opposed to summative assessment which is managerial in character and is assessment *of* learning. Formative assessment must happen continuously for teaching to be effective.

> It is rooted in self-referencing; a pupil needs to know where s/he is and understand not only where s/he wants to be but also how to 'fill the gap'. This involves both the teacher and the pupil in a process of continual reflection and review about **progress**. When teachers and peers provide quality feedback, pupils are empowered to take the appropriate action.
>
> (QCA 2001a)

The framework classifies assessment as short-term, medium-term and long-term (DfEE 2001a). Short-term assessments are an informal part of every lesson and do not need to be recorded as they are for immediate action and attention rather than for longer-term planning. Ideally, most short-term assessments should become out of date by the end of the lesson or unit of work as the pupils progress.

Medium-term assessments are more summative in character and review pupils' progress over a longer period such as a half-term or term, but may still have some formative characteristics if they are used to plan the work for the next half-term and set pupil targets.

Long-term assessments are summative and more managerial in character. They may review pupils' progress against national standards or key objectives for the year or key stage, allowing managers of the system to hold teachers, schools or LEAs accountable, or for curriculum reforms to be judged. They may also provide useful information about standards for the teacher or institution receiving the pupils in the next year or key stage. However, it is through the more effective use of short-term, formative assessments that we are most likely to improve standards.

An extensive and influential survey of the research literature was conducted by Black and Wiliam (1998) to resolve three key questions about formative assessment:

- Is there evidence that improving formative assessment raises standards?
- Is there evidence that there is room for improvement?
- Is there evidence about how to improve formative assessment?

The conclusion was that the answer to each of the questions was a clear 'Yes'.

High-quality formative assessment has a powerful impact on learning. A review of approximately 250 studies into the use of formative assessment revealed significant increases in student performances on standardised tests (Black and Wiliam 1998). Such increases would be sufficient to lift England from 41st to 5th place in the TIMSS international league tables (Beaton *et al.* 1996) and would equate, for the average student, to an improvement of two grades at GCSE. Low attainers are reported to benefit even more, with an increase of three grades in comparison with one grade for higher attainers (Black and Wiliam 1998).

Unfortunately, the research also shows that high-quality formative assessment is not very common. A number of criticisms were made of assessment practices found in the UK. They did not apply to all teachers or to all schools, but we summarise a few of them here for you to judge your own practices against.

Task 6.1:   Criticising the assessment practices in your own school
Black and Wiliam made the following criticisms of negative assessment practices often found in the UK:

- *test questions encourage rote and superficial learning;*
- *the giving of marks or grades is over-emphasised, while the giving of advice is under-emphasised;*
- *an over-emphasis on competition rather than personal improvement teaches low-attainers that they lack 'ability';*
- *feedback often serves social and managerial functions, at the expense of learning functions;*
- *the collection of marks to fill up records is given greater priority than the analysis of pupils' work to discern learning needs;*
- *insufficient attention is paid to the assessment records of previous teachers.*
                                      (summarised from Black and Wiliam 1998)

Which of the criticisms apply to your own practices?
Which of these criticisms are due to the emphasis placed on high-stakes external examinations by successive government policies since 1988?

Little effective advice was offered to teachers regarding formative assessment during the 1990s. The emphasis was on external examinations, often with high stakes attached and intended to create league tables. The stress was on the managerial functions of assessment which ensured the domination of summative assessment over learning throughout the decade (Black and Wiliam 1998). In the early 1990s, much of the guidance offered to teachers about formative assessment emphasised a completely impractical 'tick-box' approach based on multiple statements of attainment (Tanner1992). This was intended to serve both summative and formative ends, but in the event succeeded in neither and was only ended through union action by teachers in the mid-1990s. You should remember this period of tick-box madness when we discuss record-keeping and reporting later in this chapter.

QCA have taken note of the research and emphasise that effective formative assessment is a key factor in raising standards. They offer advice on the features which should be found in effective formative assessment:

> Central to formative assessment, or 'assessment for learning' is that it:
> * is embedded in the teaching and learning process of which it is an essential part;
> * shares learning goals with pupils;
> * helps pupils to know and to recognise the standards to aim for;
> * provides feedback which leads pupils to identify what they should do next to improve;
> * has a commitment that every pupil can improve;
> * involves both teacher and pupils reviewing and reflecting on pupils' performance and progress;
> * involves pupils in self-assessment.
>
> (QCA 2001a)

Research has identified the use of questioning and discussion, the involvement of pupils in the assessment process, and the quality of feedback as key elements for effective formative assessment.

Assessing through questioning and discussion

During teaching, assessment is an informal activity as you absorb and react to how the class are responding to the tasks and to your input. You can assess the pupils' understanding of and involvement in the lesson in a variety of ways: by observing their facial expressions, by looking at their written work, by listening in to discussions, or by direct questioning. However, for such assessments to be formative there must be feedback into the learning process. In response to such continuous informal assessments, you adapt your teaching, speeding up or slowing down the pace, introducing a new metaphor, abandoning one track in favour of another, making continuous judgements and decisions about how to proceed.

However, the process is not all one way. As children participate in a lesson, they are continually receiving information; either they process it by assimilating that which confirms previously held concepts and ignoring that which does not fit, or they accommodate by developing new concepts to organise and explain the new idea. As they build new concepts they continually check their version of events against the official version being presented by the teacher or other pupils, modifying and adapting it as necessary. In order to do this they need both time to think and feedback on their tentative constructs. Ideally, they should be given the opportunity to articulate their thoughts and have them confirmed or modified in a thoughtful, reflective discussion. In reality there is not usually enough time for every pupil to receive personal oral feedback during the lesson, but good teachers ensure that sufficient pupils have opportunities to express their ideas for the majority of opinions to be evaluated.

As we discussed in Chapter 4, the most effective teachers observed in the RSN project (Tanner *et al.* 1999) planned to address misconceptions directly during such sessions, ensuring that the most common were clearly evaluated as incorrect. Clearly, some questions are much more effective than others in providing teachers with opportunities to assess children's mathematical development. Wiliam (1999a: 16) recommends the use of 'rich mathematical questions' which provide 'a window into the pupil's thinking'. For example, we observed a student teacher ask her Year 9 class:

'If the answer is –0.5, what was the question?'

The responses included:

–50 written as a decimal
–1 – 0.5
–0.5 × 0

The open nature of the question, together with the careful choice of values, invites pupils to indicate their underlying misconceptions which may then be modified during the ensuing discussion.

Similarly, one of the successful teachers in the RSN project used the following statement as a stimulus for discussion as part of a warm-up to assess pupils' understanding of their work on squares and square roots in the previous lesson:

The square root of a number is always smaller than the number itself.

He asked the class to think about the statement in silence for two minutes before discussing it in small groups. Pupils were then invited out to the board to give their opinions and justify their conclusions. Initially, these were accepted without confirmation of their validity, but with an invitation for other pupils to question or comment. This approach revealed misconceptions about decimal multiplication always making numbers larger and multiplication and ordering of negative numbers. As the discussion progressed, however, the teacher was able to focus the attention of the class on key issues raised by pupils. This led eventually to the class reasoning their way collectively towards a correct solution in which they believed.

Both these challenges were useful in providing opportunities for discussions during which formative assessment and effective learning could occur. However, the success of the activity depends crucially on exactly how the teacher intervenes in the discussion to support learning through questioning. We hope that you noticed that both the format of the task and the use of focusing questions (see Chapter 3) were critical for the success of the activities.

In order for the task to be effective as a vehicle for formative assessment based on discussion it must be sufficiently open to include a problem, that is an 'unresolved or not trivially resolvable problem' which induces some purpose or tension to sustain a discussion (Ryan and Williams 2000).

However, in addition to the problem, the discussion must be supported and developed through questioning by the teacher. This should be indirect in character, so as not to steal the problem by funnelling strategic thinking. The pupils must be left with a sufficient gap to fill using their own powers of reasoning. Support from the teacher comes from focusing questions and encouragement to engage in collective reflection. The resulting dialogue should be thoughtful and reflective, designed to explore understanding, giving all pupils the opportunity to think and to articulate their thoughts (Tanner 1997; Black and Wiliam 1998).

A recent research report from QCA on using assessment to raise achievement in mathematics (QCA 2001b) suggests that changing the way a question is phrased can make a significant difference to:

- the thought processes pupils need to go through;
- the language demands made on pupils;
- the extent to which pupils reveal their understanding;
- the number of questions needed to make an assessment of pupils' current understanding.

(QCA 2001b: 11)

The following are offered as examples of types of question which can be effective in providing assessment opportunities:

1. How can we be sure that …?
2. Is it ever/always true/false that …?
3. Why do —, —, —, all give the same answer?
4. How do you …?
5. How would you explain …?
6. What does that tell us about…?
7. What is wrong with …?
8. Why is — true?

(QCA 2001b: 12)

The common characteristic of these questions is that they are sufficiently open to develop a genuine problem and demand reasoning and argument from pupils. The report continues by providing examples of how traditional tasks can be developed into effective assessment opportunities.

Task 6.2:   Developing effective questions for formative assessment
Consider the following closed, direct questions. How might you rephrase them to create opportunities for formative assessment?
What is 23 + 13? What is 13 + 23?
Are these two triangles similar?
23.6 + 4.23 = ?
What is the probability of getting a head if you flip a new euro coin?

There is no right answer to this task, but here are some of our suggestions:

> Why do 23 + 13 and 13 + 23 give the same answer? Does it work for all the four rules?
> How could you prove that these two triangles are similar?
> John added 23.6 to 4.23 and got 65.9. What do you think he did wrong? How would you explain to him?
> I flipped a euro 400 times and got 221 heads. Does this mean that the coin is biased?

More examples of questions which teachers might use for effective formative assessment may be found in *Better Thinking, Better Mathematics* (Tanner and Jones 1995a). However, as we discussed earlier, the communication involved in formative assessment should be two-way. A recurring theme in the research is that children should be actively involved in their own assessment (Schoenfeld 1987; Gipps 1994; Tanner and Jones 1994; Black and Wiliam 1998).

Involving children in their own assessment

It is claimed that the feedback which is provided in formative assessment requires three elements to be present if learning is to be improved (Black and Wiliam 1998). First, pupils must have sound metacognitive knowledge in the area in question: they must know what they know already. Second, they must know what they are trying to achieve: they should know their learning objectives. Third, they need a strategy to help them to close the gap, a form of metacognitive skill. From this analysis, the value of beginning lessons with a review or warm-up of preliminary work and the sharing of learning goals with pupils is clear. However, there is another aspect, which is significant here, which arises regularly in the research literature: children need to develop skills of self-assessment if they are to learn efficiently.

> For formative assessment to be productive, pupils should be trained in self-assessment so that they can understand the main purposes of their learning and thereby grasp what they need to do to achieve.
>
> (Black and Wiliam 1998)

Explaining the learning objectives at the start of a lesson to clarify to pupils what it is that they are meant to be learning has long been recommended as good practice and is included in the QCA suggestions above. Similarly, sharing the assessment criteria for a task helps pupils to focus on those aspects of their learning which you consider to be important.

However, early attempts to introduce an element of self-assessment into the SAT examinations were unsuccessful. The feedback was not positive; pupils did not know how to assess themselves.

Task 6.3: **What is necessary for successful pupil self-assessment**
Why do you think that the early attempts at including pupil self-assessment in the SATs failed?
What is necessary for successful pupil self-assessment?

Many pupils lack a clear overview of their own learning and become confused because they do not understand the criteria against which they are being assessed (QCA 2001b: 5). We found a similar problem in the PAMP project (see Chapter 5). In order to assess themselves children must be aware of the nature of a good solution to the problem: they must have internalised the assessment criteria for the task. In the early stages of the PAMP project, we found few pupils who were so aware. Furthermore, it was clear that self-assessment was a novel concept for many pupils; they needed to learn *how* to assess themselves (Tanner and Jones 1994).

This is where peer-assessment proves to be so valuable. We found that participation in peer-assessment helped to teach pupils both about the nature of a good solution and about how to assess.

With the open-ended, problem-solving tasks which are found in coursework, the assessment criteria are often difficult to interpret. Showing pupils examples of good quality work produced by other pupils can be helpful in illustrating how the criteria are interpreted, and can be used to develop skills of peer- and self-assessment (Jones 1992).

During the PAMP project, we found the effective use of the plenary to be critical when tasks involved open-ended problem solving. In plenaries, groups can present their draft reports to the class for peer-assessment. Clear 'ground rules' and good discipline are necessary to ensure a safe environment for presenting pupils. We tell pupils to ask for explanations of points which they did not understand: 'Will that always be true?'; 'How can you be sure they are equal?'; 'Why is __ true?'; but demand that any criticism must be justified and accompanied by suggestions for improvement. The aim was to create a community of enquiry which was mutually supportive rather than competitive.

Reporting back in the plenary has a dual purpose. Overtly the purpose is to improve the write-up of an activity through discussion and constructive criticism. However, this is also an opportunity for learning the skills of peer-assessment and thus self-assessment through collective reflection. In the early stages pupils did not know what sort of question to ask, or what aspect of the report was significant. Teachers asked the key questions which focused the attention of the class on the most significant aspects of an investigation. However, gradually the pupils began to realise the form of discussion which was appropriate and began to copy the teacher's style of question. More importantly, in time it became clear that pupils were asking themselves such questions prior to their presentation and preparing their responses. This is when self-assessment begins to pay back in terms of learning.

The criteria against which Attainment Target 1 is assessed appear complex even to teachers. Pupils need to learn how such criteria are interpreted in the context of tasks which they have attempted. Collective peer-assessment of other pupils' work helps children to understand how the criteria are interpreted. Sometimes we allowed pupils to redraft their work after the plenary which was then submitted for formal marking. The grades achieved following redrafting were usually higher than would have been achieved unaided but this formative assessment was part of the teaching and learning process, not a summative judgement for external examination (Tanner and Jones 1994).

A key aspect of the plenary is collective reflection. Thus we always asked, 'If I were to do this task again what would I do differently?' This focused attention on the problem-solving process itself and allowed consideration of the elegance of different solutions. Assessing the work of others helped to identify the nature of a good solution and hence helped pupils to concentrate on what was important in their own work. By learning to assess the work of others, students learned to reflect on and assess their own work (Tanner and Jones 1994).

Although the PAMP project was focused on Ma1 and problem-solving processes, many of the techniques which we described are directly applicable to lessons which are targeted at more straightforward mathematical content from the other areas of the programme of study. In fact, in the second phase of the project we discovered that classes who had engaged in collective reflection through peer- and self-assessment were significantly better than their matched control groups in the content areas of mathematics (significance $<0.1\%$, effect size 0.2, Tanner and Jones 2000b).

Although we recommend that a sufficiently challenging problem is required for useful discussion, there are a number of effective strategies which can be used with less demanding work which encourage self-assessment. Many of the successful teachers in the RSN project had devised reflective assessment activities which they used in their plenaries at the end of most lessons. These include asking pupils:

- to identify warnings which they would give to other pupils about to start the same task;
- to mark the work of an imaginary pupil which contains standard errors and to explain why the errors were made;
- to identify what is important for them to remember from today's lesson.

(Tanner and Jones 2000b)

One of the RSN teachers regularly ended units of work by asking the pupils to write a question to test their understanding of the topic. They were then asked to present their ideas to the class and a discussion followed about which questions best tested the assessment criteria for the topic. To add interest and motivation she claimed that the best questions would be used in the end of year examinations. This not only provided an opportunity for both teacher and pupils to assess the learning which had occurred, but also ensured that the class had a good set of summary notes for revision later. More importantly, the pupils were forced to reflect on the extent of their own learning compared with the assessment criteria.

Other successful strategies include appointing a pupil to act as a 'rapporteur' during the plenary to summarise the main points of the lesson and to answer any questions from other pupils; and asking pupils to indicate, perhaps by using tick boxes, the degree to which they feel that they have understood each of the lesson objectives (Wiliam 2000a). This second strategy has the advantage of providing the teacher with a written record of the pupils' perceptions of their understanding.

It is often helpful to ask children to assess the extent to which they feel they have properly understood the key concepts in a unit of work *independently* of their success in the tasks set in the unit. If you think back to when you were learning mathematics as a pupil, you can probably recall occasions when you successfully completed all the exercises which had been set by the teacher, but had a nagging feeling that you did not really understand what you were doing. In such situations, learning is often transitory, and melts away as a routine based on an unsound foundation is quickly forgotten.

QCA (2001b) reports a school using 'traffic light' self-assessment when reviewing half-term tests. On their record of attainment sheet, they indicate the extent to which they feel they have understood the learning objectives associated with particular questions using a green blob to mean 'I understood this and feel confident.' A green blob can be used next to an incorrect answer if the error was trivial. An amber blob indicates that they have some understanding but are not confident, feeling 'not sure' about the topic. This might be used even if the question was correct in the test. A red blob means 'I don't understand at all.' Self-assessment using a system of traffic lights or smiley faces can help teachers to identify areas of work which need review. More importantly, it forces children to reflect on their own learning, developing their metacognitive knowledge and helping them to identify suitable targets for improvement (Wiliam 2000a).

Some teachers follow up 'traffic light' self-assessment sessions with a peer support session in which pupils with green blobs help pupils with amber blobs to correct work where necessary, allowing the teacher to focus on the pupils with red blobs. Ideally such sessions should end with pupils having appropriate attainable targets for future work.

Pupils can only set appropriate targets for improvement and find strategies for achieving them if they have received feedback of sufficient quality. To be effective, feedback must be sufficiently direct to enable children to identify errors and misconceptions with precision. However, it must also include advice on how to improve the work which is sufficiently explicit for a learner to act on it.

Feedback and marking strategies

Teachers spend a great deal of time and effort providing feedback to children in a variety of ways.

Task 6.4:   Providing feedback
List five different ways in which you provide feedback to children.
What advantages and disadvantages do you see in your approaches?
Do any of your approaches meet the two conditions listed above?

We group feedback under three main headings:

- oral feedback on classwork or homework during teaching;
- written feedback on classwork or homework;
- written feedback on tests or examinations.

Much feedback which is provided to children is oral and immediate, arising in the normal flow of teaching, either in interactive dialogues which are occurring during whole-class teaching or with individuals or small groups as teachers circulate during exercise or task sessions. This form of feedback should always be formative in character, as its overt aim is to support the learning process. Most research indicates that oral feedback is more effective than written feedback (QCA

2001a). However, not all oral feedback is good (Wiliam 1999b). The quality of the dialogue is important.

Children need to be given sufficient opportunity to reason things out for themselves. A limited response which demands that they complete some of the reasoning for themselves is far better than presenting them with a completed solution. Interventions should be interactive and based on supporting and developing pupils' own ideas rather than a repeated explanation of the teacher's method (Tanner 1997). 'Just enough help and no more' should be the guiding principle. Often when children are 'stuck' on a problem, the best response is simply to ask them to read the problem out loud or copy down the diagram, building confidence and creating time for them to think for themselves (Wiliam 1999b).

Pupils need to feel able to ask for help and the ethos of the school should encourage them to do so (QCA 2001a). It is also important for children to realise that to get questions wrong is a natural part of the learning process. The most successful teachers in the RSN project emphasised that a wrong answer was an opportunity to learn, rather than a cause for teacher displeasure. To encourage this view it is important to dissociate criticism of an incorrect approach or misconception from criticism of the child.

> Feedback to any pupil should be about the particular qualities of his or her work, with advice on what he or she can do to improve, and should avoid comparisons with other pupils.
>
> (Black and Wiliam 1998)

While competition can be a powerful motivator, particularly when it is between evenly matched teams or classes, it has strong negative side-effects when associated with the assessment of individual pupils. The losers in the competition often begin to believe that they lack natural ability, leading them to 'retire hurt', losing the motivation to learn. The danger then is that they try to build up their self-esteem in other, less appropriate ways (Black and Wiliam 1998).

Oral feedback often makes use of praise, which is often regarded as an obviously good thing. However, research (Good and Grouws 1975; Brophy 1981) shows that this is not the case. Although praise is a motivator, it is addictive and seems insincere when overused. If used carelessly, it encourages children to associate their success or failure with factors which are out of their control such as innate ability (Wiliam 1999b). It is more effective to use praise sparingly and associate it with specific actions and qualities of work which are within their control such as effort, accuracy or persistence.

Checking and grading pupils' work is a significant part of a teacher's workload and is a powerful vehicle for communication between teacher and pupil to provide feedback about individual work. You may offer feedback on written work in a variety of ways:

- a mark out of a given total, e.g. 7/10;
- a grade, which may be related to NC levels, GCSE grades, or school descriptors, e.g. B3, meaning good standard of mathematics, moderate presentation and effort;
- a general comment, e.g. 'Untidy work', which may be oral or written;
- an instruction, e.g. 'Show your workings';
- a specific target which indicates what needs to be done next in order to improve, e.g. 'Try to show why your formula always works';
- correction of errors, e.g. in calculation, spelling, method, by showing a correct version alongside;
- an indication that a problem needs to be discussed, e.g: 'See me about this exercise.'

It is surprising that so much effort goes into providing pupils with marks and grades. A mark or grade represents a summative judgement which tells the pupil how well they did and nothing more. Pupils receiving high marks are encouraged and show increased interest in work. Pupils receiving low marks are discouraged and begin to lose interest (Butler 1988). A mark out of ten tells you nothing about your errors or how you might improve.

Research suggests that feedback based on grades or marks fails to change future performance (see Butler 1987; 1988; Wiliam 1999b). In Butler's (1987) research, pupils whose feedback consisted of praise and grades increasingly attributed their performance to their ability in mathematics, and performed no better on subsequent tasks than pupils who were given no feedback. However, pupils who received just comments on their work improved their performance in later lessons. Where pupils were given both grades and comments, the impact of the grade appeared to dominate and no benefit was found.

The aim should be to encourage children to take the view that their mathematical ability is not fixed, but can be improved through their own actions. To this end, feedback should always indicate what is wrong with the work and what needs to be done to improve. To be helpful, such advice needs to be precise, indicating the steps to be taken, e.g. 'Draw a bigger diagram and use a ruler' rather than general comments such as 'You are too untidy!' The aim should be to create a classroom culture where all pupils believe that they can improve their performance through their own efforts and know how to apply themselves to succeed.

Setting clear, short-term targets for pupils has been shown to be effective in improving learning (Tanner et al. 1999). Target setting can motivate pupils by reducing what initially may appear as an impossible challenge into a series of small, clearly specified and achievable steps. Again, the intention is to convince the pupils that they can improve their performance through their own efforts. In the longer term the aim must be to teach them that they are in control of their own learning. To this end pupils should be closely involved in setting their own targets and not be treated as passive recipients of teacher-set targets.

Many schools test pupils at the end of units of work. The purpose of such assessments is often unclear. Formative comments and suggestions received after the end of a unit of work are usually too late for pupils to act on; that topic is over and a new one has started! If pupils are formatively assessed and receive helpful feedback prior to the end of a unit of work, they may be able to act on the advice before moving on to new work.

Assessments at the end of a unit of work are summative in nature and often seem to serve little purpose other than to provide data for entry into pupils' records. Unfortunately, such records often seem to serve little function beyond filling up filing cabinets!

Recording and reporting

In the early days of the National Curriculum, vast amounts of teacher time, effort and good will were wasted on creating records which could not be used for any sensible purpose (Tanner 1992). We begin from the premise that if distinctive records are to be kept, over and above the contents of pupils' exercise books and teachers' day-to-day mark books, they should be:

- valid, in that they assess children against appropriate learning objectives;
- reliable, in that they can be trusted to indicate knowledge which is secure, and not forgotten shortly after the assessment;
- useful for communication with parents about children's progress;
- helpful when making judgements against National Curriculum and other external criteria;
- useful for long-term planning.

Few records that we see meet any of these criteria. Furthermore, we doubt that the recording system recommended in the framework is likely to meet them.

The problem which we have to face with all assessment and recording procedures in the medium to long term is that people *forget*. All assessments are snapshots of a moving target. If you save a data file to the hard drive of your computer and leave it for the next six months, you expect that when you reopen that file the contents will be unchanged. People are not like that. They learn new knowledge (even when they are not in your lessons). If their current knowledge is not used regularly it decays away and becomes inaccurate. Can you remember the mathematics you learned in your final year at university? If only we could convince the pen-pushers and bureaucrats that people are not computers!

Pupil records based on tick boxes set against statements of attainment quickly became discredited among teachers, not only due to the high administrative burden they created, but more importantly, because they were so unreliable that they were useless. Some LEAs created complex systems which demanded for example: one line in a box to mean 'has met the topic', two lines to mean 'can use the knowledge to solve problems' and shading in the box when 'real understanding has been achieved'. Unfortunately, even children whose boxes had been shaded in persisted in forgetting things! Teachers who received such records with a new class and tried to use them for planning their teaching quickly discovered that they could not be trusted to indicate children's current knowledge (Tanner 1992).

Unfortunately the framework begins the section on recording by claiming that 'pupils' progress towards the key objectives needs to be recorded'(DfEE 2001a:1.41) and suggests that a class record sheet be updated every six weeks. They give no reason for doing this beyond creating a useful aide-memoire for parents evening. They suggest that you date the record when an objective is achieved. Why the date would be useful is unclear, although you would be able to say, 'He might not know it now, but he knew it on Tuesday 17th October.' We suggest that this is a pointless exercise and that you should maintain records which are useful instead.

We subscribe to the principle that you should not record any information twice. If the departmental scheme of work is written according to the guidelines we described in Chapter 4, there should be little need for detailed records of the teaching which has occurred to individual pupils beyond that which is usually found in a teacher's record and mark book. If whole-class teaching approaches are used, then only exceptional performances need be recorded. Most record keeping can be done by adding notes to your mark book as an integral part of your marking and preparation for teaching.

A limited selection of other aspects of pupils' work, e.g. coursework tasks, test papers, examination results, etc. which may be required for formal summative assessments should be kept in a portfolio. Pupils should be involved in selecting the sample of their best work and this should be an integral part of the target-setting process. Pupils' self-assessments and their agreed targets might also be included, although it is important that pupils keep their own copy of their targets, perhaps in their homework diaries or personal organisers. Pupils' portfolios are very helpful when discussing progress with parents and can provide useful evidence when assessment against external criteria is demanded at the end of a key stage.

We have suggested that pupils' portfolios should contain the scripts from the periodic summative tests and examinations, however, if such tests and examinations are to fulfil the criteria we listed above, certain conditions must be met.

First, to ensure that the assessment is valid, we suggest that test or examination questions subsume the key objectives for appropriate years. However, as we argued in Chapter 5, although these are necessary they are not sufficient. Your aims for teaching mathematics should be wider than this.

The supplement of examples in the framework provides an excellent source of ideas for both teaching and assessment. Objectives should be chosen from the years above and below the target year to differentiate and provide appropriate challenge. Care should be taken to ensure that the questions include objectives from AT1 as well as the content targets. To be valid, questions should demand more than instrumental recall of an algorithm. Genuine problem contexts are required.

You should also recall the importance of making connections which we discussed in Chapter 4. To be valid, the test and examinations should include questions which demand the use of mathematics from more than one aspect of the subject. Remember, what you test is what you get, so if you want children to make links you should assess their ability to make links in your key examinations.

Second, to ensure that assessment is reliable, assessment situations should be sufficiently distant from teaching to allow insecure, instrumental knowledge to decay away. We suggest a delay of at least two weeks after teaching before a topic is summatively assessed. Similarly, a test or examination based on a single topic is too simple a context to assess whether knowledge is robust. Tests on single topics may be useful for immediate, formative assessment for learning, but often produce unreliable data for records intended for medium- and long-term planning. We suggest that your periodic summative assessments include at least two or three new topics. You should also periodically assess significant key objectives from older work.

Third, to ensure that the record is useful, results should be analysed to identify persistent misconceptions and areas where understanding is weak. A summary mark is not helpful for planning teaching or discussing targets with pupils. It is important for pupils to analyse in detail their performance in tests and examinations, distinguishing between careless errors, poor revision and genuine misunderstanding. The 'traffic light' system which we described above, creates a very useful record which can help you or the next teacher of the class plan for the next block of teaching. It also provides a very helpful document for target setting with pupils and parents.

Conclusion

The over-emphasis on the use of summative assessment for managerial purposes during the 1990s led to genuine formative assessment or assessment for learning remaining under-developed. However, the research evidence is clear about the potential for significantly improved learning which formative assessment techniques offer.

Formative assessment requires the use of questioning and discussion, the involvement of pupils in the assessment process, and high-quality feedback. To this end you should ensure that your teaching strategies include opportunities for pupils to articulate their ideas about the concepts they are developing and to test them out in discussion.

A sufficiently demanding and open problem is necessary to initiate and sustain discussion, which should be supported and developed through indirect questioning by the teacher. The resulting dialogue should explore children's understanding and encourage thinking and reflection.

The use of self-assessment encourages pupils to reflect on their own learning to identify which aspects are most important, what they have not fully understood and how to make progress. However, pupils need to be taught how to assess themselves. Involvement in peer-assessment helps in this process by providing a mirror for the pupil's own thought processes.

Formative assessment can enhance learning through the provision of effective feedback which conveys an image of mathematical ability as trainable and clearly identifies steps which the pupils can take to improve their performance. Feedback based on grades or marks fails to change future performance. Specific comments alone are far more effective. When grades/marks are combined with comments, the grades/marks dominate and remove the value of the comments.

Too much assessment and testing in schools seems to have the sole aim of generating marks for records. Although records are clearly necessary for medium- and long-term planning, we feel that you should ensure that any records you maintain for this purpose are valid, in that they assess children against appropriate learning objectives; and reliable, in that they can be trusted to indicate knowledge which is secure, and not forgotten shortly after the assessment. We recommend basing such records on portfolios of significant work which are maintained at intervals by the pupils themselves.

When periodic tests and examinations are used for summative purposes, pupils should be encouraged to analyse and reflect on their results. The 'traffic light' system encourages such reflection and generates a useful record for target setting and planning future teaching.

SECTION 2

Numeracy in practice: lesson ideas from the classroom

Each of the four chapters in this section is structured in a similar fashion and is underpinned by two themes.

The first theme exemplifies tried and tested ideas for developing numeracy within the programmes of study for Number, Algebra, Shape and Space, and Handling Data. Guidance is included on the common misconceptions held by pupils, strategies for overcoming these, lesson activities, worksheets, teacher guidance and strategies for assessment. There is no separate chapter on Ma1. An investigative approach permeates all topics and each chapter indicates how pupils may be encouraged to develop their mathematical thinking skills.

The second theme relates to the more generic advice given by the framework. In Chapter 7 we explore the opportunities offered by the use of the three-part lesson. In Chapter 8 we focus on algebra lessons which offer opportunities for significant pupil articulation of their ideas and strategies and consider how ICT can be used to support learning. In Chapter 9 we exemplify the use of techniques of formative assessment to improve learning. We illustrate how plenary activities may be used within the teaching of topics in shape and space to facilitate reflection and so contribute to the development of peer- and self-assessment. In Chapter 10 we examine the development of links within mathematics. In particular we consider examples of lessons involving practical and extended tasks in which the mathematical thinking skills associated with Ma1 may be developed.

CHAPTER 7

Developing numeracy within number and calculations

Introduction

In this chapter we describe lessons which encourage the development of numeracy within the context of the number and calculations programme of study. We have chosen the two lessons described here to illustrate the use of the three-part lesson structure recommended by the KS3 Framework when teaching decimals.

The lessons were taught in one of the RSN schools which showed a particularly high 'value-added' content in mathematics. They are described by the head of the mathematics department.

The lessons were planned following a review of the topic in the light of the framework. Decimals was chosen as the first topic to review because concerns had been expressed in departmental meetings that although Year 8 pupils had apparently performed well in classwork and homework, they had displayed significant misconceptions in end-of-term assessments. Collaborative planning was a common procedure within the department, intended to facilitate the sharing of good practice and to encourage common standards and approaches, and the description illustrates how a topic might be reviewed to introduce some of the key ideas from the framework to overcome common misconceptions.

Objectives

By the end of this chapter you should:

- be aware of some of the most common misconceptions in children's understanding of decimals;
- understand how a department might collaborate to review the teaching of a topic;
- understand how the three-part lesson structure can be applied to a lesson on decimals;

Warm-up

- understand how a warm-up session can be used for formative assessment and the identification of misconceptions in decimals;
- be aware of how techniques such as 'mathematical rumours' can be used to generate discussion involving mathematical reasoning and justification;

Main activity

- understand how mathematical discussions can help to address misconceptions;
- be aware of how trial and improvement can be used to investigate mathematical structure;

Plenary

- be aware of techniques which can be used in the plenary to generate collective reflection; to formalise the knowledge which has been gained and to make links and prepare for the next lesson.

Starting the review process

As a first step it was announced that time would be set aside in the next departmental meeting to review our teaching of decimals in Year 8. Each member of the department was allocated a task in preparation for the next meeting. For example, collecting together the resources currently recommended in the scheme of work, researching common misconceptions relating to decimals, analysing and summarising the questions asked in the end-of-topic test, reading and summarising suggested approaches to decimals from the KS3 Framework, etc.

This information was then distributed to each team member a few days before the next department meeting. We all familiarised ourselves with it so that time could be spent constructively during the meeting in planning the sequence of lessons and writing rich questions and tasks which would stimulate discussion and expose misconceptions, providing opportunities for formative assessment and effective teaching.

The misconceptions we hoped to address

As we discussed in Chapter 4, there are many common misconceptions associated with decimals. Many of these are based on an incomplete understanding of place value. In particular:

- *decimal point ignored*: when comparing decimals, pupils ignore the meaning of the decimal point and order them as if they were whole numbers, so, for example: 0.4 is assumed to be less than 0.16 because 4 < 16;
- *largest is smallest*: the size of the decimal is erroneously related to its length; as the number of decimal places increases the place value of each digit decreases and, therefore, it is argued that the value of the decimal becomes smaller;
- *line up the right-hand edge*: this is a specific example of 'decimal point ignored' in which previously learned algorithms for arithmetic are erroneously extended from whole numbers to decimals;
- *perform operations separately*: pupils often treat the digits on the left and right of the decimal point as if they are separate numbers. Thus 8.9 + 0.1 = 8.10.

$$\text{(see also Foxman 1985)}$$

The prevalence of these errors is indicated in the responses of 15-year-old pupils to the following question from the APU survey:

Which of the numbers below has the *smallest* value?

		Response rate	Error type
A:	0.625	4%	
B:	0.25	2%	
C:	0.3753	36%	largest is smallest
D:	0.125	43%	correct answer
E:	0.5	3%	decimal point ignored
Question omitted		2%	

(Taken from Foxman 1985: 54)

Not surprisingly, pupils' methods of calculating with decimals also display errors based on seemingly logical but flawed thinking. What errors would you expect to arise from these questions?

5.07 + 1.3 =

40 ÷ 0.08 =

In questions involving addition or subtraction, the APU found two prevalent errors (Foxman 1985). The decimal point might be ignored and the calculation performed as for whole numbers – the 'ignore the points and perform the operation' (IPO) error. Alternatively, pupils considered the decimal point to separate the number into two parts and the calculation was performed independently on these parts – the 'notice the points and perform the operation separately' (POS) error. Before reading on you might like to try out some of these questions with your own classes and compare the response rates with those obtained by the APU.

APU found the following pattern of responses:

	Response	Error type	Response rate for 11-year-olds
5.07 + 1.3 =	6.37	Correct	46%
	6.1(0)	POS	16%
	5.2(0)	IPO	6%
	7.(0)	IPO	8%

(After Foxman 1985: 71)

With tasks involving multiplication or division, pupils over-generalise from their knowledge of calculating with positive integers and assume that multiplication always results in a larger answer and division in a smaller. Frequently, pupils will obtain the correct numerical answer to a calculation but misplace the decimal point. For example, only 40% of 15-year-olds could calculate the correct answer to $^{4}\%.8$, and a further 14% gave answers such as 5 or 500 (Foxman 1985: 94). More recent analysis of pupils' responses to KS3 test papers indicate that such misconceptions are still prevalent (Ryan and Williams 2000).

We are sure that you will have recognised many of the misconceptions listed above. They were certainly familiar to us as a department. However, when we compared the types of question asked in the end-of-topic test with those asked during classroom activities a number of fundamental differences were revealed. The test questions were, in the main, more demanding than the questions set for practice during lessons. For example:

Test Question A   Write down the number that is halfway between 5 and 5.7.

Figure 7.1 shows the corresponding worksheet question

Write down what numbers the arrows point to:

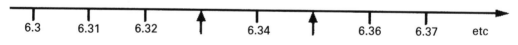

Figure 7.1   Simple worksheet question on the number line

Test Question B   Arrange these numbers in ascending order.

5.4   5.417   5.14   5.104   5.41

Corresponding question from the class text   Arrange these numbers in ascending order.

3.17   3.26   3.04   4.31   4.33

It was clear that many of the questions available in class texts and on a number of worksheets were repetitive in nature. They demanded no more of pupils than simply to follow a pattern or a set, routine method to arrive at correct solutions. Pupils did not need to think about the significance of the place value of the digits in the numbers used. An addition question, for example, would typically be set out in a vertical format:

```
    3.54
  + 4.07
  _____

  _____
```

Issues such as 'lining up' decimal points were avoided rather than confronted (see Chapter 4). We were not challenging pupils to develop strategies for dealing with questions such as:

3.54 + 14 + 2.7

After careful analysis of the types of questions and discussion of the main misconceptions associated with decimals we concluded that we needed:

- a carefully planned sequence of lessons on decimals (to include place value and calculations);
- a range of questions and activities to target common misconceptions;
- planned opportunities for pupils to give reasons for their answers and explanations of their thinking;
- questions to develop links between decimals, fractions and percentages.

We spent the following three department meetings planning sequences of lessons on decimals. We worked in pairs initially, then as a team, to link the lessons together. Extracts from two of these lessons are discussed in the next section.

Extract 1   Comparing and ordering decimals beyond two decimal places, including negative values

This topic was taught to my Year 8 class of 29 pupils; 15 boys and 14 girls. Over half of these pupils had achieved Level 5 in mathematics in their Key Stage 2 Tests with the remainder of the class having achieved Level 4. The extract below is taken from the fourth lesson taught in a sequence of six. In the first three lessons, number lines had been used to develop pupils' understanding of decimals to three decimal places. Pupils had been involved in estimating the position of a range of decimals; accurately positioning decimals on a wide range of number lines and using number lines to 'zoom in' to three decimal places. Figure 7.2 shows the number lines and calculations which we used to show how to zoom in. Volunteers were asked to read off the values at the arrows and the end-points of the new interval.

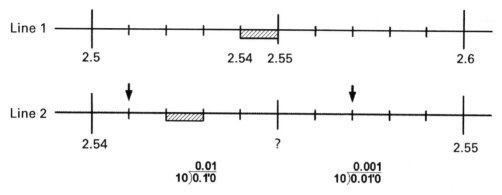

Figure 7.2   Using a number line to 'zoom in' to three decimal places

We worked on ordering a set of numbers (including decimals to 3 decimal places) in ascending and descending order, and developed mental and written strategies for adding, subtracting, multiplying and dividing decimals. Figure 7.3 shows how we used a number line to show decimal subtraction.

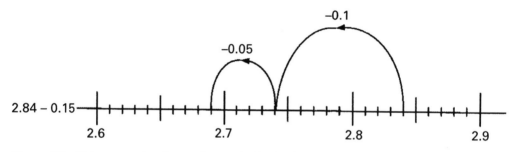

Figure 7.3   Using a number line to show a decimal subtraction (2.84 – 0.15)

For the fourth lesson, my objectives required pupils to learn to:

• compare decimals with different numbers of decimal places;
• order decimals in ascending and descending order, including negative values.

I also wanted to make some formative assessments of the class's understanding of place value in order to begin planning the next two lessons in detail. The importance of asking probing questions in order to make sound, formative assessments and to move pupils' thinking forward cannot be over-emphasised. Good teachers ask good questions. Such questions help them to understand how individual pupils think and to establish whether there are any 'gaps' in their understanding or if there are any underlying misconceptions. This implied a lesson in which I would need to 'think on my feet' in order to deal with misunderstandings as they arose, to encourage pupils to offer reasons and explanations for their thinking, and to reflect on what they had learned. Table 7.1 shows the outline lesson plan.

Number lines would form a valuable aid for this lesson. I intended to ask pupils to use them to explain their methods and to justify their answers. Each pupil would be given an A4 sheet with ten 'blank' number lines on it.

Table 7.1   Outline lesson plan: Hannah's homework

Activity	Description	Time
WARM-UP	A TRUE or FALSE statement written on the whiteboard for discussion 3.16 + 5.3 = 8.19 TRUE or FALSE?	10–15 min
Whole class	Pupils to discuss whether the statement is true or false. A short question and answer session to explore ways of convincing someone that it is false.	
MAIN ACTIVITY	Assessing Hannah's homework. Pupils asked to mark another pupil's homework giving reasons for any mistakes found in the work.	30–35 min
Pairs	Class to work in pairs, reporting their findings to the class after around 10 minutes and towards the end of the activity. Pupils to focus on ways to convince their teacher and the class of why their answers are correct.	
PLENARY Whole class	Summarising and consolidating the key points of the lesson focusing on misconceptions. Setting a short homework task to write some advice for Hannah that will help her answer similar questions correctly next time.	15 min

The warm-up activity

Written on the board before the class entered the room was a mathematical question for pupils to ponder:

3.16 + 5.3 = 8.19   TRUE or FALSE?

I chose this type of lesson starter and this question in particular because:

- it allowed me to make an initial assessment of the class's current level of understanding and to target two pupils whose work was causing concern. This would also help me formulate good questions to use later in the lesson to move pupils' thinking forward;
- the board prompt targeted two potential misconceptions: line up the right-hand edge, perform operations separately;
- I intended to ask pupils to supply reasons for their responses in order to convince me (and their peers) that they were correct. This would encourage discussion between pupils and create a culture of oral participation in readiness for the main activity.

I began briskly soon after the pupils arrived and settled down.

Teacher: I need you to work in pairs to decide whether the statement that I've written on the board is true or false. No guessing however, because I'll need you to convince me and the rest of the class why you decide whether it's TRUE or FALSE. You have around five minutes. Begin.

Pupil 1: Can we write things down?'

Teacher: If you need to. I'll leave that up to you.

Pupils began to work quietly at first, many considering the problem on their own.

Teacher: Once you've thought of your own answer, you might like to try to convince your partner first before I ask you to convince the whole class.

The noise and activity level rose at this point with pupils making tentative attempts at explaining their thinking to each other. After about five minutes I brought them to order:

Teacher: Right then, Gareth and Andrew, you can start us off; tell us whether you think the statement is true or false.

Gareth: We're not absolutely sure, but we think it might be true.

Teacher: Why, Andrew?

Andrew: I added the numbers up and it worked!

Teacher: Which numbers did you add?

Andrew: The five and the three, and the sixteen and the three.

Teacher: Does anyone else agree with the boys?

Siân: We don't. The answer is eight point four six.

Teacher: How do you know you're right?

Siân: Add the five and the three. Then add the decimals.

Following some discussion on what Siân meant by the decimals, I quickly recapped on place value of each digit in the 3.16.

The lesson continued:

Siân: I must be right because the answer has to be bigger than 8.1 something because you had a point 3 in the 5.3.

Teacher: Good. Does everyone understand Siân's reason? Put your hand up if you do.

Most of the class responded positively. At this point I drew this rough sketch of a number line on the board (see Figure 7.4 below) and asked 'Do you agree that the answer is greater than 8?' A loud response of 'Yes!' followed. I then continued by suggesting that we now only need to add 0.16 and 0.3 on to 8. Most pupils seemed at ease with this and, following some further discussion as to the value of each division on the scale, we proceeded to use the number line to show this addition.

Two pupils were then invited out to the board to estimate the position of 8 + 0.16, which they did by marking it with a cross and finally adding on 0.3 (shown as a series of three 'jumps')

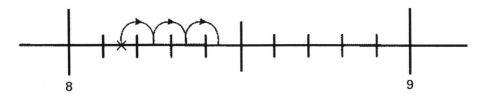

Figure 7.4   Using a number line to correct a misconception (3.16 + 5.3 = 8.19)

Andrew: It's eight point four six.
Teacher: Yes, well done.

We ended the warm-up by working out another question: 5.31 + 2.9 and used the number line again to show that the answer was 8.21 and not 7.40.

The warm-up had served its objectives well. It had proved to be a valuable tool for formative assessment, revealing which pupils held the expected misconceptions and had provided a useful stimulus for mathematical reasoning and discussion.

The main teaching activity

The main activity in this lesson asks the pupils to mark and assess the work of a fictitious student, Hannah. 'Hannah's homework' contains a number of errors and possible misconceptions planted there by me. The task offers pupils a chance to consolidate and improve their own learning by encouraging them to reflect on their own understanding of decimal place value as they try to find reasons for Hannah's errors.

In the previous lesson, pupils had begun to order numbers with three decimal places on number lines. Hannah's homework (see Figure 7.5) would offer them the opportunity not only to refresh their thoughts on this but also to order a set of numbers with differing numbers of decimal places. This would be an additional challenge.

I began the activity by setting the scene and introducing the task.

Teacher: I came across a piece of unmarked homework yesterday. Somebody called Hannah must have been late handing it in and just left it on my desk. I don't teach anyone called Hannah this year, but I thought I'd get it marked this morning so that I can find out who she is and return it to her as soon as possible, before she starts to worry about losing it. Since it's homework on decimals, I thought it would be a good idea if you helped me to mark it. I need two volunteers to hand out copies of the homework to everyone …

Name: **Hannah**   Class: **8C**   **DECIMALS HOMEWORK**

1. Choose either the < (less than) or the > (more than) sign in order to make each statement **true**.

0.3 $\boxed{<}$ 0.34   2.03 $\boxed{>}$ 2.1

0.08 $\boxed{<}$ 0.071   30.228 $\boxed{>}$ 30.3

2. Arrange these **DECIMAL** numbers in **ASCENDING** order.

0.132,   0.401,   0.625,   0.123,   0.041

0.041   0.123   0.132   0.401   0.625

0.12,   0.201,   −0.1   0.102   −0.09,   0.19   −0.109

−0.109   −0.09   −0.1   0.12   0.19   0.102   0.201

3. Add together:

3.4, 5.3 and 10.2

$$\begin{array}{r} 3.4 \\ 5.3 \\ 10.2 \\ \hline 18.9 \end{array}$$

4.6, 5 and 3.08

$$\begin{array}{r} 4.6 \\ 5 \\ 3.08 \\ \hline 7.19 \end{array}$$

4. Write down a number that is ³⁄₁₀ less than 3.1.   2.8

Write down a number that is ³⁄₁₀₀ less than 3.1.   3.97

5. Write down **5 numbers** between 5.6 and 5.65.

Now mark your numbers on this NUMBER LINE.   5.61 , 5.62, 5.63, 5.64, 5.6

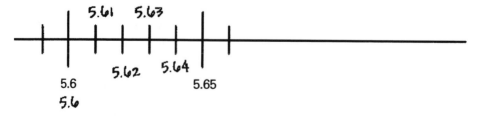

Figure 7.5   Hannah's homework

The copies were distributed quickly. I could hear some whispered speculation as to whom Hannah might be. A few pupils were busily searching for red pens! I felt confident that they were already interested in the task.

Teacher: Right then, who can tell me what I usually do when I mark your homework? What feedback do I give you? How do you know whether you've done well or not?

Pupils responded with:

- a percentage, a mark or a grade;
- a comment telling us what you thought of it;
- sometimes you write out some corrections showing us where we went wrong;
- you give us a target telling us what to do next in order to get it right.

After some further lively discussion on some of the reasons why I felt a grade was only important sometimes, and why I set targets for them, we agreed as a class that when marking Hannah's homework they would:

- work in pairs taking one question at a time;
- place a tick, a cross or a question mark next to each answer; the question mark would indicate either that they didn't agree with each other or that they were both unsure of the answer;
- find reasons why Hannah had made the mistakes, and write these down.
- think of ways of convincing the rest of the class and me that their marking was accurate and that their reasons were sound.

Pupil: Do we need calculators?
Teacher: If you feel at some point that a calculator might help or that you can't carry on without one then put up your hand and we'll talk about it.

As we discussed in Chapter 1, my intention here was to encourage the pupils to use calculators to support their mathematical thinking rather than to avoid doing simple mental arithmetic.

Teacher: Begin then and remember to listen to each other. Everyone will need a chance to say what they think.

The activity began quite noisily, some pupils getting paper, others moving chairs so that they could sit opposite each other. Some pupils were speculating on the outcome, 'I bet you it's all right, it doesn't look that hard ...' One or two quietly queried my motives, 'I wonder why she hasn't just marked it herself?'

After one or two minutes they settled to work with many pupils preferring to 'have a go' themselves first. They needed some time to look at the work and think about the answers themselves. Thinking time is important. I stopped them after approximately ten minutes to check how far everyone had got with the task. Most, by now, had read, attempted and marked most of the questions.

Teacher: Does anyone have something to report yet? Is there something you'd like to share with the class?

Some pupils said they suspected that parts of question 1 were wrong. Other pupils commented that question 4 looked difficult. One of the most able pupils in the class predicted that Hannah wasn't likely to do well if she'd got parts of question 1 wrong. Two of the quieter girls said that they thought that they'd use a number line in question 3 in order to prove that they were right and not Hannah. During this discussion a number of pupils wrote down some of the points made. I praised the class for working so well and for sharing their thoughts with the rest of the class. After reminding them to work in pairs I encouraged them to continue, and warned them that we would have another reporting back session in about 15 minutes time.

The classroom became very busy. I decided to focus my attention on two boys who had displayed some misunderstandings during the warm-up session. By the time I reached them they had marked the homework and were discussing question 1:

Pupil 1:   She's got the first two right I think, but I'm not sure really about the others

Pupil 2:   She thinks 0.071 is bigger than 0.08 … Maybe she's just mixed up the signs.

Pupil 1:   But she put them in the right place for the first two …?

Another, longer pause followed so I joined in the conversation:

Teacher: What makes you think that $0.08 < 0.071$ is wrong then? Can you convince me that it's wrong?

They thought about this for a while. I asked them to tell me the value of the digit '8'. They agreed it was 8 hundredths. I proceeded to ask them to tell me how many hundredths there were in 0.071. They thought about it and agreed it was seven although David argued the 1 thousandth made the number bigger than 7 hundredths. They eventually concluded that 0.08 was greater than 0.071.

Teacher: What mistake could Hannah have made then?

Pupil 1:   Maybe she got confused because one number had two decimals and the other number had three decimals?

Pupil 2:   She might just have thought that 71 was bigger than 8.

Before leaving them to move on to another pair, I asked them to draw me a number line that showed that 0.08 was greater than 0.071 and promised to return in a few minutes to see what they'd done.

During my discussions with a number of groups I judged that:

- almost all pupils had successfully marked questions 1 and 3, using their knowledge of place value to compare digit values in question 1 and to line up the decimal points accurately in question 3;
- a number of pupils had difficulty in placing the negative values on a number line;
- question 4 had, indeed, stretched the most able but a few pupils had succeeded in developing a sound strategy for performing these subtractions mentally.

I used this knowledge to drive the plenary.

The plenary

In order for the plenary session to help pupils to summarise, consolidate and reflect on what has been learned during the lesson, it should:

- be planned, with one or two clear objectives;
- be considered as important as the warm-up and the main activity;
- occupy a significant proportion of the lesson, often between 10 and 15 minutes;
- not include the few minutes needed to pack away and return equipment at the end of the lesson.

I had planned a plenary of 15 minutes in which to focus on one or two common errors or misconceptions and to ask pupils to write down some advice for Hannah to help her improve her work.

The following extracts taken from the lesson illustrate how these key objectives were accomplished in practice.

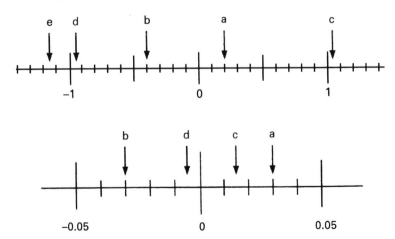

Figure 7.6   Using a number line in the plenary

I asked a number of pupils to come to the board to write down the numbers they thought the arrows pointed to and to share their strategies for working them out, for example: working out the 'halfway' number first, counting on and counting back. This allowed me to probe misunderstandings and to reinforce knowledge of directed numbers. It also provoked a useful dialogue on the infinite nature of the number line.

Finally, the class was asked to write down two pieces of advice for Hannah to help her improve her work. This had to be done for homework and pinned to the assessment wall before the next lesson. In the next lesson we would read them and select the best.

Review of the lesson

The number line provided a visual representation of decimals and assisted pupils to develop their concepts of place value. The true/false lesson starter prompted pupils to analyse their own understandings of decimals and hence to confront any misconceptions. The discussions required pupils to articulate and justify their strategies and answers. As they marked Hannah's work pupils were encouraged to compare her answers with their own approaches. An exercise in which pupils are asked only to perform calculations does not require this degree of analytical thinking. Some pupils may choose to reflect on their thinking processes but, in order to teach them to learn effectively, we should be encouraging all pupils to do so. In the next lesson extract we shall explore how similar approaches were used to extend pupils' understanding of calculations involving decimals.

Extract 2   Calculating with decimals

This lesson was taught to a Year 9, Set 2 class of 30 pupils: 17 boys and 13 girls. I suggested to a colleague that we might plan the lesson together. During the two previous lessons pupils had been dealing with approximations, emphasising estimation and the appropriate use of calculators. Some pupils had expressed surprise at the results of some of the calculations; for example, when multiplying 72.5 by 0.85, many had not anticipated the answer being smaller than 72.5. A few pupils were also unsure with approximations, particularly when required to approximate numbers with many digits after the decimal point, for example:

> Use a calculator to work out 15 divided by 7 and approximate the solution to 2 decimal places.

As a result of our discussions and the progress made by our pupils we decided that the main aim of the next lesson would be to investigate the effect of multiplying and dividing by decimals. In particular, the lesson objectives would be:

- to explore the effect of multiplying and dividing numbers by decimals greater than zero;
- to use a method of trial and improvement for refining solutions;
- to practise approximating solutions to a given degree of accuracy making sensible use of a calculator.

The outline lesson plan is provided in Table 7.2.

Table 7.2 Outline lesson plan: Grand Prix decimals

Activity	Description	Time
WARM-UP Whole class	*Multiplying makes numbers bigger.* *Dividing makes numbers smaller.* The warm-up activity will be a question and answer session to determine the validity of these statements. Pupils will be encouraged to try whole numbers, decimals and negative numbers in their investigation.	10–15 min
MAIN ACTIVITY Pairs	*The main activity will involve pupils playing a game:* Grand Prix Decimals. They will need to predict, estimate and use a method of trial and improvement to make progress and win the game. Short interactions between teacher and pupils will be used to check on progress, target misunderstandings and encourage estimation and checking of results.	30–35 min
PLENARY Whole class	Pupils will be asked to decide whether the statements are valid, summing up the key ideas during the lesson and using these as part of their argument. Teacher will draw the class's attention to common errors and misconceptions.	15 min

The warm-up: mathematical rumours

As the class entered the room, I had just finished writing two 'rumours' on the board:

Multiplying makes numbers bigger.
Dividing makes numbers smaller.

As I greeted the class and encouraged them to settle quickly, I noticed that some were already reading the prompt and drawing other pupils' attention to it. I began:

Teacher: Someone has started these rumours and apparently they're beginning to spread like wildfire. I don't know if any of you have heard them yet. Year 10 is beginning to believe them too! Do you think there might be any truth in them? Should we believe these rumours?

I asked the class to read the rumours to themselves quietly.

Teacher: OK, who believes the first rumour? Put your hand up if you do.

Most of the class raised their hands. A few held back, unsure.

Teacher: Well, I think we need to find out the truth. Let's get to the bottom of it. We'll look at the multiplication one first. I'd like you to think of a pair of numbers that will show that the rumour is true and then try to find a different pair of numbers that might show that the rumour is false. Keep an open mind; just try out some numbers. Work in pairs please. You have three minutes.

After a few minutes, the first volunteer to report back suggested the numbers 2 and 100:

Pupil: 2 × 100 = 200 so the rumour is true.

Most pupils offered whole numbers only so I decided to move the discussion forward.

Teacher: Only whole numbers? What about decimals?

The next suggestion was 3.2 × 2 = 6.4, again proving the rumour to be true.

Pupil: If you multiply by 0.5, it's false.

The class fell silent looking at me, waiting for my response.

Teacher: Ah! Let's work out 3 × 0.5.

For the next few minutes, pupils began trying out multiplications with a range of numbers.

We rounded off the warm-up with pupils calling out higher or lower to a number of calculations that I wrote on the board.

7 × 4	Higher or lower than 7?	Higher!
0.2 × 5	Higher or lower than 0.2?	Higher!
5 × 0.2	Higher or lower than 5?	Lower!
0.3 × 1	Higher or lower than 0.3?	…?

The last question resulted in a mixed response. Someone called out 'It stays the same.' The class agreed that if you multiply a number by 1 it would stay the same.

We decided that the first rumour was certainly not true.

A similar discussion followed on divisions. The class found these considerably harder, particularly examples such as

Is 5 divided by 0.2 higher or lower than 5?

We ended the warm-up without forming any solid opinions on the second rumour. I warned the class that I planned to return to it in the plenary.

The main activity

The main teaching activity was a game. We had used 'racing' type games previously in a variety of contexts: racing to the top of a pyramid, racing to complete a mathematical obstacle course, etc. This time we selected motorcar racing – 'Grand Prix decimals' (see Figure 7.7).

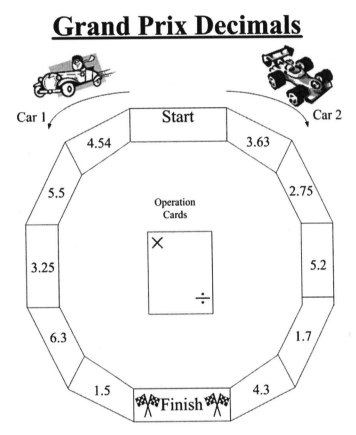

Figure 7.7   Grand Prix decimals worksheet

Pupils were encouraged to use rough paper to record the numbers they tried in order to refine their guesses.

Laminated card copies of the Decimal Grand Prix were handed out. Pupils were asked to form pairs and to quietly read the rules and instructions of the game. I projected an OHT copy of the game onto the board.

Rules of the game

- Play in pairs. You need a counter each, some rough paper and pencils, and one calculator.

- Decide who drives each car. You follow different arrows to reach the finish line.
- You must pick up an operation card for each turn. This tells you whether to multiply or divide.
- You must successfully multiply (or divide) the number you are on to equal the number in the next space. If your solution matches the number to 1 decimal place, you may advance. Otherwise, wait for another turn and then try to improve your operating number.

Teacher: I need a volunteer to help me demonstrate how the game works.

I chose a volunteer (David) and moved to the back of the class so that I could focus on the game and see the rest of the class at the same time. David stood by the board.

Teacher: David, you can be Car 1. Now, pick up an operation card.

It was multiplication.

Teacher: Right then, your challenge is to choose a number to multiply by 7 in order to make 4.54. Take a guess.

While David was thinking, I prompted the class to predict whether he would need a decimal greater or less than one.

David: I'll try 1.3.

I asked the class whether they thought this was a good starting number. One or two raised their hands, most were unsure.

Teacher: Think carefully. Does he need to make a number bigger than 7 or less than 7?
Class: Less than 7.

A number of pupils now stretched up their hands. They decided he would need to multiply by a number less than one. I asked David to think again.

David: I'll try 0.6 then.
Teacher: Why?
David: Half of 7 is 3.5, so it needs to be just a bit bigger.

I asked the class whether they thought it was a sensible starting number. They agreed that it was. David proceeded to work out 7×0.6 on a calculator giving 4.2.

Teacher: Could he have worked that out without a calculator?

A loud response of 'Yes' followed! We established a sensible procedure for using the calculators. Multiplying a decimal by a whole number should be done without and any easy divisions also.

Teacher: His target number was 4.54, did he match it to one decimal place?

The class agreed that he hadn't. I explained that he'd now have to wait for another turn.

Before setting them to play the game on their own, I asked them to give me a reason why David gave 1.3 as his first guess. They agreed that he must have tried to make 7 starting with 4. He had done the calculations the wrong way around.

During the activity, as I moved around the class, I detected an obvious feeling of enjoyment among pupils, with many getting 'stuck in' to the game quickly, sorting out the counters, positioning the operation cards and calculator, reaching for paper and pencils etc. I only needed to nudge one or two of the slow starters along. I called out that we'd take a 'pit stop' after ten minutes to see how everyone was getting along.

I decided to spend this time observing one pair in particular. I chose them because they were the reluctant starters. I wanted to assess whether they could make sensible predictions of the numbers to calculate with. I suspected that they would find the division demanding (along with many others in the class). Developing a 'feel' for these calculations would take time. I waited a few minutes and then sat quietly by their side, observing and listening to them playing the game.

Katy: I'm on 3.63 and I need to hit 2.75 by dividing.

She paused, and then looked at me.

Katy: These dividing sums are harder, I don't know what to start with. The only thing I can think of is trying any number like 5 and then going from there.
Teacher: Let's see if we can think of a way of starting with a better guess. What if I divide by 1? What will I get?
Katy: 3.63
Teacher: What if I divide 3.63 by 2?
Katy: A bit more than 1.5 because 3 shared by 2 is 1.5.
Teacher: Now take a guess at what I should divide by to get 2.75.

Katy shook her head. I sketched a number line (see Figure 7.8) on to some rough paper.
   Katy marked 3.63 and 2.75 on these lines.

Teacher: We agreed that 3.63 divided by 1 is 3.63 and 3.63 divided by 2 is just over 1.5, Katy, can you mark these on the number line?

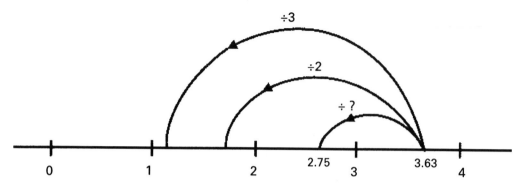

Figure 7.8   Using a number line to estimate the answer to a decimal division

Teacher: Now look at the numbers we have on the line and see if we can use them to take a guess at a number to try for 2.75.

Katy: I could try 1.5.

Teacher: Why?

Katy: It looks about halfway.

Teacher: Try it.

I watched as Katy worked out the solution and rounded it to one decimal place.

I observed the pair for the next few minutes, prompting them to use a number line to help them with their guesses.

During the pit stop I discovered that a number of pupils were experiencing difficulty with the divisions. I asked Katy to come to the board to explain how she divided 3.63 to get 2.75.

The plenary

In the plenary we planned to ask pupils to highlight the key ideas of the lesson while we would focus attention on misunderstandings. The teaching approaches used here are very similar to those described in the first lesson in this chapter. Questioning is again a key teaching strategy and we used it to probe understanding, to push pupils towards making predictions and to check whether answers were reasonable. Calculators were to be used throughout the lesson with pupils being encouraged to estimate before calculating. I stopped the class 12 minutes before the end. A few audible moans were heard. One or two pupils, I suspected, were on the verge of winning. Six pupils had finished already and were helping their partners along. Two of the most able pupils had started again, racing from the finish line back to the start.

I reminded them that we needed to decide whether the rumours we examined at the beginning of the lesson were true or false. I asked the least able in the class for their thoughts first. It was important that they came to their conclusions and shared them with us. Together, as a class, we summed up the 'Key Ideas' for positive numbers:

- If you multiply by a decimal less than 1 the answer will be smaller.
- Multiplying and dividing by 1 leaves numbers the same.
- Dividing by a decimal bigger than 1 makes a number smaller.
- Dividing by a decimal less than 1 makes a number bigger.

I was pleased with the responses. The last statement was still considered to be the most difficult, indicating that some pupils still had a limited concept of division. I made a mental note to pursue this further in future activities. We ended the lesson looking at the summary on the whiteboard and suggesting examples for each one.

Changing the focus: looking for mathematical structure

I was very happy with the way the lesson had progressed, with the children gaining insight into the effect of multiplying and dividing by decimals and learning to estimate answers. However, there is a mathematical structure underpinning the activity – inverse operations – and that had remained hidden by the trial and improvement process. I didn't want to let the opportunity to offer that insight pass so at the very end of the lesson I set a challenge homework to prepare the pupils for the next lesson.

'Now I'll let you into a secret. While you were *guessing* what to multiply or divide by in order to make your targets, I knew how to *calculate* the answers. For your homework I'd like you to try to think what calculation I might have been doing. We'll discuss your ideas next lesson.'

Discussion

In these two lesson extracts we have, we hope, described activities that your pupils would find interesting. Their main value, however, lies in the quality of the teaching and learning opportunities they provide. Starting the lesson with the 'prompts' posed challenging problems for pupils to consider. As pupils compared their views, both they and the teacher were alerted to underlying difficulties or misconceptions. The prompts were chosen to exemplify mathematical generalities and hence to encourage understanding of mathematical concepts.

The purpose of the main activity should be to extend pupils' conceptual development. Practice can be undertaken individually at home but interaction with the teacher is necessarily limited to lesson time. The activities were devised to require pupils to articulate their thinking, and to test the validity of their mathematical reasoning by trying to convince others. The teacher can then intervene to focus attention on significant issues or difficulties. During these discussions, pupils may take the opportunity to reflect on their knowledge and to identify which aspects are still not securely understood.

The main opportunity for reflection, however, is during the plenary. The tasks here were chosen to encourage pupils to consider what they had learned during the lesson and how this related to what was already known. It is in this phase of the lesson that implicit understanding of the type acquired as you busily apply an algorithm is formalised into accessible metacognitive knowledge of why that strategy is appropriate for that particular problem. As the teacher listens to the pupils' contributions, informal assessments can indicate which topics will require further attention.

Conclusion

One of the most publicised features of the KS3 Framework has been its recommended lesson structure and here we have illustrated how a three-part lesson can be used to assist with the effective teaching of decimals. However, it is important to recognise that although the three-part structure can provide a convenient format, the teaching and learning occurs during the interactions between pupils and teacher. Such interactions are not dependent on a particular lesson format but on the provision of opportunities for the development of mathematical thinking. In order to develop this type of thinking pupils have to articulate and compare their mathematical strategies, and to reflect on what they have learned, within a supportive classroom culture. The three-part lesson is but one of a variety of strategies which supports this. We shall explore these further in the next few chapters.

CHAPTER 8

Algebra

Introduction

Anecdotal and research evidence indicates that of all the areas of mathematics, algebra is regarded with considerable dislike (see e.g. Cockcroft 1982: 60). It is considered to be difficult to understand and, all too often, the tasks that are set, such as algebraic manipulation, appear to have no obvious purpose. The power of algebra rests in its ability to represent general functions and relationships succinctly through the use of symbols. This same power, unfortunately, is also the source of pupils' difficulties. When we use algebra we move away from working with particular numbers or contexts towards operating with the underpinning general patterns and relationships. This requires thinking at a higher level or, in Piagetian terms, the employment of formal, abstract thought. However, many pupils in lower secondary school are still developing their abilities to think at such a level. If algebra is to be taught effectively then pupils' learning must be scaffolded as they develop these new thinking skills.

Because algebra is so abstract, many teaching approaches resort to the use of metaphor and analogy. However, as we saw in Chapter 4, not all of these provide a sound basis for mathematical understanding. Inappropriate teaching strategies can contribute to the growth of restricted mental models and encourage misconceptions, which hinder the development of true algebraic concepts and formal thought.

In this chapter we describe lessons which use the teaching strategies recommended by the framework to teach algebra. In particular we focus on algebra lessons which offer opportunities for significant pupil articulation of their ideas and strategies.

Objectives

By the end of this chapter you should:

- be aware of strategies for teaching algebra which encourage significant pupil articulation of ideas and strategies;

- be aware of the levels of understanding which can be identified in pupils' algebra development and some of the key misconceptions associated with those levels;
- understand how ICT can be used to help develop the concept of a variable;
- understand how show-me cards, target boards and board prompts can be used as lesson starters to encourage pupil articulation and mathematical discussion.

Misconceptions

As we mentioned in Chapter 4, Küchemann's (1981) original analysis of algebra identified six levels of understanding.

1. Letter evaluated. Equations such as $x - 2 = 7$ can be answered from knowledge of number facts, without recourse to algebraic manipulation.
2. Letter ignored. Comparison of the two expressions is sufficient to complete the task, e.g. if $x + y = 6$ then what does $x + y - 2 = ?$
3. Letter as object. Fruit salad metaphors lead to letters being interpreted as objects such as apples and bananas, rather than as numbers (see task 4.5 in Chapter 4).
4. Letter as specific unknown. A letter is understood to stand for a single number, allowing the solution of tasks such as: if $e + f = 8$ then $e + f + g = ?$
5. A generalised number. Letters are understood to be able to take a range of values, so that pupils can answer questions such as: if $c + d = 10$ and c is less than d, what can you say about c?
6. Letter as variable. Pupils can analyse the relationship which exists between the variables, and can answer questions such as: which is larger, x^2 or $2x$?

(after Küchemann 1981: 104)

Pupils working at the first three levels do not demonstrate any understanding of algebra as a formal system. Only from level four and above, when they begin to interpret letters as, at least, representing a specific unknown, can they be said to have an understanding of algebra. Worryingly, Küchemann found that only 17 per cent of 13-year-olds interpreted letters in this way. This may be partly due to the type of tasks sometimes set during Years 7 and 8 in which misconceptions are not challenged but avoided, and correct answers can be obtained without the use of algebra, as in Level 1 above.

Algebra is often introduced by asking pupils to express instructions in words, for example through the use of 'I think of a number' games and 'Number machines', before moving on to represent the variable by a letter. It is tempting to use alliteration to suggest the letter. Consider this example:

In a dice game the instructions say to multiply the score on the dice by 2 and subtract 4.

= dice score multiplied by 2 and take away 4

= dice score $\times$ 2 – 4

= $d \times 2 - 4$

(taken from QCA 2000: 15)

The use of 'd', the first letter of 'dice', invites pupils to misinterpret its meaning as 'd = dice' thereby reinforcing the misconception that letters represent objects. Surprisingly, the example is taken from the QCA's 'Bridging Unit in Algebra'! We consider that alliteration is best avoided, at least in the early stages of developing the concept of letter as variable.

In addition to pupils needing to interpret letters as representing variables, the introduction of algebra also requires a more general interpretation of the equals sign. Until pupils reach tasks such as that exemplified in Level 4, the equals sign is often interpreted as an instruction to carry out an operation. For example, $x - 2 = 7$ can be read as 'what number take away 2 **makes** 7?' rather than a statement of equivalence between the two sides of the equation. Pupils who interpret the equals sign in this way will be unable to cope with the 'lack of closure' required by expressions such as $8 + g$ in Level 4. The desire to 'finish off' the sum leads to answers like $8g$ or even 8.

In Chapter 4 we identified the need for questions to be set which targeted misconceptions and provoked discussion in order to enhance learning. We have found activities which target misconceptions to be effective lesson starters which provide the teacher with an opportunity for formative assessment. We have also used ICT to provide valid and generalisable mental models for algebraic concepts. In the rest of this chapter we shall examine ways in which lesson starters and ICT can be used to teach algebra effectively.

Lesson starter activities in algebra

Since we introduced these lesson starters into our teaching we have found that such activities generate a buzz at the beginning of the lesson. Many of the tasks have an element of challenge, which the pupils enjoy. That is not to imply that the tasks are competitive in the sense of the slower learners ending up, yet again, at the bottom of the heap but rather that the challenge is self-directed; pupils are expected to use the activity to check on their understanding and recall of the topic. As the starter often leads into the main theme of the lesson, pupils have realised that if they miss out on this activity they find it harder to understand the new work. This has led to an eagerness to participate as pupils seek to clarify any uncertainties before the lesson proceeds. They are able to use the formative feed-back to enhance their learning strategies (see Chapter 6).

We have found show-me cards, target boards and board prompts to be useful activities to challenge misconceptions and to stimulate discussion in order to extend learning.

'Show-me' cards

'Show me' activities are now commonplace in primary classrooms and are used increasingly in secondary mathematics lessons, particularly in Year 7. As we suggested in Chapter 3, wipe-clean boards (plain, laminated card is suitable) can be used with water-based markers for pupils to write down their answers and then hold up to show to the teacher.

'Show me' has several advantages over the 'hands up' strategy for class questioning (i.e. when the teacher asks a question, the pupils raise their hands and one pupil is chosen to answer). Pupils cannot 'opt out' of thinking when 'show me' is used. The teacher can detect, at a glance, which pupils are not participating or are giving incorrect responses. Skilled teachers can use this instant feedback to generate follow-up questions. These may target individual pupils to confront misunderstandings, to challenge the most able or to support the weakest. Our pupils are generally unafraid of making mistakes during this activity as their responses are not public; only the teacher can see their answers on the card. For this strategy to be used to maximise learning, however, pupils have to be required to explain or give reasons for their responses. The following lesson extract describes how we used a 'show-me' card activity to start a Year 7 algebra lesson on 'Building expressions'.

Lesson entry: Pupils remove their show-me cards and water-based markers from their folders containing their exercise books, investigative work and other resources, e.g. 100 squares, number lines, etc.

Once the class had settled, I called out these instructions:

'I have a number y. Subtract 2 from it. What number am I left with?'

I waited a few seconds for pupils to write down their answers then called out,

'Show me.'

The class held up their cards to me. I scanned the class, making mental notes of blank cards or incorrect expressions. I showed my card with the correct expression written on it to the class and then asked a pupil with the correct answer to explain how they had worked it out. After two similar sets of instructions, I increased the difficulty of the task:

'I have a number, n. I double it, then add on 5. What number do I have now?'

This time I chose three pupils to come to the front and show their cards to the class:

$$2n + 5 \qquad n2 + 5 \qquad n \times 2 + 5$$

They explained why they thought they were correct and other pupils were invited to comment on the expressions before I established the convention of placing the number before the letter. I try to help children to reason and justify their thinking. I insist that the pupils who are not speaking are listening attentively and are ready to comment on the ideas raised. My aim is to encourage mathematical debate in my classroom.

After further practice of similar expressions, I continued with:

'I start with a number n. I subtract 6 from it and then double the answer. What number do I have now?'

Most cards displayed: $n - 6 \times 2$. Discussion of this led us into the main activity of the lesson — the use of brackets.

There are numerous variations on this approach, for example:

- you could hold up a board with an expression written on it and ask pupils to call out a set of instructions to create the expression;
- you could write an expression, say $4(x - 7)$ and ask pupils to give instructions to 'undo' it.

Using show-me cards in this fashion provides feedback on pupils' thinking, challenges mistakes or misconceptions, stimulates discussion and reinforces the interpretation of letters as variables.

Target boards

Target boards are now used routinely in both primary and Year 7 mathematics classrooms. Many commercially produced target boards are made from sturdy card large enough for the teacher to hold up in front of a class for pupils to focus on the numbers. Smaller, similar boards for individual or paired activities are also available. An alternative approach is to produce a target board on an OHT to project onto a whiteboard. This allows you more freedom during the lesson starter to circulate or to focus your attention on particular pupils. The main advantage of this approach, however, is that, during questioning sessions, you can invite pupils to come to the front of the class to circle possible answers on the target board and to explain their thinking. As the technology becomes more widespread, interactive whiteboards could be used to present such activities.

Target boards are frequently used to rehearse arithmetic facts; however, they can be used more imaginatively to develop, for example, mathematical thinking skills and algebraic understanding. We offer an example of an algebra target board in Figure 8.1.

The boards provide a focus for interactive teaching activities. When used well they provide opportunities for pupils to explain their ideas and can stimulate discussion. Pupils can be called up to the board to indicate possible answers. They can be asked to demonstrate their methods for calculating and estimating using a free section of the board set aside as a notepad. Such activities allow us, as teachers, to target any misunderstandings or potential misconceptions. Requiring pupils to explain their strategies helps them to develop their powers of mathematical reasoning and communication.

Lesson starters (or longer activities) using target boards can be easily produced for use with classes of all abilities in Key Stages 3 and 4. In the next two activities we will explore how target boards can be used to teach algebra. This first activity was designed as a lesson starter for a Year 8 class. The 4 by 4 board contains 15 expressions with one square remaining blank (see Figure. 8.1). The class of 24 pupils was divided into 4 groups of 5 and one group of 4. Each group was given a whiteboard marker pen, some rough paper and some pencils.

a	$a \times 2$	$2(a-1)$	
$a-1+a+1$	$2a-3a$	$a+10-4+3a$	$2a$
$4a+6$	$2(2a+3)$	$-a$	$\dfrac{2a}{2}$
$a-1+a-1$	$-1 \times a$	$1 \times a$	$2a-2$

Figure 8.1   Algebra target board for use in Key Stage 3

The lesson started with a quick recap on the work of the previous lesson. Pupils had worked on formulating simple expressions such as $a+7$, $2a$, $2a-3$ from simple word expressions and those which required the introduction of brackets, for example:

Add 10 to my number then double the result.

Subtract my number from 20 then multiply the answer by 4.

Following this, the target board in Figure 8.1 was projected onto the whiteboard and the class was given some time to study the expressions before we continued.

Teacher: We're going to play a game. I'll start by drawing a circle around one of the expressions on the board, then Team A will have two minutes exactly to come out and circle another two expressions that are equivalent to the one I circle. They'll also have to make up another expression of their own that is also equivalent and write it in the empty square. There will be 1 point for each correct expression circled and 1 point for their own expression.

Before beginning the game, I explained that there would be bonus points awarded if a team made mistakes, so everyone would need to listen and to make up an equivalent expression in case they had the opportunity to steal some points for their team. If you look at the board in Figure 8.1 you will notice that it is made up of five sets of equivalent expressions, some easier than others. The activity can be differentiated by asking the weaker groups to circle the simplest expressions and targeting the most able with the more difficult ones.

The game took just over ten minutes to play. During the game I made mental notes of any issues which would need following up later, for example:

- which expressions had been the most difficult for the class to unravel?
- were there any interesting expressions offered?
- were there any major misconceptions evident in pupils' responses?

I rounded the starter task off by posing these three questions:

- Who can think of a way to convince us that $4a + 6 = 2(2a + 3)$?
- Why isn't $4a + 6 = 10$?
- Is $4c = 4 \times c$ or is $4c = c + c + c + c$?

As the pupils offered their explanations to the class I was able to assess how confident they were with algebraic syntax. This also provided a further opportunity to emphasise that letters represent variables and, hence, the underpinning generality of the expressions.

The target board in Figure 8.2 was used with a Key Stage 4 class working towards the Intermediate paper at GCSE. They had generated sequences from simple expressions such as $2n + 4$, ½, $50 - n$ during the previous lesson and they were familiar with using the associated mathematical language 'expression', 'term', 'nth term'. The target board provided a focus to generate sequences given an expression for the nth term.

$n + 3$	$2n - 3$	$\dfrac{n}{n + 4}$
$20 - n$	n^2	$\dfrac{1}{n}$
$2n^2$	$\dfrac{n(n + 1)}{2}$	$(2n)^2$

Figure 8.2   Algebra target board for use in Key Stage 4

I used the board to recap the work from the previous lesson, but also introduced some additional difficulties, which would lead into the main activity of the lesson. I pointed to each expression in turn, beginning with the simplest linear expression and progressing to the fractional expressions before tackling the quadratics. These are a few of the questions asked. You may like to jot down some others.

- Write down the first five terms of the sequence.
- Write down the 10th term, the 20th term, the 100th term, ...
- Explain what happens to the sequence as n increases.
- Does the number 50 (or any other number) belong in the sequence?
- Find the expression that generates this sequence 1, 3, 6, 10, ...
- Do $2n^2$ and $(2n)^2$ generate the same sequence? Why?

We expect that, by now, you have thought of several other ways in which target boards could be used in teaching algebra. We have found the target board in Figure 8.3 useful to practise the substitution of positive and negative numbers and simple fractions, and to find equivalent expressions. Which questions would you ask using this board?

We consider the target board to be a useful format within which to frame starter activities. However, it is the quality of the thought-provoking questions asked by the teacher, and the interactions to support thinking in the ensuing discussion, which ensure an effective learning experience for pupils.

Board prompts

As we indicated in Chapter 7, a board prompt is simply a statement or question written on the board at the beginning of the lesson. Its purpose is to intrigue pupils, to challenge them to think and, possibly, to confront misconceptions. We like to use board prompts to set the scene for the lesson: we pose a problem to be

a^2	$\dfrac{5(a-1)}{2}$	1		
$2(a-1)$	$\dfrac{a}{a}$	0	$2a$	
$2a^2$	$10-2a$	$\dfrac{3a}{c}$	-1	
a^3	$2a-2$	$-2a$	$\dfrac{100a}{100a}$	

Figure 8.3   Algebra target board for negative numbers and fractions

analysed, demand that the pupils start to think for themselves and expect discussion and justification of their strategies and conclusions.

Board prompts can be created for any mathematical topic. The approach you adopt when using a board prompt to start a lesson will depend on what your objectives and priorities are for the particular class. If you intend to initiate whole-class discussion then giving pupils a few minutes to think of their responses and then asking for a number of contributions before continuing may be the most suitable way forward. If you wish to encourage pupil–pupil discussion then asking pupils to scrutinise the statement or question with a partner initially and then to share their ideas with another pair before reporting back to the class may be a better option. Varying your strategies in this way helps to ensure that all pupils engage with the task and participate in discussions, as they cannot rely on being able to hide in a group.

Discussion is particularly important to expose and address misconceptions in algebra and to help pupils to develop a full understanding of the concept of a variable. Consider how your pupils in Key Stage 3 would respond to these prompts:

- $8x + 4 + 7x - 3x = 16x$ TRUE or FALSE?
- $x^2 > 2x$ TRUE or FALSE?
- $x + 10 > 10$ TRUE or FALSE?

The first prompt targets a common misconception. The other two require pupils to substitute a range of numbers for x in order to investigate fully the truth of the statements and arrive at a general conclusion. Again, by increasing the degree of difficulty of the expressions used, similar board prompts may be created to start algebra lessons for the most able pupils in Key Stage 4.

Using an algebra board prompt with GCSE pupils

As my Year 10 class of 30 pupils entered the classroom, I wrote on the board:

Arrange these expressions in ascending order:

$$\frac{1}{n}, \quad \frac{1}{n^2}, \quad n^2, \quad 2n$$

The class were working towards the Higher GCSE paper. More than half the pupils had attained level 7 at the end of Key Stage 3 ; the others had gained good Level 6s.

Teacher: Right, settle down quickly, I've written a question for you to try on the board. I'd like you to work in pairs or in threes. Take a minute or two to read the question carefully first.

After the initial noise of settling down and reaching for equipment, the class began to read the prompt from the board. Many pupils jotted the four expressions onto a clean page in the back of their exercise books reserved for rough working.

Teacher: Does everyone understand the question? Yes? Good. I'd like you all to make a prediction. Look at the expressions and write down what you think the correct order will be.

The noise level increased significantly as pupils began to discuss and argue about a possible order.

Teacher: Sarah, start us off. What do you think the correct order is?

I held up the board marker to Sarah who checked her book and made her way to the board. Sarah took the pen and carefully wrote down

$$\frac{1}{n^2}, \quad \frac{1}{n}, \quad 2n, \quad n^2$$

Teacher: Thank you. Now, explain to us why you placed them in that order.
Sarah: n^2 will be the biggest, so $\frac{1}{n^2}$ will be the smallest; it'll be a fraction. $\frac{1}{n}$ will be a fraction as well, but $2n$ won't be.
Teacher: Does anyone agree with Sarah?

Many heads nodded in approval.

Teacher: 'Who disagrees? No one?
            OK then, I'd like you to look at the question again, but this time I want you to use these numbers for n' (*and I wrote: 2, ½ , and −2 on the board*)

Some murmuring was evident as pupils began thinking of the effects of using these numbers. One pupil called out:

Pupil 1:   'I only thought of whole numbers ... didn't think to use minus numbers.'

The class returned busily to work. Some pupils put up their hands to ask for reassurance when attempting to divide by ½ and ¼.

A few minutes later, pupils were again asked to come out to fill in values into a table I had quickly sketched on the board (see Figure 8.4).

n	$\dfrac{1}{n^2}$	$\dfrac{1}{n}$	$2n$	n^2
2	$\dfrac{1}{4}$	$\dfrac{1}{2}$	4	4
$\dfrac{1}{2}$	4	2	1	$\dfrac{1}{4}$
-2	$\dfrac{1}{4}$	$-\dfrac{1}{2}$	-4	4

Figure 8.4   A table of values for ordering expressions

Pupils were asked for their observations.

Pupil 2:   '2 and ½ work in reverse.'
Pupil 3:   'The squaring with the minus 2 changes the order.'

For homework at the end of the lesson I asked them to try other positive, negative and fractional values in the expressions to test whether their observations remained valid.

We have found that starting lessons with activities such as these have a number of benefits. They help to get the lesson off to a brisk, lively start and help to create a culture within mathematics classes where pupils are prepared to participate, to discuss errors and to think for themselves. Where questioning is carefully planned, the pupils' responses provide instant feedback about the current state of their thinking and knowledge. We can then intervene to focus the class's attention on key points or misconceptions in order to scaffold learning.

Scaffolding provides temporary support while pupils are learning a new skill or developing a new concept. Sometimes the support is provided by the teacher, using carefully planned questioning, but sometimes it can be provided by the use of ICT.

Using ICT to teach algebra

ICT capability is a key skill. All teachers are expected to contribute to its development with pupils of all abilities. The use of ICT can enhance the teaching and learning of mathematics but it needs to be employed appropriately.

There are four stages of development as teachers move towards the effective integration of ICT into their teaching. The use of ICT can be viewed as:

- the end-of-term treat: a special event which is expected to contribute little to pupils' mathematical knowledge;
- teaching someone else's subject: the main aim of the lesson is to develop ICT skills;
- a teaching tool: ICT is used to enhance the teaching of mathematics;
- ICT capability: the focus moves from teaching ICT or mathematics to meeting the needs of the pupils.

(after Kennewell *et al.* 2000: 99)

We should aim for our lessons involving ICT to meet the demands of the latter two stages. Just as we consider the appropriateness and desirability of using practical equipment, visual aids or calculators in the teaching of a topic, the potential for using various forms of ICT should also be considered within our planning. We have found the following checklist to be helpful:

- Will the use of ICT actually enhance the learning of mathematics in this lesson, or will it be a time-consuming, add-on extra?
- Will pupils already have experience of using a range of software from their IT lessons? If not, can we teach them the basics of using spreadsheets or databases in order to exploit their use in algebra and problem solving?
- Should we allow pupils some autonomy in selecting ICT as a tool to use in their mathematics lessons?
- How will we encourage them to reflect on the use made of ICT and evaluate the contribution it made to their learning?

ICT offers great potential for enthusing pupils and assisting their learning. Earlier, we discussed how teachers could scaffold learning through the use of questioning. In the next lesson extract we describe how a spreadsheet was used to scaffold the learning of lower-ability pupils.

Using a spreadsheet to solve equations through trial and improvement

The remainder of this chapter outlines a lesson to solve simple quadratic and cubic equations by trial and improvement using a spreadsheet. An outline plan of the lesson is given in Figure 8.5.

Activity	Description	Time
WARM-UP Whole class	Recap on squares, cubes, square roots and cube roots. A brief activity focusing on estimation. Squares and cubes of numbers to 10^2 and 5^3, including decimals: 3.5^2, 2.1^2. Estimate the square root of 20, the cube root of 30.	5 min
MAIN ACTIVITY Individuals/Pairs	Spreadsheet task: using trial and improvement to solve: $X^2 = 60$ $X^2 = 90$ $X^2 - 20 = 18$ $X^2 + X = 80$	40–45 min
PLENARY Whole class	Summarise and consolidate the key points of the lesson focusing on strategies for trial and improvement and the use of a number line to arrive at solutions. Set the scene for the next lesson.	10 min

Figure 8.5   An outline lesson plan for solving equations by trial and improvement

This lesson was taught to a Year 11 class of 18 pupils who were aiming for foundation level at GCSE. This topic was being taught towards the end of their course. Many of the pupils found algebra difficult, particularly when asked to solve linear equations or to substitute into formulae and expressions. Their teacher was concerned that the concept of finding and refining a solution to an equation using a trial and improvement strategy would become 'lost' amid the necessary substitution and calculations. As he explained:

> 'I need them to get the hang of using trial and improvement without imme-diately getting bogged down with the substitutions. They can use calculators for dealing with the decimals, but they still need to organise their results clearly in order to make sense of them.'

A spreadsheet offered a number of advantages.

• The spreadsheet would take care of the substitution and calculations while the pupils were able to focus on the underlying process.

- The spreadsheet would provide a tabulated format for recording results that would be straightforward, uncluttered and clear for pupils to interpret.
- The substitution of numbers into formulae reinforces the notion of letter as variable.
- ICT use is still enough of a novelty to motivate pupils.

The use of a spreadsheet in this initial lesson would allow us to focus on developing the concept of trial and improvement. The task would also help the class to develop the concept of a variable by allowing them to see x taking a range of values.

A very short lesson starter was planned in order to maximise the time available on the computers. The teacher had drawn a table on the board before the lesson started for the pupils to complete by calculating the squares and cubes of numbers from 1 to 10.

Two pupils were invited to the board to complete the table with prompting from their classmates. The teacher insisted that the calculations were written down each time in order to reinforce that $3^2 = 9$ and not 6! When the table was complete, some more quick-fire instructions followed:

- Estimate 3.5^2.
- Estimate 2.1^3.
- Estimate the square root of 20.
- Estimate the cube root of 30.

Pupils used the information generated in the table to estimate their answers. One pupil asked whether 3.5^2 would be exactly between 9 and 16. A calculator was used to find this out and to check how close other estimates had been. The lesson objectives were then shared with the class

- to learn how to solve quadratic and cubic equations using trial and improvement;
- to develop the idea of x as a variable quantity;
- to learn how to use a spreadsheet to work systematically and to organise our work;
- to revise how to insert rows and formulae into a spreadsheet and how to replicate;
- to appreciate the power of the spreadsheet to perform instantaneous recalculation when data is modified.

The teacher used a data projector to show her computer screen to the whole class. She asked for a volunteer to type for her and explained how to load the pre-prepared spreadsheet. She talked to the whole class while her typist followed her instructions.

The class had previous experience of using spreadsheets and was reasonably familiar with entering formulae. The teacher quickly showed the pupils how to input more complex expressions involving powers. In order to work out the results for a number of x-values, the formula needs to be replicated. The teacher inserted values of x from 1 to 10. Some gasps of surprise were audible as the spreadsheet instantly calculated the values of x^2.

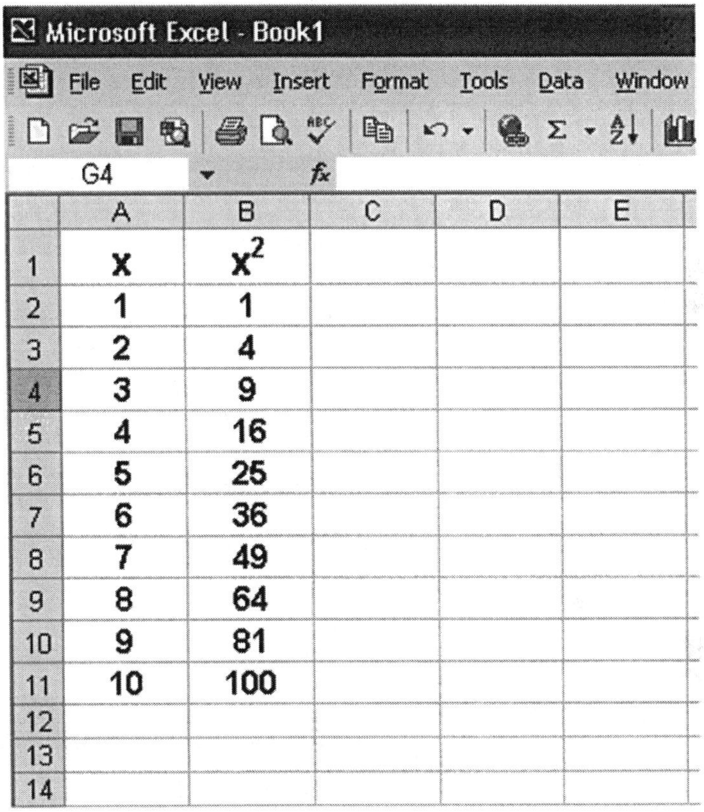

	A	B	C	D	E
1	x	x^2			
2	1	1			
3	2	4			
4	3	9			
5	4	16			
6	5	25			
7	6	36			
8	7	49			
9	8	64			
10	9	81			
11	10	100			
12					
13					
14					

Figure 8.6 Spreadsheet showing squares of numbers from 1 to 10

Teacher: Look at these values closely and remember that we're trying to solve $x^2 = 60$
Can anybody guess what x might be?

Pupil: Somewhere between 7 and 8

Teacher: Why?

Pupil: Seven squared is 49 and eight squared is 64.

This pupil decided that he'd like to try 7.5 although one or two others argued that he should try 7.6. The teacher went along with his wishes and proceeded to show the class how to insert a row to enter a value of 7.5.

This gave a value of 56.25.

Too low !

The process continued with the teacher inserting first 7.6, then 7.7 and 7.8.

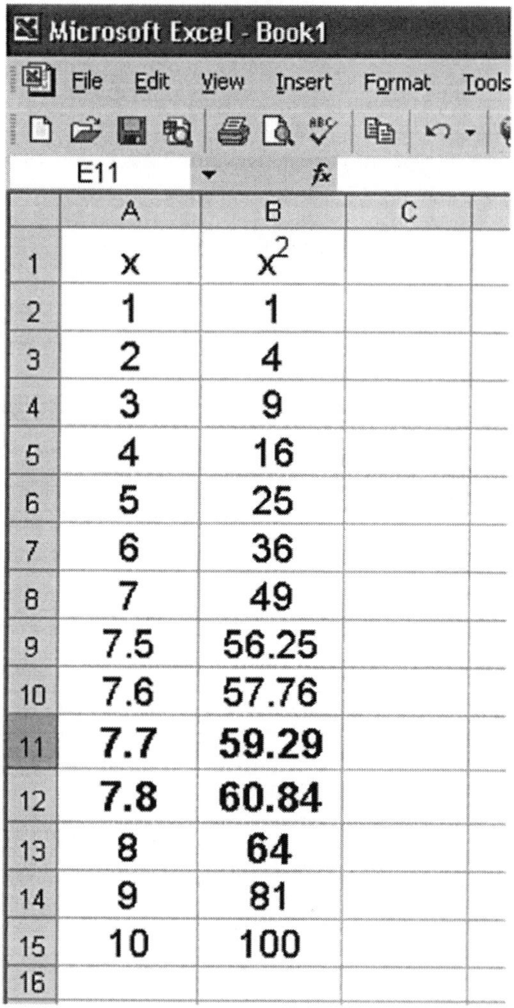

	A	B	C
1	x	x^2	
2	1	1	
3	2	4	
4	3	9	
5	4	16	
6	5	25	
7	6	36	
8	7	49	
9	7.5	56.25	
10	7.6	57.76	
11	7.7	59.29	
12	7.8	60.84	
13	8	64	
14	9	81	
15	10	100	
16			

Microsoft Excel - Book1 — File Edit View Insert Format Tools — E11

Figure 8.7   Final version of spreadsheet

Eventually, teacher inserted a value of 7.75 to help them determine whether 7.7 or 7.8 gave the solution to 1 decimal place.

At this point the teacher moved away from the computer and quickly drew a number line on the board (see Figure 8.8).

After some discussion, the class decided that 7.75 gave the solution to 1 decimal place. The class were set to work on other examples:

$x^2 = 90$ $x^2 - 20 = 18$ $x^2 + x = 80$

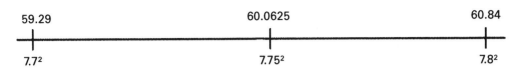

Figure 8.8   Number line showing numbers and their squares

The teacher insisted that the pupils drew a number line for each equation at the end to determine the solution to 1 decimal place.

With this small class of 18, every pupil had a machine to themselves but regularly checked their results with their neighbour's. It was a very busy lesson. Formulae were entered incorrectly and pupils needed constant reassurance that they were getting the correct results. By the end of the lesson, however, the pupils had solved between 5 and 8 equations with the most able progressing to equations such as $x^3 = 100$ and $x^3 - x = 5.5$.

After such a busy lesson a plenary is essential to help pupils to formalise their learning of the main mathematical points. Towards the end of the lesson, the teacher asked the class to sum up what they had learned:

Pupil 1:   You have to look for two numbers, one lower, one higher.

Pupil 2:   If you can guess between which numbers it'll be between, you don't have to fill in all the x values. You could just start with 7 and 8 say.

Pupil 3:   Drawing the number line helps to work out the final answer. You can get mixed up if you try to do it only from the screen.

The use of the spreadsheet had contributed to pupils developing a clearer understanding of the underlying trial and improvement process than would have been possible using paper and pencil methods or even a calculator. Part of the scaffolding that the spreadsheet provided arose from the visual, ordered display of the numbers and the facility to insert the next trial value in its correct position in the number sequence as pupils 'zoomed in' on the solution.

The help that this gave to pupils was evident in the following lesson when pupils, unprompted, set out their workings in exactly the same format as they had appeared in the spreadsheet. Pupils even left spare lines between the initial values for x so that they could insert their next estimates more easily. This suggests that the spreadsheet had provided pupils with a visual, mental model of the trial and improvement strategy. This mental model was retained into the next lesson even though the spreadsheet was no longer available.

The insertion of numbers into the spreadsheet formulae and the instantaneous recalculation of values reinforced the concept of letters as variables. Although it was beyond the scope of this initial lesson, the use of the spreadsheet could be extended to graph the functions and hence facilitate the development of different representations strengthening connections between different aspects of mathematics.

Furthermore, the lesson contributed to the development of pupils' mathematical thinking skills as they planned which numbers to select next and whether to continue to work via the spreadsheet or to represent the solutions on a number line.

Not only had the spreadsheet contributed to pupils' learning, the class had clearly enjoyed the lesson. We should not underestimate the power of ICT to motivate pupils. Their enthusiasm was contagious and the class and the teacher looked forward to the next lesson.

Conclusion

The abstract nature of algebra means that it is all too easy for pupils to develop misconceptions. These can only be challenged if they are made explicit and their deficiencies brought to the attention of the learner. Activities such as discussion, and mathematical argumentation, which require pupils to articulate their strategies and interpretations, are needed to provide opportunities for misconceptions to be identified and corrected.

The lesson starter activities described here all feature interaction, articulation and discussion as key teaching and learning strategies. The questions asked are intended to probe pupils' understanding and thus to indicate to both teacher and learner which points need further consideration before they are fully understood. Learning is scaffolded as pupils listen to the responses of others and contrast those interpretations with their own. The questions asked by the teacher should focus pupils' attention on key points and set up cognitive conflict when misconceptions exist.

ICT may also be used to provide scaffolding for learning. The use of a spreadsheet can reinforce the notion of letters as variables. The ease of recalculation means that arithmetic does not obscure the underlying principles being taught. The ease of switching between different representations helps to develop connections across areas of mathematics.

However, much of the articulation and discussion described in this chapter has been 'in the action' (Schön 1987) as part of a busy lesson and, unless pupils reflect on their learning, much of it will remain at the level of implicit knowledge. In the next chapter we shall see how plenaries can be used to facilitate collective reflection.

CHAPTER 9

Shape and space

Introduction

In this chapter we aim to exemplify the use of some of the key strategies recommended by the KS3 Framework in the context of the 'Shape and space' programme of study. In particular we talk about the use of techniques of formative assessment to improve learning.

Earlier, in Chapters 5 and 6, we discussed the value of plenary activities, which prompt pupils to reflect back on the lesson. The plenary session is intended to provide opportunities to summarise the main points of the lesson; to focus pupils' attention on what they have learned; to identify remaining difficulties and to identify what should be taught next (DfEE 2001a: 1.30). Such reflection encourages the development of metacognitive self-knowledge, by making explicit what pupils have learned and how this links with their prior knowledge, and also improves their ability to predict which aspects of a task are likely to cause difficulties.

Metacognitive knowledge is based on the skill of self-assessment. Learners have to be able to identify which aspects they have understood and which need further work. As we discussed in Chapter 6, pupils learn to assess themselves by participating in peer-assessment. As they try to assess the work of others, pupils reflect back on their own work and identify their own strengths and weaknesses. Discussion is a key element in this process. As pupils examine other pupils' work and listen to their explanations they may compare these with their own attempts and interpretations. As teachers, we can use pupils' contributions to focus attention on the features that are desirable in a good solution and thereby help to clarify the assessment criteria for the task.

Such discussions provide us with information to assess the progress made, where the pupils are, what they need to do next and so to provide formative feedback, which will help them to progress. We discussed the value of formative assessment and the involvement of pupils in the assessment process in Chapter 6. Here we will illustrate how plenary activities may be used within the teaching of topics in shape and space to facilitate reflection and so contribute to the development of peer- and self-assessment.

Objectives

By the end of this chapter you should:

- understand how formative assessment can be used in shape and space to improve learning;
- be able to identify some key misconceptions in shape and space and plan to confront them directly;
- understand how to focus attention on common errors ('hot spots') in plenaries;
- understand how pupils writing their own questions can be used to generate collective reflection on learning;
- be aware of how peer and self-assessment can be used in the context of a practical task on area.

We shall begin by considering some of the more common misconceptions which are met in the area of shape and space prior to discussing how such misconceptions may be exposed through formative assessment in plenaries.

Misconceptions and common difficulties

- Common terms and shapes are falsely associated with particular orientations. For example: triangles are always isosceles and base down, the word straight is taken to mean horizontal.
- Pupils often find it difficult to find embedded shapes within diagrams.
- Questions are significantly harder when a construction line is required or when the diagram is not provided.
- Similarly when finding areas of compound shapes, questions on squared paper are the easiest and those involving the calculation of lengths are the most difficult.
- When measuring the perimeter of a shape drawn on squared paper, pupils often count how many squares are around the outside rather than the lengths of the lines, thus adding one square on each corner.
- Pupils often confuse the distinction between perimeter and area. Associated with this is a failure to recognise the dimensional difference between length and area.
- When enlarging shapes in a given ratio, children often choose an additive rather than multiplicative strategy. Thus enlarging a rectangle with sides 4 and 10 to a new rectangle of 6 and x respectively will generate the answer 12 (10 + 2).
- Mathematical syntax is often ignored when writing algebraic statements in trigonometry. For example: $\tan x = \frac{3}{5} = 31°$.

We shall now consider how plenaries can be used to address misconceptions directly through collective reflection and discussion by taking extracts from two different lessons. In the first example, the plenary was fairly short, lasting less than ten minutes. The second plenary was used to formalise pupils' knowledge at the end of a unit of work and lasted for around 30 minutes.

Finally, we shall explore how a practical investigation into the relationship between perimeter and area of shapes can be used to develop skills of peer- and self-assessment.

Using plenaries to address misconceptions

Plenary 1:   Focusing attention on common errors (hot spots)

My Year 8, Set 3 class of 25 pupils had been working on finding areas of compound shapes made from rectangles and triangles. This is a topic pupils often find difficult, especially if the dissection of the shape into suitable areas is left up to them. Such dissections require pupils to visualise shapes within a diagram and to relate these to the formulae and strategies they know, i.e. to be aware of what prior knowledge would be applicable to the task. One of my objectives for the lesson was to develop such metacognitive knowledge.

The lesson starter had focused on strategies for multiplying decimals by whole numbers, with pupils developing strategies for performing calculations such as 5.5 × 6 and 3.4 × 8, using both mental and written methods.

During the main activity pupils had considered a number of compound shapes such as that illustrated in Figure. 9.1

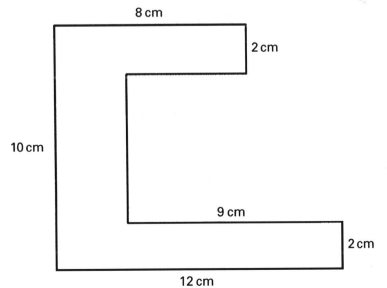

Figure 9.1   Areas of compound shapes

Ten minutes before the end of the lesson, I asked the class to stop working and to listen carefully.

Teacher: Put your hands up if you had any problems with some of the questions today.

Nearly all pupils raised their hands.

Teacher: Some of the questions were a little challenging, I agree. For the next few minutes I'd like you to work with your partner to write down some of the things that made the questions difficult for you. Write down some things that caught you out or some things that you'll need to remember in future when you're finding areas of shapes like these again. Make a list of warnings that you might give another class before they try the same questions. We'll call them 'hot spots'. Two or three will be enough.

I encouraged one or two pupils to look back at one of the questions in particular. Some pupils who had quickly written down their hot spots were instructed to share theirs with another pair.

Teacher: Right, Sarah, you begin. Read out one of your hot spots.
Sarah: You need to mark off the rectangles and triangles or you might get into a muddle.

I quickly sketched a diagram on the board (see Figure 9.2) and invited Sarah to mark off her rectangles. Sarah drew in some dotted lines explaining as she did so that this was not the only way that the shape could be divided into rectangles.

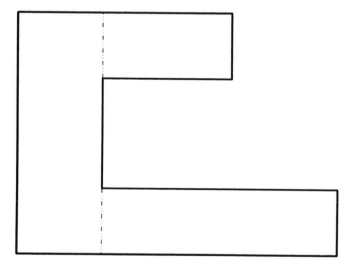

Figure 9.2   Dividing up a compound shape

Many pupils agreed that this strategy was a good idea. One pupil suggested that it was a good idea to write the areas on each shape after working them out in order to see clearly which numbers to add up at the end.

I continued to ask for more hot spots from the class. By the end of the lesson, the class had produced this list of warnings.

- Mark off the shapes clearly into rectangles, or rectangles and triangles.
- Check that you know all the lengths; you might need to work some of them out.
- Remember to divide by 2 when you find the areas of triangles.
- Make sure that you use the perpendicular height.
- You don't have to use all the numbers on the diagram.
- Check if a triangle has a right angle. If so, then one of the sides is the perpendicular height.
- Don't forget to add the areas together at the end.
- Check if you've got cm and mm. Change them all to be the same before you start.
- Get the units right: cm² or mm².

Each time a new hot spot was identified I asked the class to hold up their hands if they'd been caught out by it and used the board diagram to illustrate as many as I could. This gave me feedback on which aspects pupils had found difficult, providing a check on the impressions I had gained during the lesson.

The lesson ended with pupils being given a short task for homework (see Figure 9.3).

The Swimming Pool Task

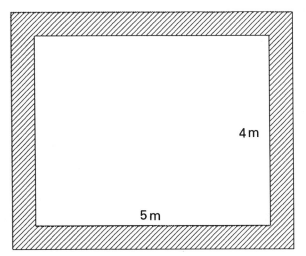

Stephen's swimming pool is surrounded by
paving 1m wide. Work out the area of the paving.

Figure 9.3   Path around the swimming pool

I expected that most pupils would divide the paved area into rectangles. Strategies for finding areas of borders and similar problems would form the main activity of the next lesson and the pupils' solutions to the homework task would be used as a starting point.

The discussion of the hot spots listed in the plenary made the most common errors explicit. This helped pupils to avoid them during the homework. In order to help pupils to remember these, I planned to revisit the list of hot spots at the end of the unit of work on area when the pupils would be asked to make a summary of the main ones in their books. An example of a pupil's summary is given in Figure 9.4.

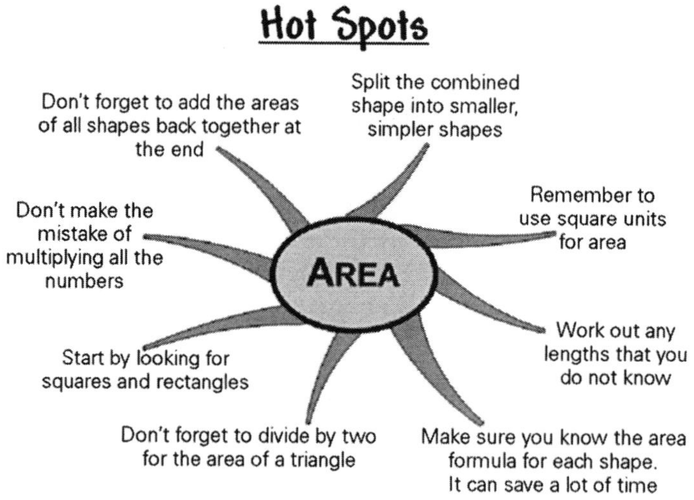

Hot Spots

Don't forget to add the areas of all shapes back together at the end

Split the combined shape into smaller, simpler shapes

Don't make the mistake of multiplying all the numbers

AREA

Remember to use square units for area

Start by looking for squares and rectangles

Work out any lengths that you do not know

Don't forget to divide by two for the area of a triangle

Make sure you know the area formula for each shape. It can save a lot of time

Figure 9.4 An example of a pupil's summary

A plenary of this type encourages pupils to reflect on their own learning but the quality of feedback to the teacher is dependent on how freely pupils will 'put their hands up' to admit to having made particular errors. An alternative strategy is to ask pupils to write notes for revision purposes at the end of every unit of work and to use the discussion of hot spots to illustrate their notes, giving themselves coaching hints in their notebooks.

Another useful strategy for helping pupils to reflect back on the key issues for learning in a topic is to ask them to try to write good examination questions on the unit. Promising to include the best examples in the final examination adds to motivation.

Plenary 2:   Concluding a topic: asking pupils to write their own questions

I used this plenary at the end of a series of lessons on trigonometry in right-angled triangles. The class of 30 Year 10 pupils were working towards the higher tier at GCSE. I planned to allow 30 minutes for this activity.

Teacher: I'm setting you a challenge. In pairs or threes I want you to write a really good question on trigonometry. Make it as tricky as you like, but take care that you can arrive at the solution yourself. I'll include the best questions in the end of year examination.

The prospect of having a question of their own in the examination (and hence some easy marks!) was all that was needed to spur the pupils into action. After a few minutes of activity, I stopped the class.

Teacher: I've just been eavesdropping on some of your discussions and I've heard a number of good suggestions for questions. Let's all think for a minute. What makes a really good, challenging question? Think back over some of the questions that you've tried during the last couple of weeks. Which ones made you think?

These are some of the suggestions made by the class:

- Questions without a diagram were the hardest. You had to concentrate on trying to see what it looked like.
- Some questions had diagrams with lots of details on them and were confusing.
- Sometimes you had to use something else to help you, like bearings or parallel lines.
- Questions where you had to find some angles and lengths first before you could get the one you wanted were harder.
- Some questions had triangles on top of each other. This made it hard to concentrate on the triangle you needed.
- There wasn't always a right angle there and you had to draw one in yourself to get a right-angled triangle that you could use.

I handed out a sheet of paper to each pair to copy out their final question as the class worked diligently for the next 15 minutes or so. I asked the class to try to incorporate one or two of these features in their questions.

As they worked, pupils discussed various approaches to designing a good question:

- Let's draw the triangles and decide which side we want them to work out. Then we can work backwards and decide what information we'll have to give them.

- We could make the numbers really big. I found those hard because you had to take more care with the calculator.
- Draw the diagram, then we'll write the question and get rid of the diagram at the end.

During such discussions, pupils made explicit the factors which they found made a question difficult. This helped them to be aware of any gaps in their understanding.

Ten minutes before the end of the lesson, I asked one pair out to the front of the class to write their question on the board (see Figure 9.5). A different pair of volunteers was invited to come out to solve the problem. One pupil was in charge of the board pen and the other the calculator. The rest of the class were told to consider the problem individually and to check the pair's method and calculations.

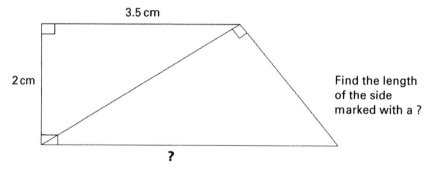

Figure 9.5 The first trigonometry question

The volunteers at the front proceeded to work out a solution to the problem. Every so often they turned to face the class, seeking their approval and, occasionally, talking through their method out loud,

> 'I'll start by drawing the two triangles separately, that might help me see the problem clearly.'

All pupils worked busily, checking each step of the solution. I encouraged the pair at the board to think out loud as this helped the class understand their approach and method. At the end of their solution, after the class had agreed that the answer was correct, I focused everyone's attention on one particular line of working:

$$\text{Tan } x = \frac{3.5}{2} = 60.3° \text{ (1.d.p)}$$

Teacher: Would someone like to comment on this line?

Pupil: I know what he means but it looks confusing. It more or less says that tan x = 60.3° but it's really x that is 60.3°.

I stressed the need to show workings clearly and logically. We agreed that the correct use of mathematical syntax was important when writing mathematics out formally. The pair at the board amended the line to

$$\text{Tan } x = \frac{3.5}{2},$$

$$x = 60.3° \text{ (1.d.p)}$$

Teacher: OK, we have a solution but could we have found x another way?

Another two valid approaches were suggested by the class and we briefly considered the relative merits of each approach.

Two more pairs were, in turn, invited to write their questions on the board and strategies for solving these questions were discussed. I stressed the different areas of mathematics involved in each problem (e.g. angle properties of parallel lines, bearings) and also emphasised the need to draw diagrams before attempting 'word' problems.

A number of challenging questions were written by the class and the best question (see Figure 9.6) was indeed included in the test.

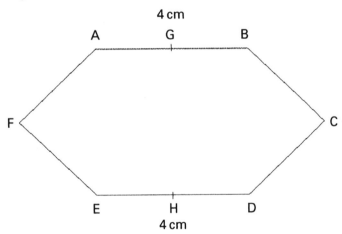

ABCDEF is a hexagon with two lines of symmetry, FC and GH. GH is 3 cm long and FC is 7 cm long.

a) Find the perimeter of the hexagon.

b) Find B$\hat{C}$D and C$\hat{D}$E.

Figure 9.6 The test question

Discussion – the value of plenaries

When pupils articulate their thinking and discuss their strategies it leads them to compare their progress with that of others, to reflect back over what they have learned, to identify what difficulties still remain and in what ways their approaches could have been improved. All of these processes contribute to greater metacognitive knowledge which, as we saw in Chapter 5, leads to improved performance in mathematics. Articulation of pupils' thinking also enables us as teachers to make more accurate assessments of our pupils' understanding and hence to scaffold their learning more effectively. Assessment is not only carried out by the teacher: underpinning these plenary strategies has been the expectation that pupils are able to assess their own work and that of their peers. In the next section we describe a task in which pupils are taught the skills of peer- and self-assessment while learning about area.

Using peer and self-assessment to encourage reflection

This task, 'Pipes and Wires' (Tanner and Jones 1995a) is shown in Figure 9.7. It was chosen for a Year 9 class during the months leading up to the Key Stage 3 National Tests for a number of reasons:

- the teaching programme for the term stated that the class should undertake an extended task, which targeted Ma1 and its associated thinking skills;
- the task was practical and would appeal to the class;
- it offered a suitable context in which to introduce the area of a circle.

All the extended tasks included in our schemes of work for Key Stage 3 focus on developing the metacognitive skills of planning, monitoring and evaluating. The evolution of these thinking skills is a major objective for pupils' mathematical development, especially when tackling tasks of this nature.

The task offers the opportunity for pupils to model real data, and to use and apply their knowledge and understanding of the areas of 2D shapes to solve a practical problem. Pupils are required to identify and control variables, to predict and test hypotheses and to explore algebraic relationships between two variables. The task yields fairly 'clean' empirical data, which can be plotted on a graph. A line (or curve) of best fit will provide a reasonable approximation to the actual function (area of the pipe plotted against the number of wires is linear, perimeter plotted against wires is quadratic).

A sequence of three lessons was planned. In the first lesson, I introduced the task. The second lesson focused on finding the formula for area of a circle. In the third lesson we returned to the 'Pipes and Wires' task with the intention of using the formula for area of a circle in the task.

My teaching approach followed the start-stop-go strategy described in Chapter 5. Pupils worked collaboratively to identify variables, to establish their question, to hypothesise and predict and finally to plan their approaches. My role

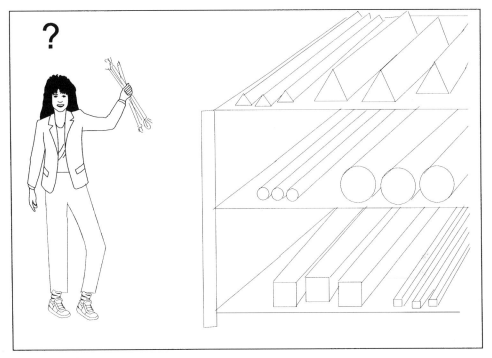

Siân has started work at Telephone Ted's company. Her job is to choose the correct size pipe to hold different numbers of wires. The pipe comes in different shapes and sizes, and the wires inside it must not be squashed but must not be loose either.

Siân's sister Susie decides to investigate in her maths lesson how many wires can fit inside a pipe using card and sellotape to make pipes and straws as the wires.

Can you help her?

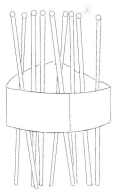

Figure 9.7   Pipes and wires worksheet

was to encourage groups of pupils to share their approaches with the class and to question pupils in detail about their plans. I had planned a number of organising questions to be asked during the lesson:

- What variables are there?
- Do you think any of them might be connected?
- How can we measure them easily?
- Can you explain your plan?
- What are you hoping to find out?
- Once you've collected your data, how will it help you?
- What will you do next?
- How will you convince someone that your rule will always work?

The aim here was to encourage pupils to develop a framework of questions to help organise their thoughts. Pupils had learned to expect to be asked these questions and frequently asked them of themselves as they worked. Pupils also began the practical data collection during the first lesson, making their pipes, counting the wires and recording their results.

In the following sections I describe some of the significant features of the lessons.

Lesson 1 The pipes and wires task

I introduced the task by setting it in a real life context.

Teacher: Have you ever counted the number of wires that are connected to the back of your TV, VHS or DVD players at home? Our systems looked like there was half a ton of spaghetti hanging out of them until my son had the bright idea of enclosing them all in a conduit. (There were some looks of bewilderment until this word was explained to them.)

Pupils responded with these remarks:

Pupil 1:   My dad did the same with our Christmas lights.
Pupil 2:   The IT room has loads of them, you'd get tangled in the wires if they were left loose.

I quickly focused the discussion on the size and shapes of different conduits, and illustrated points with a number of model pipes made from card and sticky tape in a range of shapes and sizes. Having caught their interest, I told the class to read the worksheet in silence for a couple of minutes, and to think of an interesting mathematical question to do with the size and shape of a conduit and the number of wires that would fit inside it.

Teacher: Once you've thought of an interesting question to investigate or a hypothesis to test you might like to think of a plan to follow. Write it down and discuss it in your group of three.

Pupils put forward their ideas and plans to their group energetically. Tentative plans were jotted down quickly with pupils anxious to 'get on' with it and make the pipes. I circulated, listening to the discussions.

A few minutes later, I announced that I now needed to hear some of their plans.

Teacher: We'll start by brainstorming all the variables that we can associate with this task. What things could we change? How would these changes affect the number of wires that would fit inside the pipes? Right, who's going to start us off?

A number of variables were identified by the class and I wrote each one on the board.

The shape of the pipe
The size of the pipe
The size of the straws (wires)
The area of the face of the pipe
The perimeter of the pipe
The amount of spare room in the pipe

Each variable was considered in turn. The class suggested a number of shapes for the pipes: square, triangular, circular, rectangular, and trapezoidal pipes were suggested. One very enthusiastic pupil suggested a semicircular pipe because it would rest flat against the floor with a curved 'top'. This would prevent people from tripping over it! I continued by questioning pupils further and asking them to explain some of the suggestions made.

Teacher: What did you mean by the size of the pipe, Stephen?
Stephen: I meant the size of the hole. You know, the hole that the straws will fit through.
Teacher: I'd like to hear some of your plans now. Tom, will your group start us off? Everybody needs to listen carefully. You might hear a plan that's similar to yours. You might pick up some good ideas that you can use. I'll also need to hear some of your opinions.

The class listened attentively as Tom's group explained their plan. Tom was asked to explain what they hoped to find out. What was their hypothesis?

Tom: We're going to start by looking at square pipes. We'll make a pipe that measures 2 cm by 2 cm first and count the straws that we can fit inside. Then we'll move on to a pipe that measures 3 cm by 3 cm, then 4 by 4 and 5 by 5. We know we'll get more straws each time. Maybe the number of straws each time will get bigger by the same amount.

The class was asked to comment on this plan. A number of observations were made.

Pupil 1:   I think it's a good plan and I think he's right about the number of straws getting more by the same amount. I think it'll be 4 or 5 more each time.

Pupil 2:   The perimeters go up in fours, 8, 12, 16, 20 ...
             but the areas don't – they go 4, 9, 16, 25 ...

Pupil 3:   I think you'll get more straws each time not the same.

Teacher: That's interesting. I wonder who's right? You'll need to test those ideas out. Now then ... Bethan, would you describe your plan?

Bethan: We thought we'd start by finding out which shape pipe holds the most straws. We think it might be the circle or maybe the square. Because we're going to change the shape we'll keep the perimeter the same, starting with a perimeter of 10 cm, so that it's a fair test.

Teacher: What makes you think that the circular pipe will hold more straws?

Bethan: We thought they might fit better because they're circles too. They won't fit exactly because they don't tessellate. We're going to work out the space wasted as well.

Pupils found this plan interesting and a number of hands went up to offer their thoughts and suggestions.

Pupil 1:   The wires won't tessellate anyway. I don't think it matters whether the pipe is a circle or any other shape. I think they'll hold the same number of straws.

Pupil 2:   The pipe will be pushed out as far as it will go for a circle. That's why it'll hold more wires.

After listening to the plans of four groups, I then asked the class to make changes to their plans (if they thought this necessary) and to formally write down their plans and predictions. The class then started work. Many groups worked efficiently, sharing the tasks of building the pipes between them. Some noticed that there were two different sized straws and hurried to alert other groups. The noise level in the class was quite high with pupils sorting out strategies for counting straws and for measuring and 'sticking' the pipes together. I warned the class that they had a further ten minutes to work before they would have to report back to the class again.

After ten minutes I stopped the class and asked a few groups to describe their progress. This forced the pupils to monitor their progress against their plan and also against the progress of others. It also gave me the opportunity to stress key strategies such as the need to work systematically, and the need to organise re-sults in a sensible way. Groups were encouraged to adopt strategies described by others if they thought it would improve their progress. A number of pupils commented that they couldn't make any further progress until they could work out the area of a circle accurately:

Pupil 1:   Is there a formula to help us work it out? We can use a square grid, but that might not be accurate enough.

I concluded by instructing pupils to tidy up their data by the next lesson when they would work on finding the areas of circles. Tidying away the pipes and wires took a few minutes longer, with pipes and wires being saved in empty boxes for lesson three.

Lesson 2   Areas of circles

In the next lesson, we followed up on this realisation that they need to learn a new piece of mathematics by developing the formula for the area of a circle and practising using it to find areas of circular shapes. We were then equipped ready to return to the problem of pipes and wires.

Lesson 3   Looking for connections

I began the lesson by asking the class to return to their groups and to spend a few moments refreshing their thoughts on the work carried out on the task so far. My main objective for this lesson was to encourage pupils to look for relationships between variables in their data, to draw graphs and use these to make predictions to be tested practically. The emphasis would also be on pupils explaining their thinking to me and to their peers. I explained these objectives with the class.

Teacher: Today I need you to complete your data collection, and start looking for relationships between some of your variables. You'll need to see whether your data helps you to prove that your hypothesis is true or false. Drawing a graph might be useful. If you find a connection or a rule, you'll need to test it out. I will be joining most groups during the lesson to hear you explaining what you've found out so far. At the end of the lesson you'll need to be prepared to report back to the whole class again.

   The class continued to work enthusiastically on the task. Pupils busied themselves completing their data collection and organising their data. Groups quickly moved on to scrutinising their tables of results, looking for patterns in their data. One group had decided to increase the area of their square conduits by 2 square centimetres each time and then taking the square root of the area in order to find the approximate length for the sides. They had predicted that the number of straws would increase in proportion.

Pupil 1:   It looks like we are nearly adding the same amount of straws each time. First it was 5 more, then 6 more then 5 more, but then when we increased the area again, we got 8 more, which seems a lot.

Teacher: What do you plan on doing about that?

Pupil 2:   Maybe we should set it up again and count them again. When you have lots of straws it's difficult to count them properly. I think we might have made a mistake.

The pupil filled the pipe again with straws, taking care not to 'push' the sides out, but to keep the shape of the square.

Pupil 1:   It's 6 this time. That's better.

Teacher: Can you draw a graph to show your results? What variables are you going to compare?

Pupil 1:   We'll compare the area of the pipe with the number of straws. Area across the bottom, straws up the side.

Teacher: What do you expect to happen to the number of straws if you were to increase the area of your pipe again by the same amount?

Pupil 2:   We should get about 5 more again.

Teacher: Could you draw a line on your graph that would help you make a prediction?

Pupil 2:   If we just join the points we'll get a zigzag line.

Teacher: What if you tried drawing a straight line to fit your points as best as you can.

The pupils discussed the best position for such a line. They eventually drew a very acceptable line of best fit. I encouraged them to use this line to make further predictions, which they could then test practically.

Most of my time was spent in this way, encouraging pupils to explain their results to me and pointing them in the direction of finding connections and rules. I issued a warning towards the end of the lesson that it was time to gather their thoughts in order to report back to the class.

Teacher: We need to hear if you've got anything interesting to report. I saw some groups drawing some interesting graphs and writing down some rules. Who'd like to share their findings with the class?

A number of volunteers raised their hands. Some interesting theories emerged.

Pupil 1:   Every time we increased the area by 2 cm^2 the number of straws increased by about the same amount. We drew a graph with a line of best fit. Our rule was something like number of straws is 4 times the area and add two. This seemed to work when we tested it.

Pupil 3:   We looked at the different shapes with the same perimeter. We found the areas of each one and counted the number of straws. We were right: the circle held the most. We also worked out the amount of free space in each shape. We then started working on circular pipes only, increasing the area each time. We need to do more work on this before we can say anything else.

By the end of the lesson, I was pleased that all pupils had made significant progress with the task. The task had required pupils to analyse their findings and predict and test relationships. They had been encouraged to give reasons for their thinking and to explain their work in detail. They had also learned how to find the areas of circles and had used this convincingly when working out the areas of their pipes and, indeed, the area of the straws (which had a diameter of 0.4 cm!) They had converted cm^2 to mm^2 and worked out the percentage of wasted space inside their pipes. A few had written their rules in algebra. One able pupil attempted to work out the equation of the line of best fit by using the coordinates of two points on the line.

For homework, all pupils were asked to write a formal report on their investigation into Pipes and Wires and to complete a pupil self-assessment proforma for the task (see Figure 9.8). They were allowed into class during lunchtimes to

PIPES and WIRES Self-assessment	Name: Bethan

☐ I thought of a simple hypothesis to test.
☐ I worked in a systematic way, increasing the perimeters
  or areas in equal steps.
☐ I took more than 4 sets of measurements.
☐ I recorded my results in a sensible way.

☐ I looked for patterns in my results.
☐ I explained unusual results.
☐ I looked for a rule connecting perimeters and the number
  of straws.
☐ I drew a line of best fit on my graph.
☐ I used a graph plotter to find an equation for the line of best fit.
☐ I wrote my rule in algebra.

☐ I made predictions and tested them.
☐ I explained how my formula or rule works.

☐ I investigated something else **how much free space ?**

What went well?	What problems did you encounter?	What would you do differently next time?
Using the graph plotter Drawing the graphs	The straws fell out sometimes so you didn't know if your results were right	Check results Try to explain my formulas.

Figure 9.8   A pupil's self-assessment sheet

complete any outstanding data collection. Three groups were invited to report back their major findings to the class a week later.

Pupils took the presentation of their reports seriously with many choosing to write 'scripts' to help to convey their findings clearly. Tables and graphs were drawn out carefully to be shown to the class. Sometimes we videoed the presentations; clips from the video are useful for discussion at department meetings and also provoke great interest at parents' evenings. Sometimes we would invite other staff to attend a presentation, a teacher from another set or the head of year, to impress them with how well the group had worked.

As each group presented their report, I used questioning to focus attention on key aspects — systematic working, reasoning, testing of hypotheses, justification of conclusions — and to relate these to the assessment criteria. Pupils were encouraged to ask similar questions and to contrast the presentation with their own reports. As pupils listened and participated, they compared their own work and self-assessments with those being approved through the public discussion. This helped them to understand the assessment criteria and to identify their individual areas of strength and any aspects that could be improved.

Conclusion

Formative assessment is an integral part of effective teaching and learning. However, assessment should not only be undertaken by the teacher. Involving pupils in the assessment process can help to develop their skills of peer- and self-assessment and thus to improve their metacognitive knowledge. A key element in the process is the opportunity to reflect on what has been learned and what is still not fully understood. One of the main purposes of a plenary activity is to facilitate such reflection.

Reflection should not just identify what mathematics has been learned within a given topic area. Learning mathematics requires links to be made with other mathematical topics and with other subjects. The explicit awareness of such connections is part of metacognitive knowledge. In the next chapter we shall consider how such links can be developed.

CHAPTER 10

Data handling and probability

Introduction

As we discussed in Chapter 5, for pupils to be described as numerate they must be able to apply their mathematical knowledge to the solution of novel problems. These problems may be found within mathematics itself or be drawn from real-life situations. The 'Handling data' programme of study (Ma4) relies on pupils being able to use and apply their knowledge of other mathematical topics such as fractions, percentages and graphs. The teaching of this aspect of mathematics, therefore, may make a significant contribution to the development of pupils' numeracy.

In games of chance, such as the National Lottery, pupils need to understand probability in order to be able to make informed decisions about their chances of success. Similarly, with the results of surveys and opinion polls increasingly being used to support media headlines, pupils have to be able to analyse statistics critically.

The thinking skills of information processing, reasoning, enquiry, creativity and evaluation should be learned across the curriculum, but have a particular relevance in mathematics. They underpin Ma1, 'Using and applying mathematics', and are significant for both the learning of new mathematics and the application of mathematics which is known. Although mathematical thinking should be taught throughout mathematics, the 'Handling data' programme of study is a particularly rich area in which to develop all of these skills.

Within 'Handling data' pupils can be asked to design their own experiments. Initially, these may be short tasks involving familiar equipment such as dice, spinners, cards or counters. Later pupils should progress to more extended tasks where sampling, significant data collection to test a hypothesis or the calculation of relative frequencies are needed in order to solve problems. For example, pupils may be required to devise surveys to investigate real issues, devising and testing hypotheses or to conduct experiments to obtain an estimate of the probability of a drawing pin landing point up or point down.

The current regulations for GCSE demand that each scheme allocates 20% of the marks to internal assessment or coursework. This must be split between a data-handling project assessing Ma4 and a task assessing Ma1 in the context of one of the other two programmes of study.

Experiments and investigations take on more meaning for pupils if they can relate them to everyday events. Data handling and probability tasks may often be derived from real-life situations so that pupils have the opportunity to use and apply their mathematics for problems of personal relevance to them.

In this chapter we describe lessons within the context of Ma4 and the making of links within mathematics. In particular we consider examples of lessons involving practical and extended tasks in which the mathematical thinking skills associated with Ma1 may be developed.

Objectives

By the end of this chapter you should be aware of:

- some of the more common misconceptions in data handling and probability;
- ways in which the teaching of data handling and probability can contribute to the development of pupils' numeracy;
- opportunities within 'Handling data' for pupils to develop the knowledge and skills required for Ma1;
- strategies to support pupils undertaking extended tasks;
- the value of using practical and real-life contexts;
- some of the ethical issues inherent in this area of mathematics.

Misconceptions and difficulties

Some of the difficulties and misconceptions associated with probability arise from everyday life, for example:

- Most pupils have had experience of playing board games that require the throw of a six to start or finish. As they sit awaiting this six, they intuitively compare the probability of getting a six with that of getting any of the other five numbers on the die. This often leads to the misconception that a six is harder to throw.
- As most everyday games involve events that have equal probabilities, pupils assume that all outcomes are equiprobable.
- The mathematical terminology associated with this topic is used in everyday contexts with less precise meanings, for example, 'that's a certainty' or 'you have no chance of doing that'.

Other difficulties relate to:

- an incomplete understanding of the infinite nature of probability, for example, 'recency': the notion that dice, coins etc. have memories – 'we haven't had heads for ages so we must get a head next throw';
- the calculation of probabilities relating to combined events when the outcome table is not provided but must be generated by the pupil.

(See Foxman 1985; Green 1984; Ryan and Williams 2000)

Within statistics, pupils need to appreciate the ways data may be misrepresented through the incorrect selection of scales or charts. They often fail to appreciate the need to select a scale which facilitates the plotting of intermediate points (e.g. steps of 5 or 10 rather than 3 or 7).

Difficulties also arise regarding the distinction between discrete and continuous data. The size and nature of the sample required for valid inferences to be made is also a complex and challenging topic.

Practical tasks often offer opportunities for pupils to collect data that challenge their naive misconceptions and create cognitive conflict. As we discussed in Chapter 4, these conflicts may then be resolved through discussion. In the rest of the chapter we shall illustrate how such tasks can be used in the classroom.

Devising a game of chance for The Christmas Fayre

This task was set to a class of Year 9 pupils during the early part of the Autumn Term. Most pupils were working at Level 6 of the National Curriculum. Their teacher had taken responsibility in departmental meetings for planning opportunities for pupils to engage in meaningful practical activities in their mathematics lessons and at home. One of the activities created for probability was called 'The Christmas Fayre – Games of Chance' to raise money for the school.

The teacher had planned to incorporate the activity as part of the series of six lessons on probability. The task demanded that the class use and apply the mathematical knowledge which was being taught in the probability lessons. It was presented in a sufficiently open form for the pupils to be able to make strategic decisions for themselves, to plan and evaluate their work. The intention was to develop knowledge and skills associated with Ma1 as well as Ma4.

The teacher decided to introduce the task during the first lesson of the probability unit of work. This would ensure that:

- pupils would begin to brainstorm some initial ideas early on;
- the teacher would be able to monitor their progress on a regular basis over the six lessons;

- key ideas introduced during the lessons would be highlighted and pupils encouraged to use and apply the new mathematics learned during the lessons to help them analyse their game.

At the end of the lesson she set aside 20 minutes to set up a task to be completed for homework.

Teacher: The headteacher has asked all the staff to start thinking of ways in which we could help in the Christmas Fayre this year. I know it's a little early to be thinking of Christmas but we need some new attractions to raise more money than we did last year.
Anyway, I came up with the idea of getting Year 9 pupils to invent some games based on their probability work and setting these up in the Christmas Fayre to make some money. What do you think? Can we do it? Are we all up to the challenge?

The Christmas Fayre

You have been asked to invent a game of chance to play at this year's Christmas Fayre in order to raise money for the school.

Your challenge:
- The game must make money
  - ➢ You'll have to decide how much to charge to play the game and how much prize money you'll give.
  - ➢ You'll need to work out the theoretical probablities of winning.
  - ➢ You'll need to play your game and compare your experimental results with the theoretical probabilities.
  - ➢ Finally, suggest an improvement to your game (make a change that will help you make more money).

Figure 10.1   Christmas Fayre worksheet

The class began to 'buzz' with initial excitement at the idea.

Can we work as a group?

Can we make our games attractive by decorating them?

Can we run the stall ourselves?

Can we charge people anything we like to play?

The teacher demanded that they think about the problem individually in silence for a few minutes.

Teacher: Does everyone have some idea at this stage of what the task is about?

The class agreed that they did. Many wanted to explain their ideas, but the teacher decided not to hear suggestions yet. However, she asked the class to work in groups of three or four and to think of two games per group by the next lesson. Their instructions were to write down a simple description of the game, the rules of the games and what it would take to win. In particular the group had to be able to justify that the game would make money rather than lose it!

The class worked on their ideas outside the lesson, during breaks and lunchtimes.

Fifteen minutes before the end of the following lesson, the teacher asked the class to sit in their groups and to get ready to describe and explain their games to the rest of the class.

Teacher: I need you all to focus on these points when you report back
  • Give a quick description.
  • Explain what someone needs to do to WIN.
  • How much will you charge?
  • What about prizes?
  • What will you need to do to convince me that it will help us to raise money?

Teacher: OK then, Jenny's group, your game first. Talk about your best game.

The group proceeded to describe their game. They were very enthusiastic; each member of the group wanted to contribute to their mini-presentation. Their game was based on spinners and dice.

'You get a chance to spin the spinner' (referring to a spinner with the numbers 11,12,13,14 and 15 on it), 'if you get a prime number then you can roll the dice. If you get a prime on the dice as well then you win. We're going to charge 20p to play and give £1 to every winner.'

Teacher: How will you show the total number of outcomes for your game?
Pupil: We'll probably draw up a table or maybe a tree diagram.
Teacher: Do you think you'll make money?
Pupil: Yes, there are two primes on our spinner and three prime numbers on the dice. That must be less than 50–50.

The teacher congratulated the group on their game and asked them to draw up their table of outcomes before the next lesson, when she would ask them the same question again. Another three groups were given a few minutes each to describe their games. The teacher asked each group the same two questions as she'd asked the first group. She also encouraged groups not to over-complicate their games and keep them to equipment that could be borrowed from school, brought in from home or easily made. Before the class was dismissed each group was asked to work out all the possible outcomes for their game by the next lesson.

The class followed their usual unit of work on probability. The teacher had planned, however, to incorporate some discussion of the 'games' project during each lesson. The sixth lesson was dedicated entirely to experimenting with the games for the Christmas Fayre. Each lesson ending was used to discuss how the new mathematics being learned would be used to help them convince their teacher that their game would make money. At each stage, the class was asked to carry out a small amount of homework on their game in preparation for the next lesson.

By the time the sixth lesson arrived, most groups had displayed the total outcomes of their game and had worked out the theoretical probability of winning and losing. They had also worked out expected profit and loss figures based on a range of charges and prizes.

The lesson started with a short warm-up activity on strategies for converting fractions to decimals. The teacher then recapped the main points of the previous lesson.

- Working out relative frequencies after a set number of trials, using a data collection table and grouping the number of trials.
- Plotting these accurately on a graph.
- Analysing the effect of increasing the number of trials on the shape of the graph.

The class was then encouraged to use the main part of the lesson to play their game, collecting their data in a similar way to the previous lesson, using a data collection table to record their experimental results. They were warned that they had around half an hour to complete this.

The lesson proceeded with groups setting about conducting their experiments, taking care to record their results systematically. The teacher circulated listening to group discussions and encouraging pupils to convert relative frequencies from fractions to decimals without the aid of a calculator, reinforcing and practising the strategies discussed at the beginning of Lesson 5 and Lesson 6. Groups were encouraged to share the work of these conversions. As the lesson went on a number of interesting points arose and the teacher jotted these roughly on a piece of paper to form the basis of the plenary.

- Some pupils were still experiencing difficulty plotting the decimal on graph paper.
- One group had commented on the fact that the probability of getting a six on their die and a factor of six on their spinner worked out to be less than either probability of the separate events.
- A group working faster than the others had decided to improve their game by amending the rules.

Fifteen minutes before the end of the lesson, the teacher announced that their time was up for now and that any outstanding experimentation would have to be completed at lunch-time. The plenary began with the teacher projecting the OHT in Figure 10.2 onto the whiteboard. A volunteer was given a pen and asked to plot the value 0.15 on the graph. Further volunteers were asked to come to the board and plot various values, each time explaining their strategy for deciding where to plot their value.

Games of Chance

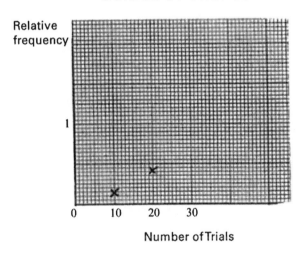

Figure 10.2   Recording experimental probability values on an OHT

Pupil 1:   I worked out where 0.1 was and 0.2, then went half way.

Pupil 2:   (When plotting 0.44). I worked out that 0.1 took up two small squares, so I counted up eight small squares for the 0.4, then 1 more square would have been 0.45, so I put my mark just under this.

Graeme's group were asked to describe to the class why they were surprised at some of their probabilities.

Graeme: We found that the probability of getting a six on our dice and a factor of six on our spinner worked out as about 0.05. But the probability of getting six on the dice is ⅙ and the probability of getting a factor of six on our spinner was ⅓. We expected the probability to be bigger.

Teacher: Do you all understand what Graeme just explained to you? No?

The teacher explained again, drawing a picture of Graeme's spinner on the board.

Teacher: Now then can anyone think of a reason why the probability of getting a six and a factor of six was smaller than either the ⅙ or the ⅓?

A number of pupils attempted to justify why the probability was smaller and not bigger, basing their explanations mainly on the fact that there were a large number of total outcomes for the combined event.

One boy offered this explanation:

Pupil 3: There must be less of a chance of getting both things than getting just one, like Manchester United have less of a chance of winning both the league and the champions' league than they do of just winning one of them.

After quickly calming down some heated arguments from rival football fans about Manchester United's prospects for the season, the teacher moved on to set the coming week's homework!

Teacher: I need you to complete all your experiments and graphs by next week. I also need you to work out the profit you expected to make and to compare this with the profit you actually made when playing your game. Joanne's group changed their rules slightly so that they would make more money. I'd like every group to do the same and use probability to explain why you'd increase your profits.

A week later at the end of a lesson the teacher checked each group's progress and set them the task of presenting their results and anticipated profits on a poster by half term. Figure 10.3 shows an example of one group's poster.

The posters were displayed for a week to allow the class time to read everyone's contributions. The teacher then set aside 20 minutes at the end of a lesson for peer-assessment. For each poster, the class were told to think of any questions they wanted to ask the group. For the purposes of assessment, they were told to consider how well each group had done under the following headings:

- accuracy of the mathematics;
- justification of the likely profit;
- communication and presentation;
- originality of the game.

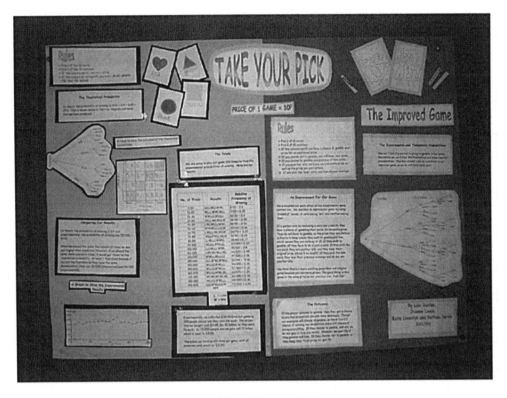

Figure 10.3   'Take your pick': a poster (School Fayre activity)

They were also asked to identify the best feature in each poster and any suggestions for improvement. The class took the exercise very seriously, making sensible, supportive comments which would help their peers in future activities of this type. Some of the games were very good and were used in the Fayre.

The teacher was pleased with the peer-assessment session and explained that she always tried to encourage the pupils to reflect back on their work and to consider how it might be improved. The delay before peer assessment meant that the activity was a helpful piece of revision a few weeks after the end of the original series of lessons. This also represented an opportunity for the teacher to assess how much of the work had been understood well enough to be remembered after the unit was over and to make a note of any areas which required revisiting.

She judged that significant learning had occurred and explained that the class had been enthused by the practical and believable nature of the problem. This task related to issues which pupils have met in everyday life when playing games of chance. Activities such as this provide opportunities to discuss the ethics of gambling as well as the mathematics. Real-life problems such as this may often motivate pupils, but the best motivation arises from problems which they have generated for themselves.

The next task was developed from an issue which was raised by the pupils in one of the RSN schools and is described by the class teacher.

Using data as a means of persuasion

Pupils of all abilities need to be presented with the opportunity to collect data that is relevant to them and in which they are interested. The following describes an activity undertaken with a small Year 8 class of pupils with Special Educational Needs. Again, the task targeted some of the skills associated with Ma1 in addition to those of Ma4, although because of the ability of the pupils, their strategic thinking was heavily scaffolded by the teacher.

For weeks, the class had been arriving at their Wednesday afternoon lesson hot and bothered. Their mathematics lesson immediately followed their games lesson! They often made comments like:

> I'd feel better if we had something cold to drink.
> My friend's school has a cold drinks machine outside the sport area.
> I think everybody would like a cold drinks machine.

I decided to help them to present their ideas to the head in a constructive way, hoping to motivate them with an issue of genuine interest to them. I planned to build the activity in over a period of two weeks (six lessons). The normal routine of the lesson would continue with the first twenty minutes concentrating on developing number work orally. The remainder of the lesson would be spent looking at various ways of collecting, summarising and representing data e.g. simple questionnaires, tally charts, tables, pictograms and a variety of bar charts. The drinks machine survey would be included in this work each lesson. I planned to include the following activities in the warm-up to support the main activity:

- Using a counting stick to:
    - count in different step sizes;
    - estimate numbers on the number line;
    - interpret interval lengths on different scales.
- Grouping in twos, fives, tens and hundreds.

The intention was to address some of the misconceptions associated with selecting and constructing scales on graphs in preparation for presenting the results of their survey.

Using the counting stick

The first three lessons started with a counting stick activity. I stood at the front of the class holding a counting stick with ten equal intervals marked clearly (see Figure 10.4).

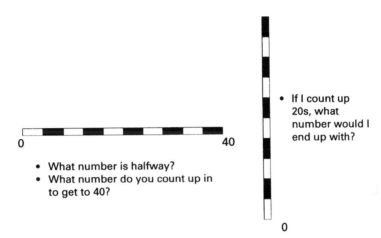

Figure 10.4   Using a counting stick to teach about scales on graphs

We began counting as a class in steps of two starting at zero. I pointed in succession to the interval markers as we counted. We proceeded to count up in fives again starting at zero, followed by intervals of ten and then 100. Having provided initial scaffolding by counting as a class, individuals were then invited to try on their own.

Michael:	Start at 50 and count up in fives.
Robert:	Count backwards in steps of two from 30.
Andrew:	Count up in steps of 20, starting with zero.
Stuart:	Count backwards in steps of three from 30 etc.

It was easy to target pupils with a range of differentiated questions. All pupils participated actively in the lesson with support readily available from two Learning Support Assistants who prompted on occasions, having been briefed about the task beforehand.

The activity was developed over the three lessons to include questions that required pupils to interpret and to make predictions.

The main activity

I discussed the issue of the drinks machine with the class and suggested that they ought to conduct a survey of pupils' opinions so that they could approach the headteacher with a reasonable proposal. We designed a short questionnaire to collect the information.

Teacher: We need to think of some questions to ask in our survey. What should we ask?

Pupil 1:   Do you want a drinks machine?
Pupil 2:   What drinks do you like?
Pupil 3:   Where shall we put the drinks machine?
Pupil 4:   Do you like cans or cartons of drink?
Pupil 5:   Do you want fizzy drinks or still drinks or both?
Pupil 6:   Do you want sports drinks?

As the pupils called out their suggestions, I quickly wrote them on the board. After the brainstorming, we considered the questions one at a time and categorised them as follows:

• questions that will help us decide whether pupils want a drink machine;
• questions that will tell us what drinks pupils like;
• questions that help us decide where to put the drinks machine.

These were the final selection of questions:

Would you like to have a drinks machine in school?

Yes ☐   No ☐   Don't mind ☐

Where shall we put it?

In the hall ☐   In the foyer ☐   Next to the sportshall ☐   Other ☐

What is your favourite drink?

Coke ☐ Pepsi ☐ Fizzy orange ☐ Still orange ☐ Energy drink ☐ Other ☐

Teacher: Well done, we now have our questionnaire. There's only one more thing to think about. Who shall we ask?

It took quite an effort on my part to focus the discussion. Everyone had a different opinion. One wanted to ask every pupil in the school. Another was only interested in the opinions of Year 8 pupils. Robert thought we should ask some pupils from every year group.

Teacher: Are you going to ask boys and girls?
Robert: I suppose so.

We finally decided on ten boys and ten girls from each year group. The pupils took turns to stand outside the main hall during morning assemblies to collect their data.

We summarised the data together. With such a small group of pupils, it was possible to sit together around some tables to deal with each questionnaire one at a time. I called out the responses to each question and the pupils created tallies of the results.

In the lessons which followed, I focused on analysing the data. The remaining lesson-starters were dedicated to grouping numbers. For example:

> If we have 17, how many groups of ten can I make?
> How many groups of five can I make etc.?

A few of the less able pupils in the class were encouraged to use counters for the activities initially, physically grouping the objects into different group sizes.

All pupils were encouraged to give reasons for their answers.

Teacher: How can I tell quickly how many groups of ten there are in 43?
Andrew: The number tells you, you've got four tens.
Teacher: OK, work out how many groups of ten and how many groups of five you can make with these numbers.

I wrote the numbers 23, 44, 28 and 37 on the board. The class began working on the numbers quietly, helped by the two Learning Support Assistants.

Teacher: Stuart, how many groups of ten can you make from 23?
Stuart: Two, with three left over.
Teacher: How many groups of five could you make?
Stuart: Four, with three left over again.

During the discussion that followed pupils were asked if they could see a connection between the number of groups of ten and the number of groups of five that could be made.

Robert: You can make more groups of five, double the number sometimes.
Teacher: What about 28? You made two groups of ten, and five groups of 5. Did you make double the number of groups this time?
Robert: No.
Teacher: Can you explain why?
Robert: There was another five, because eight is bigger than five.
Teacher: Can you give me a different number where you'll get double the number of groups of five?

A number of pupils thought about this and called out their suggestions.

Teacher: Michael, you give us a number.
Michael; Forty-one.
Teacher: Why have you chosen 41?
Michael; You won't be able to make another five ... see ... one isn't enough.

Over the three lessons, the work was developed. Most pupils began grouping numbers between zero and 100 accurately into groups of 2, 5, 10 and 20; many observing connections between the number of groups made, e.g. twice the number of groups of five as groups of ten, twice the number of groups of ten as groups of 20 etc.

The main focus of the next few lessons was transferring our knowledge of counting and grouping in twos, fives and tens to help us construct accurate diagrams and charts. During one lesson we looked at the question dealing with the location of the drinks machine.

I began by addressing directly some of the most common misconceptions about scale and the labelling of axes. I drew a bar chart which included many deliberate errors (Figure 10.5) and pasted it on to a large sheet of stiff card.

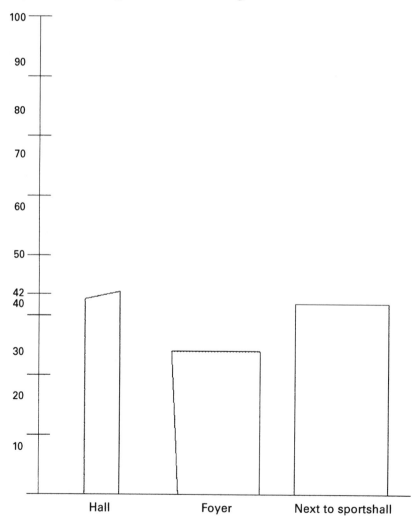

Figure 10.5   A graph demonstrating common errors and misconceptions

I then sat down with the group and we examined the chart together. Discussing a badly drawn diagram can be useful if the teacher:

- focuses clearly on the error and ensures that pupils understand why it is wrong;
- replaces the faulty diagram with a diagram drawn correctly;
- highlights the differences between the two.

Following our criticism of the badly drawn diagram, the group proceeded to draw a corrected version. During the final lesson we drew our conclusions. All that remained was to convince the headteacher that we wanted a drinks machine and, to his credit, he eventually agreed!

I was very pleased with the learning which had occurred during the task. The pupils were very motivated by its personal relevance and practical character. Addressing the misconceptions directly and in detail led them to understand their errors. With very low-ability pupils such as these, much scaffolding is necessary to ensure success and confidence building. Developing confidence in their own ability to use mathematics effectively is a significant element in building numeracy.

Similarly, low-ability children need to learn how to use and apply their mathematics at least as much as the more able. Inevitably I had to support them in this process, but I tried to present them with choices and to structure and guide their thinking rather than just tell them what to do.

The counting sticks and number lines provided much-needed scaffolding support for their learning and helped them to develop key concepts about number and scale. However, the use of such scaffolding tools to support concept development should not be restricted to only young or low-ability pupils. They can also support learning at a higher level as we will see in the next example.

Birth weights and number lines

Number lines are a very useful tool in the mathematics classroom that can illustrate explanations and support mathematical thought. We should exploit their potential wherever their use helps pupils to explain their thinking and reason mathematically. The following lesson extract illustrates the use of a number line to help pupils develop an understanding of standard deviation as a measure of dispersion.

The main aim of the lesson was to introduce the concept of standard deviation. The class had previously been using the median and inter-quartile range to compare sets of data. I wanted to use a data set which was personal for the pupils, but which avoided potentially sensitive measurements such as height or weight.

During the week leading up to the lesson described here, the class of 28 top set Year 11 pupils had been asked to find out their own birth weight and, if needed, to convert this to kilograms. All pupils succeeded in doing this and I used their data to prepare some overhead transparencies (OHTs) for the first lesson on standard deviation.

I began the lesson by displaying an OHT with all their birth weights on it (see Figure 10.6). I then asked the class to suggest some ideas on how we could analyse the data. Following this initial discussion, I proceeded to introduce and explain the idea of standard deviation as a measure of dispersion from the mean. We began by finding the standard deviation of a small set of measures (the heights of the five pupils sitting in the front row).

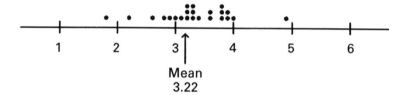

Figure 10.6   An OHT of children's birth weights on a number line

Once familiar with the technique of working out the mean distance away from the mean value, we proceeded to explore the use of calculator functions to help us deal with a large number of values (we had collected 25 birth weights). I displayed the OHT in Figure 10.6 and each pupil was given a photocopied version. This showed all the birth weights in kilograms on a suitable number line. We used calculators to evaluate the mean and standard deviation and marked the mean value with an arrow on the number line.

We then used the number line to help to analyse the data.

Teacher: Who'd like to come out to the board to show us the weights that lie within one standard deviation of the mean?

An eager volunteer was chosen. He carefully counted on from the mean weight, and marked this interval with a curved line (see Figure 10.7). The class counted the number of weights that fell in this range.

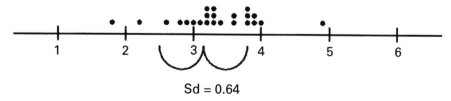

Sd = 0.64

Figure 10.7   Using a number line to show dispersion of birth weights about the mean

Teacher: OK then, using your own diagrams, work out the percentage of birth weights that fall within two standard deviations of the mean.

The class worked silently for a few minutes, carefully counting another interval in both directions and making the necessary calculations to find the percentage.

After checking that the class had arrived at the same answer, I then asked them to use their number line to estimate how many standard deviations it would take to enclose all the data.

I proceeded to ask them to make a number of predictions.

What if one other weight of 4.2 kg was added, how would this affect the mean? How would it affect the standard deviation?

What if we added a weight of 2.3 kg? What effect would this have on the mean and standard deviation?

What if we added a weight that was equal to the mean value? What would happen then?

I encouraged pupils each time to mark the value on their number line in order to supply them with a visual model of the additional data and to analyse what was happening. When would the mean increase? When would the mean and standard deviation remain the same? They were asked to explain their answers to each other and then selected individuals were asked to explain their ideas to the class. Some interesting and thoughtful responses followed.

Pupil 1: If you add one value that's equal to the mean then it won't affect the mean because you can imagine that you're dividing it by one and it stays the same.

Teacher: Look at the OHT again. What if I added 3 kg on to each birth weight? What do you think would happen then to the mean and standard deviation?

Pupil 1: They'll get bigger.

I then slid the overlay along the scale to demonstrate adding 3 kg to each value (see Figure 10.8).

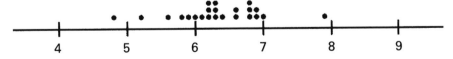

Figure 10.8   The effect on the distribution of adding 3 kg to each weight

A few pupils responded immediately.

Pupil 2:   The standard deviation stays the same.

On closer examination the class agreed that there would be no change in the standard deviation and that the mean weight would increase by 3 kg. One pupil offered this explanation.

Pupil 3:   If you add on 25 lots of three and divide by 25, the mean is three. That's why it increases by three. The standard deviation stays the same because all the weights are still the same distance away from the mean, although the mean is bigger.

Teacher: Well done. Now I want you to predict what will happen if we were to double all the weights. Write your predictions down. You can then use your number line and calculator to test your predictions for your new data.

The class worked on this for the remainder of the lesson.

The plenary

At the end of the lesson, pupils were asked to write a summary of what they'd learned during the lesson into their books. A brainstorming session followed in the last few minutes, drawing out all the key points.

Conclusion

Children are often motivated by the use of practical or real-life contexts in which to apply their mathematics. However, motivation is not the only reason for using practical or real-life examples in our work. Our pupils need to learn how to apply their mathematical knowledge and we help them to do this by demonstrating some of the ways in which mathematics can be used.

Numerate people choose to apply their mathematical knowledge to real-life situations and to interpret the world in mathematical terms. We need to help our pupils to make links between their mathematics and the world outside of school. When real-world contexts are chosen for study, misconceptions are often exposed.

The data handling and probability programme of study is a particularly appropriate one for making such links. Our children will grow up in a world in which they will be expected to make sense of statistics and make decisions in the light of probability data. The numerate person should be able to apply their mathematical knowledge to such real-life contexts.

Within this area of mathematics lie some contentious ethical issues. Probability theory underpins all games of chance from raffle tickets to the casino. As mathematicians we know that the payback is set so that the 'house' is always the winner overall, not the punter. Partly for this reason, some people and several religious groups object strongly to any form of gambling. On the other hand, many pupils will have parents who enjoy playing bingo or buying lottery tickets. We have therefore to approach the teaching of this topic with sensitivity. However, one of the aims of teaching probability is for pupils to understand the mathematics which governs their chances of success in such games.

Similar concerns may arise when using other real-life contexts such as conducting a survey to elicit public opinion about the location of a new power station or calculating the likelihood of illness arising from pollution, etc. Care must be taken not to alarm young pupils who have little control over their lifestyles. Yet if pupils are numerate, they should be able to use their mathematics to make an informed judgement about any risks or the quality of any inferences made from data. Teachers of other subjects, RE, geography and PSHE, for example, share similar concerns and we may benefit from working collaboratively with them on these topics.

The numeracy key skill underpins learning in real life and in other subject areas. The numerate school must consider the development and application of number across the curriculum as well as within mathematics and it is to this that we now turn.

Plenary: developing numeracy across your own school

In the spirit of the three-part lesson recommended by the Numeracy Framework, we feel it is appropriate to end this book by inviting you to reflect on what you have learned and to consider how you will use your new knowledge and ideas to implement change in your own school.

Numeracy, like literacy and IT capability, is one of the key skills which underpin teaching and learning across the curriculum. The key skill of numeracy demands that students actively seek and recognise opportunities to use their mathematical knowledge in other subjects and everyday life. Strategies for supporting the development of numeracy in a cross-curricular context are described in Chapter 11.

The final chapter is based on the results of the Raising Standards in Numeracy (RSN) project and describes the characteristic features of particularly successful schools at the level of the whole school and the department. It is intended to be useful to any teachers who wish to improve their own practice, but is specifically targeted at those who have some managerial responsibility for implementing change in their institution: numeracy coordinators, heads of department and senior managers.

Numeracy requires far more than basic arithmetical skills and techniques. It requires that pupils have the confidence and desire to seek opportunities to apply their knowledge on their own initiative. In order to develop such knowledge and attitudes, we believe that success in the key skill demands that children experience the effective use of numeracy as a tool or resource in all subjects in the curriculum. The aim is more than to support the teaching of another subject, although clearly this is one of our aims; it is also to apply mathematical knowledge in a range of contexts to generate the links which will make it useful and applicable. (You might like to review our comments about links within mathematics and between subjects in Chapter 5.)

CHAPTER 11

Developing numeracy across the curriculum

Introduction

Links between subjects and cross-curricular skills are far harder to develop in the secondary school than the primary school. Primary school teachers are inclined to view themselves as generalist teachers of children, who are able to emphasise links between subjects in a natural and authentic manner. However, secondary school teachers are far more inclined to view themselves as teachers of their subject. Most secondary schools are built both socially and academically around the subject departments and most secondary school teachers build their professional identities around their subject.

When they work well, departments may form closely-knit teams of collaborative and mutually supportive teachers who routinely share discussions about pedagogical issues and difficulties. However, if they are too isolated and parochial, they may also become 'bastions of curricular conservatism' which restrict professional development and fail children's needs (Siskin and Little 1995: 2). In particular, they may fail to deal effectively with key skills, social, and vocational education. Such cross-curricular issues are always in danger of being viewed as *someone else's subject* encroaching into one's own subject's precious time allocation. Hargreaves (1995) refers to schools in which subject boundaries have grown to be so strong that they impact negatively on education as 'balkanised'. Fortunately, balkanisation is not inevitable, and reforms aimed at developing key skills may in themselves encourage a more extended form of professionalism.

All secondary school teachers have a responsibility to teach key skills in addition to their own subject. We are not, however, equal partners in this. Subjects such as history are dependent on, and so may make a greater contribution to, the development of literacy. In subjects such as science, geography and technology, however, numeracy underpins much of their teaching and learning. Yet, even in these subjects, teachers must be convinced of the importance of numeracy if it is to become an integral part of their lessons. In this chapter we explore ways of working with colleagues from other subject disciplines to ensure that the numeracy key skill is developed across the curriculum.

Objectives

By the end of this chapter, you should:

- understand some of the issues associated with initiating and sustaining the development of numeracy across the curriculum;
- understand how a numeracy coordinator can initiate a programme for numeracy across the curriculum;
- be aware of effective ways of collaborating with colleagues who teach other subjects;
- be able to identify possible links between mathematics and other subjects, and be able to devise and use activities in other subject contexts which develop numeracy.

Initiating and sustaining the development of numeracy across the curriculum

The use of mathematics arises naturally in many subject areas. Science, design technology and geography are the most obvious examples but mathematics may also feature within art and design or even physical education. Coursework tasks in several subjects may require pupils to carry out surveys of opinion or to collect data to test simple hypotheses. The National Curriculum and the KS3 Framework indicate the mathematical content within other subjects and some opportunities for using and applying mathematics in the learning of those subjects. One of the challenges in developing numeracy across the curriculum is to find ways to incorporate mathematics into the practices of other subject colleagues so that the teaching and learning of that subject is enhanced as well as benefiting mathematics itself.

Numeracy across the curriculum must incorporate four main strands:

- the teaching and learning of mathematical knowledge, skills and attitudes in mathematics lessons;
- the further development of mathematical knowledge, skills and attitudes in other subjects across the curriculum;
- the use and application of mathematical knowledge and skills in other subjects, forging links between subjects;
- the development of the necessary skills, knowledge and attitudes in mathematics to support effective teaching and learning in all areas of the curriculum.

Each of these strands must be addressed if numeracy is to be developed effectively.

The interactive approaches to teaching and learning which we described in the first part of the book assume that pupils will be encouraged to think for themselves, to try to understand rather than merely memorise, and to develop their own approaches to mathematical problems. Often pupils will develop valid but idiosyncratic ways of working. This spirit of enquiry will quickly be crushed if when they come to apply their knowledge in another subject area they are told that their methods are wrong and an instrumental, mechanical line is taken. It is necessary for *all teachers*, not just the maths teachers, to understand the teaching style encouraged by the framework.

If a school-wide, consistent policy on numeracy is to be developed, significant changes in teaching approach may be demanded in a number of subject areas. Many secondary schools have appointed numeracy coordinators to drive the change. However, changes are likely to remain superficial unless they meet the aims of teachers' own subject cultures.

Pedagogy in secondary schools is driven to a large extent by the examination system. Teachers are under pressure to achieve good results and pragmati c conditions dictate the extent to which they will modify their practices to accommodate numeracy:

> Is the development of the numeracy key skill a syllabus requirement?
> Will the development of numeracy produce a better grade in my subject?

If the introduction of numeracy is to make a sustained impact within subject teaching, the first step must be to convince subject teachers of its value in terms of their own needs. The numeracy coordinator must work collaboratively with teachers to develop appropriate lesson ideas, which meet their subject-based needs and then to support their implementation in the classroom.

Collaborating with colleagues who teach other subjects

The role of the numeracy coordinator includes:

- monitoring the development of numeracy capability across the curriculum;
- encouraging the development of consistent attitudes and approaches;
- staff training;
- departmental support.

Most significantly, they are expected to work with the senior management of the school and with heads of subject departments to plan and guide the effective use and development of numeracy across the curriculum.

Success often depends on the personal qualities of the coordinator. Typically, an effective coordinator needs to understand the subject cultures and teaching styles of other staff. Furthermore, they need to be personally respected in the staff-room for their teaching ability.

However, the most numeracy-friendly schools do not rely on their coordinators being charismatic super-teachers. They support their coordinators by setting up managerial structures and procedures to facilitate two-way communication, backed up by clear messages from the senior management team that the development of the numeracy key skill across the curriculum is a priority for the school.

Successful school-based curriculum development demands supportive relationships among teachers. Curriculum development is best served by a collaborative culture which encourages trust, support and open channels of communication (Fullan 1985). Such collaborative cultures are usually spontaneous, voluntary, development-oriented and unscheduled. Unfortunately, they are also comparatively rare (Hargreaves 1994). However, the best subject departments that we found in the RSN project exhibited precisely these characteristics (Tanner and Jones 1999b). In fact, one of the major strengths of the RSN schools was that they had developed a culture of collegial collaborative teams, which could initiate and sustain change. What follows is a case study of the development and implementation of a successful whole-school numeracy policy as described by one of the RSN numeracy coordinators.

Developing and implementing a whole school numeracy policy: a case study

When I was given the role of numeracy coordinator my first feeling was one of dread. I was worried that introducing the numeracy key skill across the curriculum would turn into yet another one of those initiatives that is dead before the external speaker's car has left the car park!

Mathematics teachers have a vested interest in teaching numeracy and clearly there was potential for a great deal of added value if I could persuade my colleagues in other subjects to join us in that aim. But how? What would be in it for them?

Well, some subjects are obvious users of mathematics, and over the years we have all heard them complain of the failure of pupils to apply their knowledge outside of the mathematics classroom. A whole school numeracy policy should result in increased support for such departments and improve learning in their subject. Even in subjects that are not the most obvious users of numeracy, there might be something to gain if only I could think of the right ideas to offer; after all, as a mathematics department we had benefited from the literacy initiative last year. And, in the end, a successful policy was bound to help the pupils.

I began by getting up to speed on the latest ideas in numeracy teaching and research. I went to a number of sources: obviously the official documents like the framework, but I also searched the web and talked to the mathematics education tutors in my local university.

The cadre group

The head had designated numeracy as the theme for the coming school year. I started in September by setting up a cadre group to devise ideas and to steer the initiative. Each department was invited to send a representative to the group. Some were heads of department, but not necessarily; what I asked for was someone who was keen, someone who was interested in developing numeracy in their subject. There were 11 people in the group. I was very lucky: no department failed to send a representative. The head had made it clear that he supported the initiative and teachers in our school are always willing to work together and cooperate for the good of the pupils.

In most schools it is the science department which traditionally is the most reluctant to collaborate with mathematics over common approaches. They sometimes think they have numeracy 'sussed'. Because mathematics accounts for a fair proportion of their syllabus they think that they don't need to be supported by initiatives like this. However, I was very keen for the science department to be involved. It was important for the initiative for them to be closely involved in the development of common approaches so that they would feel a sense of ownership over strategies and commitment to the project's success. Fortunately, our science department was positive and sent a representative to each meeting of the group.

We met twice during the autumn term. In the first meeting, I gave an overview of the numeracy framework and some of the developments which were taking place in the mathematics department. Obviously there was an emphasis on mental methods and interactive teaching, but I also tried to make it relevant to them and we talked a lot about analysing data.

At the end of the first meeting they all went away with the task of looking through their schemes of work and national curriculum documents to pick out areas where mathematics might be relevant to their subject. This audit of mathematics across subject would inform the next cadre group meeting.

The cadre group representative was also responsible for raising numeracy as an issue at their next departmental meeting. I offered that I, or another member of the mathematics department, would be willing to attend departmental meetings to offer advice and support if a numeracy issue was being discussed. The head gave the initiative his full backing and demanded that every departmental meeting should include an item on the teaching of key skills and the sharing of good practice. Monthly reports on developments in relation to key skills had to be sent to him by heads of departments. Two years later this demand is still in force and members of the mathematics department are regularly invited to attend meetings of other departments.

Some of the results of the initial audit are shown below:

Sport and culture
Measurement of heights, lengths, distances, time, position, direction, fitness-related data.
Using data and making comparisons, e.g. cricket averages etc.
Proportion, enlargements, measurements, symmetry in art.
Measurement, scale drawing and the interpretation of 2D instructions to 3D actions in drama.

Design and technology
Measuring lengths, angles, areas, volumes.
3D shapes and their nets (developments).
Enlarging or reducing designs, use of scale and proportion.
Working out times, costing of materials.
Analysing foods, e.g. finding the percentage of carbohydrate and using this information to make comparisons.
Weighing and reading a variety of scales including decimals on electronic scales.
Adapting recipes for different numbers of people using ratio and proportion.

English/Media
Spelling of key mathematical vocabulary.
Interpretation of graphs and charts from the media.
Reading of non-fiction in which mathematical vocabulary charts and tables have to be interpreted.
Using data, its representation and analysis in a piece of persuasive writing.
Analysis of opinions on reading habits or preferences of books, e.g. percentage of people who liked sci-fi, crime, comedy, novels etc.
Comparing the language used in different texts, e.g. analysing word lengths in novels, newspapers, magazines etc.

Humanities
Collecting data by counting, measuring and surveys.
Measurement and units.
Maps, coordinates, angles, directions, scales and ratios.
Use of numerical data when making geographical descriptions and comparisons, e.g. comparing populations or areas.

Investigative and problem-solving work in field studies.
Calculations, averages, percentages etc.
Understanding, analysis and interpretation of a wide range of statistical evidence including secondary source data.
Analysing historical evidence numerically where appropriate by finding averages and percentages, e.g. analysis of the number of deaths in different regions during the Black Death, comparing a town or region's growth in population from one century to the next etc.
Chronology using a time line.

IT
Collecting and classifying data before entering it into data-handling software.
Selecting appropriate forms of data representation.
Interpretation of graphs and charts.
Discussing and criticising the features of graphs and charts generated by software packages that may be misleading.
Distance and angle in control.
Use of formulae in spreadsheets in modelling activities.
Use of transformations, 2D and 3D drawing in desk-top publishing.

Modern foreign languages
Planning holidays, transport timetables.
Dealing with numbers.
Currency conversions (euros and others still in use).
Shopping.
Data collection to make comparisons, e.g. girls' and boys' heights etc.
Surveys, e.g. hobbies, pets.
Telling the time.
TV programme times and calculations.
Measures.

Science
Making and recording measurements with appropriate precision.
Performing mental calculation of simple sums (including multiplying and dividing by powers of ten).
Using an appropriate range of units of measurement and considering the degree of accuracy.
Recalling the approximate magnitude of appropriate physical quantities in order to make sensible comparisons.
Representing data accurately using appropriate graphs and charts, identifying patterns and trends, interpreting effectively and predicting.

Counting, classifying, estimating, ordering numbers (including decimals and negative numbers).

Calculate means and percentages.

Standard form.

Use of algebra, including formulae and substitution and changing the subject of a formula.

In the second meeting, our discussion of the audits revealed that several departments required pupils to undertake surveys but felt that they did not usually get very far with the results. Consequently, we spent quite a lot of time discussing how a survey should be conducted and how the results should be analysed. The careers teacher, for example, had obtained detailed data about the work/ education destinations of our children after they left school. We used this to design a task in which the pupils were required to analyse the data and present their findings. (The careers department subsequently received an award for their use of key skills in careers teaching!)

Involving the whole school

Having started to explore the potential for numeracy across the curriculum via the cadre group of enthusiasts it was now time to involve the whole staff on a more formal basis. A whole school INSET day was organised for the start of the spring term. No external experts were booked; we wanted it to be a home-grown collaborative event at which we would find our own answers. I organised and planned the day using the feedback from the cadre group meetings.

We gathered the whole staff together in the school library. The seating plan forced departmental colleagues to split up and work across the curriculum areas. Senior staff, including the head, were distributed around the groups and participated on an equal footing throughout the day.

I started with a short update for the whole staff on the numeracy strategy, and some recommendations on interactive teaching, which had resulted from an action research project between the mathematics department and the university.

The whole day was interactive. I gave out cards with ticks on one side and crosses on the other to encourage participation from the start:

Who wants to be here today? Show me the tick or the cross.
Who knows what went on between Mr X and Ms Y after the Christmas party? I'll see you later to find out!

Each table had a tray full of materials including mini-whiteboards and pens, number fans, number lines etc. and we did what we would do with the pupils. I set some mental questions, they had to write their answers and show them. Then I got some staff out to the front to explain their methods on a flip chart. I had primed a couple beforehand and some of the first out to have a go were the head and the deputies.

Some staff were very keen on the idea from the start and immediately began to explore ways of using the technique in their own teaching. The Welsh department were keen to call out numbers in Welsh and have the children show them on a whiteboard. I suggested a refinement to this and they moved on to calling out mental calculations in Welsh. The natural extension was then to try to explain your method in Welsh if you could. This has become an integral part of Welsh and MFL lessons and represents a higher-order skill in language learning.

In the audit, several departments had said that they used measures and estimation in their teaching. I asked the shortest teacher in the school out to the front and asked the staff to estimate her height in centimetres. Most didn't have a clue. They could only estimate in feet and inches. I got her to hold a metre stick and then they began to give sensible answers. Then I got the tallest teacher out and had them estimate his height. This emphasised how pupils would also need something to compare with. To round this off, each tray had a bag of sweets. Each group had to estimate the weight in grams. Good estimators got to eat the sweets, but the others were taken back in!

Data-handling had also been identified as a common cross-curricular topic. We discussed the most common misconceptions which children have about scales and ways of dealing with them. The science department had a selection of scales drawn out on strips of card. The pupils could fit each scale against their axes to help them choose an appropriate scale. There was some debate about the use of such tools. Some staff felt that they actually avoided the issue and left children no better off. Others felt that they gave children insight into why certain scales worked better than others. We decided that they were useful only if they formed the basis of an interactive discussion about the reasons for choosing a specific scale over others. For example, why is a scale rising in steps of 3 or 7 difficult to use?

The morning concluded with an emphasis on the need to develop common approaches to numeracy. We discussed when it was appropriate to use mental methods, when to use calculators, and how to use calculators effectively. The focus was on encouraging flexibility and understanding rather than a demand for specific algorithms. It is all very well for the mathematics department to have policies on such matters, but they lose their impact if they are not followed through in other subjects when mathematics is applied. There was also a fair amount of mathematics revision for the staff alongside a range of new approaches. It was gratifying to overhear as staff went to lunch: 'If only I'd been taught like this I'd have understood what I was doing in maths and have done much better in school!'

Lots of activity on numeracy had arisen from the cadre meetings prior to the

INSET day and so the afternoon was spent sharing good practice across departments. Four people from different curriculum areas explained to the staff some of the approaches they had tried. For example, one of the music teachers talked about rhythms and pattern in number. The head of English had been keen to be involved because mathematics had supported the literacy year and he described how they drew graphs to track the state of Macbeth's temper during the play, using time on the horizontal axis and a measure of temper on the vertical axis.

By the end of the day the spirit was that we were all in it together and we all intended to develop numeracy as best we could in our own areas. At this point each department was sent away to come up with an action plan to achieve as much as was appropriate for their subject. The instruction was to not go over the top, but think of one or two year groups with whom departments might reasonably expect to develop numeracy-based activities.

The action plans were collected in at the end of the following week. I analysed the results and produced a summary to send around all departments. I also offered to attend their department meeting to discuss their action plan and the ways in which the mathematics department might support its implementation. During the next two terms I attended at least one meeting in every department.

We discussed mathematical language and I gave each department a mathematical vocabulary booklet (DfEE 1999b). Every numeracy task we devised included a list of key words to be emphasised when teaching. For each task we tried to focus on the main mathematical misconceptions and errors which would be likely to occur and strategies for dealing with them.

By the end of these meetings we had agreed a number of key activities for each department. Each activity was summarised using a form to identify the agreed methodology, key language to be used, resources needed and implications for the mathematics department (see Table 11.1 for an example).

These were presented and discussed at the middle management meetings which occurred each half term

The numeracy policy

It is worth pointing out that the school numeracy policy did not appear until 18 months after the start of the numeracy year. In many schools we know, policy documents are written by the coordinator alone and are only ever read by the head and the inspector. Members of staff rarely know of their contents or take any note of their recommendations. This form of policy document makes no impact on the education of children.

The only policy document worth having is one which is written after a period of consultation and negotiation. It is a statement of what is believed and

Table 11.1 An example of a numeracy activity for the RE department

Year 7 numeracy activity: The Christmas survey

	Agreed methodology	KEY language	Resources	Implications for the mathematics department
Data collection	Pupils to use TALLYING as a means of collecting and reducing their data and create FREQUENCY tables of their results.	• questionnaire • tally • frequency • bar chart • scale	Squared paper, graph paper, rulers.	Data handling to be taught during the first half of the Christmas term.
Data representation	BAR CHARTS where bars are of equal width. Pupils will need to be encouraged to use sensible SCALES for each axis, and to LABEL information clearly. PICTOGRAMS Pupils to choose a suitable symbol and KEY.	• axis, axes • horizontal • vertical • labels • pictograms • symbol • key		
Interpretation	Pupils to be encouraged to interpret their diagrams and to make comparisons.			

acted on by the staff. We believe that you should establish good practice first, and describe it later.

In the next section we describe how one department was able to implement the principles of the numeracy policy with the support and advice of the numeracy coordinator.

Policy into practice: the Zakat

You might expect the religious education classroom to be one of the last places in a secondary school to find pupils using and applying mathematics as an integral part of their work within the subject. The example that follows shows how the mathematics department and RE staff produced tasks that:

- pupils found interesting;
- teachers felt comfortable to teach;
- allowed pupils to use their mathematics in meaningful contexts;
- became the vehicle for establishing sound links between the RE teachers and the mathematics team.

Following the production of their action plan, I was invited to a scheduled RE departmental meeting during the spring term. The head of department met with me briefly before the meeting. He explained that they were currently undertaking a unit of work on Islam and were planning to study the Zakat as part of this work. (The Zakat is one of the pillars of Islam, where the faithful pay a percentage of their remaining income each year, normally 2.5 %.)

> Normally, we only mention that people pay different amounts depending on what they earn and have left at the end of the year. We give some worked examples usually, but this year we thought it would be a good idea to ask pupils themselves to work out the amount of Zakat paid by various members of the community.
>
> (Head of RE)

He expressed concern about the best approach to working out percentages with Year 9, especially as the groups were mixed ability. Could they all use mental strategies or would calculators be needed?

The enthusiasm of the three members of staff at the meeting took me by surprise. Not only were they keen to place a greater emphasis than usual on the numeracy aspect of the task, but they were anxious to approach it in a way that would help Year 9 pupils to consolidate and apply their knowledge of calculating percentages using mainly mental strategies. As mathematics teachers we were just as enthusiastic, not least because the SATs were fast approaching.

During the meeting, I used the Year 9 scheme of work for mathematics to provide examples of the work we taught on percentages and the strategies which would be familiar to the pupils. We discussed the range of abilities there would be in a mixed-ability class.

We talked through the types of question which the weaker or the most able pupils could be set and I used a number line to show how to develop pupils' strategies for working out any percentage. The RE staff thought this was a useful tool and tried it out with a range of examples.

We also considered the implications of working with decimals and the need to approximate answers to two decimal places in the context of money.

Throughout the meeting we discussed the importance of asking pupils to explain their strategies for working out the percentages. One or two teachers were a little apprehensive at the thought of dealing 'on their feet' with a range of possible methods, but were determined to try it out.

Finally we drafted a worksheet (see Figure 11.1) and agreed on a lesson plan that introduced the Zakat and involved pupils in working out some percentages. We had also discovered an interesting website on the Zakat. The department went away to explore this before arriving at their final plan for the lesson.

% ZAKAT %

ALL Muslims honour the third pillar of ISLAM by giving ZAKAT. The minimum they give is 2.5% of the money they have left at the end of the year. Often they give more than this.

DISCUSS what you think is the best way to work out 2.5% of £80 (without using a calculator). Write your final answer and explain your method here:

Use your method to work out how much ZAKAT each of the following people must pay:

✓ A Muslim doctor has £1000 left at the end of the year. He gives 2.5% ZAKAT

✓ A market trader has £450 left at the end of the year. He gives 2.5% ZAKAT

✓ A teacher has just £60 left at the end of the year. She gives 2.5% ZAKAT

✓ A wealthy shop owner has £8400 left at the end of the year. He gives 17.5% ZAKAT

✓ A Muslim office worker has £1250 left at the end of the year. She gives 8% ZAKAT.

✓ The market trader has the same amount of money left the year after and decides to give 17.5% ZAKAT

✓ The doctor has an additional £1200 left the year after, and decides to give £100 more ZAKAT than the previous year. What percentage did he give?

✓ A shop worker had £1800 left after paying 5% ZAKAT. How much did he have before he paid the ZAKAT?

Figure 11.1   The Zakat worksheet

A week or so later I met informally with the department to evaluate the lesson. The teachers felt that the inclusion of the calculations had added to the lesson and had not diverted from the main learning objectives. They were so positive that they had decided to add the task in its amended form to their scheme of work. The pupils had also enjoyed it, many of them reporting delightedly to their mathematics teachers that they had helped their RE teachers to work out percentages when finding the Zakat!

Conclusion

In summary we offer our success criteria which we determined as a cadre group following the first INSET day:

- the school has a long-term view of numeracy development;
- whole-school planning for the development of numeracy takes place;
- numeracy is a strand within every department's development plan;
- each department and teacher accepts responsibility for developing numeracy;
- departmental documentation and schemes of work make reference to numeracy content and the strategies to be used, including a policy on the use of calculators and other mathematical equipment and resources;
- all teachers are confident in the use of a range of teaching approaches for numeracy;
- pupils are confident and accurate in their use of mathematics across the curriculum and are able to make links between the mathematics they use in subject areas and the mathematics they are taught;
- subject teachers experience on-going, regular, quality INSET in numeracy which includes both theory and practice and is used to formulate whole-school approaches;
- classrooms exhibit displays related to numeracy;
- good practice is shared within departments and across the school.

All of these criteria are contingent on the effective management of the school by the head and the senior management team. Many of the successes listed above are due in no small part to the ethos of the school and the professional spirit and ambitions of the staff. These conditions did not arise by chance and in the final chapter we examine some of the whole-school issues which affect the development of a numerate school.

CHAPTER 12

Improving numeracy in your own school

Introduction

In the first two sections of the book we have tried to describe and illustrate what constitutes good practice in the teaching of numeracy. We drew evidence from a wide range of research studies and the guidance offered by the Numeracy Framework, but particularly from our experiences in the Raising Standards in Numeracy (RSN) project. In that project we identified schools in which pupils achieved standards significantly higher than would have been expected from their prior attainment according to an analysis of value added in mathematics. Our lesson observations and discussions with teachers and pupils in those schools led us to recommend a number of effective teaching practices. Some of these were described in Section 2.

In this chapter we intend to focus on the common features of good practice which we observed outside the classroom at the level of the whole school and the mathematics department. The key features were remarkably consistent from school to school, enabling us to make a number of key recommendations about how to improve numeracy in your own school.

Objectives

By the end of this chapter you should be aware of a number of features of successful schools at the level of the whole school and the department.

At whole-school level, factors which create conditions to support the development of numeracy include:

- the development of a positive school ethos;
- the use of assertive discipline to create a safe environment for learning;
- a management style which empowers heads of department.

At the level of the mathematics department, you should be aware of the contribution to the development of numeracy to be made by:

- the management styles of heads of department;
- effective teamwork and delegation of tasks within the department;
- the strategies used to encourage and sustain pedagogical change;
- planning and the development of an effective framework for teaching;
- strategies for monitoring and evaluating teaching and learning;
- the development of a self-evaluating team.

Common features of good practice identified at the level of the whole school

Ethos

> *Task 12.1:   The ethos of your school*
> *Ethos is difficult to define precisely. Before reading our comments about the positive features of ethos which we observed in the most successful schools, think about the messages which your school sends to children and staff. How do children react to each other, to teachers, to visitors?*
> *Try to identify some positive features of the ethos of your own school, which might contribute to success in numeracy teaching.*

In nearly all the schools visited, the ethos of the school was judged to be a significant factor in its success. Heads of department reported consistently that they were proud of their staff, their hard work, dedication and commitment to the school. In nearly all cases, the physical environment was well cared for; sometimes in very difficult circumstances.

Teachers talked about the messages sent to children by their environment. In most cases there were displays of pupils' work and achievements prominently placed around the buildings in public areas as well as in classrooms. Work in corridors was often protected behind perspex to prevent accidental damage in crowded conditions. The work displayed was generally recent, confirming teachers' claims that it was changed regularly. The mathematics department had often tried to make its presence felt in an area of the school. Signs saying 'Welcome to Mathematics' were common, as were displays of interesting mathematical applications or patterns. Wherever possible teachers were allocated their own room and took responsibility for the condition of their room and for the area in the immediate vicinity.

There was a clear focus in all the schools on academic achievement and standards. In some cases this was a fairly recent and deliberate change (to become more 'hard-nosed' about the purposes of school as one head put it). This had led to a change in the focus of the pastoral system and tutor time. The role of the form tutor now emphasised the proactive monitoring of homework and progress in academic subjects. Tutors were aware of targets which had been negotiated with particular pupils and monitored progress towards their attainment. In two mathematics departments we saw detailed curriculum planners on classroom walls showing how units of work would progress week by week through Key Stage 4 up to the examination.

There was evidence from both teachers and pupils that teachers liked their pupils and knew and cared about them as individuals. There was a sense that all pupils, not just the high achievers, were valued for themselves and that the school had a sense of community in which members were supposed to care for each other. Pupils' opinions were listened to and were taken seriously. This was sometimes evidenced in formal whole-school structures through which pupils could express their views. For example, two schools had school councils. More often, however, it was observed in pupils making extended verbal contributions to lessons and being listened to seriously by teachers and other pupils. When wrong answers were given there was no shame. 'If you don't get things wrong you never learn' was on a poster on one classroom wall.

> *Task 12.2:   How 'safe' is it to take a mathematical chance in your classroom?*
> *What is the ethos like in your classrooms? If a child asks a question, do other pupils behave supportively or with disdain?*
> *If a child makes a mistake on the board, do other pupils respond with derision and belittling comments?*
> *How do you respond if a pupil's comments are mocked?*
> *Is your discipline strong enough to protect them?*

In most, although not all, of the classes in the high value-added schools, there was a sense in which it was 'safe' for pupils to make verbal contributions in class without fear of humiliation. There was an expectation that the class and teacher would support tentative attempts to express ideas. For example, in one lesson we observed, the whole class waited in anticipation while a pupil struggled to explain how to complete a task on the board. On success, the class burst into spontaneous clapping. However, in one atypical secondary school where we considered the ethos to be a negative indicator, a teacher who had just encouraged a contribution from a pupil at the board said: 'I can't do as much oral work as I'd like with my top set classes; they poke fun at each other at break if they make a mistake, so the weaker ones won't try.'

Clearly such an ethos would have a negative impact on many of the strategies associated with the framework. However, in the majority of successful schools community spirit and discipline combined to create a safe, supportive environment for teaching and learning and pupils appeared eager to interact and make oral contributions to lessons.

The ideal mathematics classroom should be a community of learners in which conjecturing and taking mathematical chances are encouraged and supported. Ideally such an atmosphere should be a natural consequence of a teaching style which encourages imaginative oral contributions from all pupils and demonstrates respect and care for individuals. However, we are realistic and have taught in situations where such an ethos certainly did not exist at a whole-school level. In such circumstances, although individual teachers can create 'safe' classrooms, the playground culture may exert a negative impact on learning overall. If your school is in this situation, we feel that the starting point for change should be through the development and application of a whole school policy on discipline and learning.

Discipline

> *Task 12.3:   A common approach to discipline and learning?*
> *Does your school have a common approach to dealing with minor misbehaviour?*
> *How would you react if a pupil persisted in talking while you were talking?*
> *How would you react if a pupil mocked a comment made by another pupil?*
> *Would other teachers react in the same way?*

Most schools have clear procedures for dealing with major infringements; however, what we are interested in here is whether there is a consistent policy with respect to the day-to-day minor incidents which are routinely dealt with inside the classroom and which contribute significantly to the ethos of the school. Such school-wide policies only operate effectively if staff know and understand them, believe in their validity and are prepared to work within them

Most of the successful schools we visited had assertive discipline policies, which had been developed collaboratively by the staff rather than 'bought in' as a package. The school's discipline policy was often the result of significant consultation and collaboration within working parties. The development of a consensus over such matters is a long, slow process, and represents a major initiative for any school. In the majority of successful schools we observed, a major investment of time and creative effort into the development of a common policy had resulted in teachers expressing agreement with its principles and claiming to operate it consistently. Such policies included a clear structure of rewards and punishments and in most cases a system of positive and negative consequences was published in classrooms.

Discipline was not usually an issue for concern in the lessons we observed, with most schools presenting pupils with a clear expectation of social behaviour. For example, in only two cases did we meet pupils who were less than polite on meeting visitors in the car park, and it was not unusual to be asked 'Can I help you?' by a passing pupil. In most successful schools we were struck by the polite and helpful behaviour of the pupils. It should be noted that the schools were not all in the 'leafy suburbs', and the comments apply to some schools in areas of high social deprivation. Such polite and civilised behaviour was not a fortunate accident: rather it was the result of a deliberate policy on the part of the school, based on common high expectations and demands from all staff. Clearly for such a policy to operate effectively the whole staff had to operate as a team with a common purpose and the leadership role of the head and the senior management team was critical.

Management of staff

In nearly all the schools visited the professional skills of teachers were respected, responsibility was delegated and initiative encouraged. Management styles were generally corporate or collegial rather than autocratic and there was an emphasis on collaborative planning at all levels. In the majority of cases, interviews with teachers indicated that there was a sense of shared ownership of policies and a sense of common purpose.

In nearly all schools, effective use was made of middle managers, to whom significant responsibility had been delegated. Middle managers such as subject coordinators and heads of department were given 'freedom within fences'*. That is to say clear aims and guidelines were agreed, but within those guidelines middle managers operated with significant autonomy. For example one head of department said, 'I used to have to go running to the last head over every little thing, but this head is great; he trusts me.'

To develop numeracy is necessarily a complex and ill-defined task. The teaching required is not mechanical or formulaic, but requires creative decision making on the part of skilled professionals. The form of curriculum management which is most appropriate for such a task has been characterised by Holt (1996) as the Casablanca model after the famous movie. The head of Warner Brothers studios, Jack Warner, knew that making good movies demanded initiative and creativity. He monitored the progress of each film by watching the rushes but left the artistic control in the hands of his directors and actors.

The script was written from day to day as the filming progressed and no one

---

*Managing Director of the revitalized Harley Davidson Motorcycle company in interview on CNN International 12.3.99.

knew how the film would end until the airport sequence was filmed. It is worth noting that many of the best lines in Casablanca were unscripted, being made up by Bogart and Bergman as they interacted, e.g. 'Here's lookin' at you, kid.' We think the parallel with the management of effective teaching and learning is very close indeed, in spite of the overly precise planning suggested by the framework.

The best teaching involves interaction. Teachers bounce off pupils, making immediate decisions in response to the continuous feedback they are receiving (ad-libbing). Effective curriculum planning allows teachers to modify plans for tomorrow's lesson in the light of today's within an overall framework of general aims and principles (day-to-day script writing).

In most of the successful schools we visited the Casablanca model of curriculum planning operated: clear aims, clear frameworks, a hands-off attitude to those with devolved responsibilities, but close monitoring of ongoing teaching and learning, and detailed monitoring of trends in the final outcomes of learning. For example, one head (who had previously been a mathematics teacher herself) said: 'I can't be an expert in everything, even in a subject as important as mathematics, so I have to trust and support the experts I have appointed.'

However, heads who delegated in this way also monitored systematically and held staff accountable for their results. It was interesting to note that in the most successful schools the head was aware of, and able to discuss in some detail, the policies and practices in mathematics, but made a point of giving the head of department space to talk for themselves.

In most schools managerial structures existed to make teachers accountable for learning outcomes at all levels. Systematic testing and target setting was often used in intermediate years, not just the end of a key stage. In the most successful schools the head, senior managers and subject leaders were involved in systematic monitoring of pupils' work, the marking of books, and the setting of homework. In some cases this consisted of the head reading out a list of pupils' names in assembly to come to the office with their books. In other cases, the head of department was responsible for selecting pupils' books for checking. In some schools stickers or stamps were used which said: 'The head has seen this book.' This sent strong messages to pupils about the importance of homework. However, more importantly it allowed senior managers to monitor standards being achieved in a systematic manner.

Heads often claimed that they were trying to place emphasis on teaching and learning rather than administration. One head demanded that a pedagogical issue should appear as an item on the agenda of every departmental meeting and monitored the minutes of these meetings.

Successful schools were 'data-rich'. Head teachers and middle managers monitored learning outcomes early enough to allow intervention and recovery from poor performance, for example one school gave 'mock examinations' in Year 10 rather than Year 11 to allow pupils and teachers time to modify their work practices if the examination results were disappointing. In this school, the head of mathematics wrote to the parents of any pupils who had under-performed in the mock examination to enlist their help in modifying performance.

Statistical data was used carefully but openly to raise staff expectations of pupils' potential. Data was often presented in a digested form to focus attention on key features and be easily usable by staff. Effective head teachers used data from league tables about similar schools to challenge complacency and low expectations. They focused attention on significantly improved performances to stimulate competitiveness, professional pride and the sharing of good practice.

Data was used sensitively but directly to identify clearly any problem areas to those involved, for example one head used value-added data to demonstrate under-performance to a department so as to stimulate change. Although heads worked in a collegial manner, they had what one referred to as 'the edge' and 'placed children's welfare and achievement ahead of teachers' egos'.

In many cases, value-added analyses made examination-based assessments of teaching quality more acceptable to teachers, allowing heads to hold staff accountable for learning outcomes and to set challenging targets. In such cases, the role of the head of department was pivotal in the negotiation, between subject staff and senior managers, of targets which were both credible and challenging. The key to this negotiation was data, which could be used to focus attention on the individual pupils who would have to meet their own personal targets if departmental, and hence school, targets were to be achieved. In the best cases the target-setting process involved open communication and negotiation, supported by accurate data beginning from the level of the pupil, through the class and the department up to the whole school and back down to the individual pupil.

Common features of good practice identified at the level of the department

Subject leaders and teamwork: 'leading from the middle'

The most effective subject leaders had been empowered to do the job and were supported by their line managers. They operated within the guidelines negotiated with their heads, but within those 'fences' they had the freedom to exercise their own professional responsibility.

Effective team leaders had a sense of drive and purpose and were willing to challenge complacencies to encourage the development of higher expectations. For example, some had used statistical data effectively to compare their performance with similar schools or other departments to demonstrate under-performance and the need for change.

Standards of mathematics are highest when the teachers operate as a team. As one secondary head put it: 'My maths department aren't the very best teachers in the school as individuals, but they are by far the best team, and the whole is far greater than the sum of the parts.'

The most effective teams shared common aims and values, generally the result of effective team leadership rather than serendipity. Such teams trust each other sufficiently to be prepared to act as critical friends when discussing pedagogy. The most effective teams were reflective and self-monitoring and were described as such by their heads.

Team leaders often claimed to lead from the front: 'I wouldn't ask any of my team to do anything I couldn't do myself.' as one head of department said when explaining why she would be the first to be videotaped for staff development purposes. However, they were team builders working to develop common aims and values and stimulate change through persuasion rather than dictation, aiming for hearts-and-minds conversions rather than compliance. One head of department summed this up:

> Mathematicians are very independently minded; they are used to working problems out for themselves and they don't take kindly to being told. The *only* way to manage a mathematics team is through collegiality. I lead from the middle. Different team members take point [the lead] at different times.

'Taking point' – the art of delegation

One of the ways in which team leaders developed a team spirit and ensured participation and collaboration was via effective delegation. In most schools the head of department had delegated appropriate responsibility for aspects of the work to each of the members of the team. Even in the case of newly qualified teachers, an expectation existed that the teacher would take on a small but significant task, which required management and leadership. For example, a newly qualified teacher might be given responsibility for managing the department's entries into a national mathematics competition, while a more experienced member of the team might be responsible for developing curriculum materials in Year 8. Each team member required the cooperation of their colleagues in order to manage their own area successfully.

The Casablanca model was followed here too, in that tasks which had been delegated in this way were under the complete control of the teacher concerned. Good managers monitored progress, but avoided interference, for example offering support rather than taking over, if a task was not progressing as expected.

Encouraging change

Several team leaders had used the introduction of a new resource or participation in a curriculum development project as a vehicle to encourage monitoring, reflection and pedagogical change. One head of department, when referring to the resources provided by a well-known project, said: 'The materials aren't that good, but I wanted us all to sit down and talk about how we'd use them in the classroom.'

One of the more unfortunate changes which occurred at the end of the 1980s with the introduction of the National Curriculum was an increase in administration. In many departments the focus was on *what* we taught rather than *how* we should teach it. Often assessment and administration dominated departmental meetings at the expense of serious discussion about pedagogy. In the worst cases teaching became driven by the collection of evidence for purposes more associated with 'back covering' than education (Tanner 1992).

Task 12.4:   *Analysing an agenda for a departmental meeting*
Find the agenda and minutes for your most recent departmental meeting.
How much of the business was about teaching and learning?
How much could have been sent around on a memo?

Effective heads of department ensured that pedagogical questions were discussed on a regular basis: often as the major items on the agenda of departmental meetings. On such occasions, different team members were often encouraged to take the lead and describe and reflect on an aspect of their teaching. In one department a regular item on the agenda was for teachers to describe their best lesson from the last week. Team leaders often focused attention on effective performance, for example an improving class, or a teacher's new successful approach, or developments within another department or school.

Routine communication of information was often relegated to memos rather than discussed in meetings. One head of department said: 'My departmental meetings are far too valuable to waste on administration. We discuss how to overcome misconceptions when teaching decimals not when to fill in the record cards. I send routine stuff like that round by memo.'

Effective subject leaders ensured that a framework existed within which their team members were able to operate with professional freedom and responsibility.

Planning and the development of an effective framework for teaching

In the most successful mathematics departments the schemes of work structured the progression of teaching and learning experiences but were flexible enough to

KS 3

Year 7: Set 1   **TOPIC: AREA**

TIMING	RESOURCES
8 - 9 lessons	Squared paper Square grids Worksheet – True / False ST(P) 7A Keymaths 7(1)
USE OF CALCULATORS	MENTAL ARITHMETIC
Most of the work should be undertaken without the aid of a calculator. When using a calculator, pupils should be encouraged to estimate answers and check their solutions by applying inverse operations.	• Multipying – building from 1 x 1 digits to 3 x 2 digits. • Strategies for dividing • Multiplying and dividing whole numbers and decimals by powers of 10 Encourage pupils to develop their own strategies and share these with others.
KEYWORDS AND LANGUAGE	LINKS AND CONNECTIONS
Area, base, height Units, Millimetre, centimetre, metre, kilometre Parallelogram, rectangle, triangle Compound shape	Units Decimals 2-D shapes
ASSESSMENT	DISCUSSION
• Main assessment is unit test • Mental arithmetic test and KEYWORDS test • 'True or False' activity • 'Areas of letters' investigation	Do rectangles with the same area have the same perimeter?

KS3   YEAR 7 SET 1   TOPIC: AREA

NC POS

Find areas by counting and dissection methods progressing to derivation of formulae and use of formulae.

LEAD IN

Some initial work on finding and estimating areas by counting squares may be useful, leading to finding the areas of rectangles

LEARNING OBJECTIVES

- to distinguish between units of length and units of area
- to find areas of triangles and compound shapes made from rectangles and triangles
- to investigate finding the area of a parallelogram and establishing a formula
- to apply the above to problems

METHODOLOGY

A suitable approach would be to encourage pupils to find ways of calculating areas of triangles initially by completing rectangles and establishing a formula, eg:

Also, parallelograms by cutting and moving a triangle from a rectangle and hence establishing a formula:

- Some questions should contain lengths as decimals and pupils should be encouraged to measure lengths accurately in order to find areas;
- Pupils need to encounter shapes drawn in a variety of orientations and not always sitting on its base;
- Some examples should contain mixed units and pupils should be encouraged to develop ways of converting units appropriately;
- Examples should include 'inverse problems' eg: finding the height given the area and base;
- Pupils also need to be encouraged to become engaged in problem solving activities — see the 'True / False activity;
- Throughout this work pupils should be encouraged to develop their own strategies for multiplication and division.

Figure 12.1   An example of a topic from the scheme of work

allow professional judgements to be made and to accommodate individual teaching styles. The schemes of work were extremely detailed and typically offered guidance on learning objectives, possible teaching approaches, recommended resources, key mathematical vocabulary, opportunities for mental arithmetic, calculator use, discussion, possible Ma1 activities, connections to other areas and assessment. As a matter of policy, investigative approaches and problem-solving activities were integrated into the curriculum and used at appropriate points in lessons.

In spite of the detailed planning which underpinned the best schemes of work, they often looked very much like unfinished documents. In the best schools these documents had been developed collaboratively, often with different members of the department taking the lead for specific year-groups. More than this, however, schemes of work remained under continual review and discussion at departmental meetings. In some cases, parts of the scheme of work were obviously work-in-progress and were handwritten with space for staff to add material and ideas following discussion in meetings (see Figure 12.1). Schemes of work provided a framework within which creative teaching could occur and, in the spirit of our Casablanca allegory, the script could be rewritten in response to feedback as the curriculum progressed.

Monitoring

Effective subject leaders also followed the Casablanca model of management encouraging professional judgement and discretion but monitoring progress closely so that they could act quickly when necessary. Pupils' learning and teachers' assessment was monitored through the regular and systematic sampling of books (equivalent to watching the rushes). Planning was sometimes monitored through the collection of teachers' planners and record books, but more often than not, the scheme of work included sufficient detail to make highly elaborate recording superfluous. The monitoring of the work in pupils' books was often considered sufficient when combined with the content of teachers' mark books. One head of department expressed the key principle:

> We never record a piece of information twice. If a child has a target written in their book or diary it doesn't need to be written elsewhere. The scheme of work is detailed and there is no point in each teacher writing it out again. We keep notes in our mark-books, alongside the scheme of work and in the pupils' books; that's enough.

Monitoring of books was organised systematically to ensure fair and thorough coverage throughout the year. What was to be monitored was not left to chance, but was structured to gain maximum value from the process. In one school a

FACULTY MONITORING: KS4 Year 11   19/2/02

MONITORED BY: AD

General comments / actions

Marking consistent across Intermediate classes – all aspects covered although not to same degree.

Marking of Foundation classes satisfactory

Name & Form / Set	Scheme of work – coverage	Scheme of work- methodology	Pupils aware of how to do well	Marking up to date	Strengths/weaknesses highlighted	Targets set for improvement	Completion of classwork	Completion of homework	Evidence of pupils acting on advice	Spelling of key words	Comments / Actions
Ann	✓	✓	✓	✓	✓	X	✓	✓	✓	-	
Jo	✓	✓	✓	✓	✓	✓	✓	X	X	-	Lack of effort – to be monitored
Kelly	✓	✓	✓	✓	✓	✓	✓	✓	✓	-	
Mark	✓	✓	✓	✓	✓	X	✓	✓	✓	-	
Chris	✓	✓	✓	✓	✓	✓	✓	✓	✓	-	Monitored – parental request
Paul	✓	✓	✓	✓	✓	X	✓	X	X	-	Monitored – 'U' for attainment
Sue	✓	✓	✓	✓	✓	✓	✓	✓	✓	-	
John	✓	✓	✓	✓	✓	✓	✓	✓	✓	-	

Figure 12.2   An example of a faculty monitoring form

monitoring form (Figure 12.2) was constructed to cover a number of key features of departmental policy.

Teaching and learning was further monitored through regular and systematic lesson observation.

Observing each other teach

Have you been observed teaching by a colleague since you qualified as a teacher? If so, how you felt about the experience probably depended on its purpose. If the observation was by an inspector making judgements about the quality of your teaching, or a senior manager judging whether you were eligible for a threshold payment, you probably found it to be a stressful experience. The 'high stakes' nature of such examinations of your performance can make it very difficult to gain professional benefit from the event.

In the most successful schools, the aim of lesson observations by colleagues was to improve the teaching of both the observer and the observed. Such observations were intended to be non-threatening. However, in order to be professionally useful, the process had to evaluate and discuss the quality of learning and the effectiveness of teaching approaches. The development of a system of colleague-observation raises sensitive issues. Clear guidelines were established in advance

about the purposes of lesson observation, the role of the observer and the ownership of and access to any notes or evaluative comments. Procedures were established
to limit access to written evaluations, which remained the property of the observed
teacher.

Where there was a strong emphasis on the evaluation of performance prior to
an inspection, lesson evaluation forms were used which were based on those used
by Ofsted. In this context, the observation became quite judgemental, casting
the observer in the role of expert and thus limiting mutual learning. Allowing
inspection to drive the process changes its character and restricts its professional
benefits.

Our preferred model for colleague-observation is that of peer-evaluation
within action research. Under this model, peer-observation and evaluation can
be used to foster collegiality and reflection. The underlying assumption is that
both observer and observed wish to increase their understanding of the teaching and learning process and are working together in order to answer a specific
question. It is a particularly powerful tool when introducing a curriculum development such as the numeracy strategy, as both parties can claim with some
justification that they are learning about the best ways to use the techniques
involved.

Both teachers should agree about the question they wish to answer in advance,
for example, 'How should I teach mental mathematics?' They then discuss which
of the ideas from the framework they wish to try and how they intend to apply
them. During the lesson, the observer makes evaluative notes as a critical friend
and joins in, supporting the teaching, where possible. The intention is not to
make a judgement about the teacher, but to learn about teaching and improve
the performance of both parties. After the lesson they should reflect together
about their common experience and both should make suggestions about what
worked and how the lesson could be improved. If one of the teachers is more
experienced than the other, then that teacher may choose to act as a classroom
coach but, even here, the process works best when the two teachers regard each
other as co-learners. Several subject leaders in the successful schools regularly
encouraged their team to observe them, and frequently offered to act as in-class
support to encourage curriculum development.

Some schools had formalised their action research into a small project on which
they were collaborating. In one case this was initiated by a teacher studying for a
masters degree who was using the project as the basis of her dissertation. Another
school had gained funding from the General Teaching Council and had approached
a local university with a view to conducting action research in collaboration with
them. Creating collaborative projects or joining in research studies with university departments of education is an effective mechanism for initiating and
sustaining curriculum development.

> *Task 12.5:   Planning some small scale action research to improve*
> *numeracy*
> *Formulate a question you wish to answer, e.g. 'How can we introduce more formative*
> *assessment into our teaching?'*
> *Read what has been written recently about your question.*
> *Discuss with your department which ideas they might like to introduce.*
> *Is there a local university researcher who might collaborate with you?*
> *Plan a series of experimental lessons and mutual observations over the next half*
> *term, planning to report back at future departmental meetings.*
> *Discuss experiences at departmental meetings and modify approaches in the light of*
> *evaluations.*

Conclusion

The strategies and approaches which we have identified here as particularly successful in value-added terms and have recommended as good practice are in line with other research findings (e.g. Ayers *et al.* 1999; Cobb *et al.* 1997; Tanner *et al.* 1999). In particular, they further validate some of the approaches suggested by the KS3 Framework (DfEE 2001a). However, even teachers in the successful schools had generally received very little training on how to cope with their responsibilities as middle managers. Often, although heads of departments have proved themselves to be good teachers and mathematicians, the management strategies they adopt are sometimes left to chance. The key elements of the successful approaches identified here are, unfortunately, not common to all schools. Communicating those approaches to teachers in other schools is going to be a difficult task. However, the progress demonstrated by the successful schools dictates that we must do it and we hope that the discussion in this final chapter will contribute to the dissemination of good practice.

We have been very privileged over the years to work in collaborative action research projects with very many skilled and creative teachers. We would not have been able to write this book without the support of practising teachers who generously donated their time and ideas while working to develop new understanding about teaching and learning.

We believe that research which is grounded in the classroom and under the control of practising teachers is the most significant factor in improving the education of our children. We hope that you will realise the power of such action research to improve numeracy in your school and will wish to join the ever increasing numbers of teachers who feel empowered to join in researching and developing new approaches to teaching and learning mathematics.

Bibliography

ACCAC (2000) *Mathematics in the National Curriculum in Wales*, Cardiff: ACCAC.

Adhami, M. (1999) 'Two cheers for the Numeracy Strategy', *Equals* (7)1, 8–10.

Adhami, M., Johnson, D. and Shayer, M. (1998) *Thinking Maths: The Programme for Accelerated Learning in Mathematics*, London: Heinemann.

Askew, M., Rhodes, V., Brown, M., Wiliam, D. and Johnson, D. (1997) *Effective Teachers of Numeracy: Final Report*, London: King's College.

Askew, M. (1999) 'Teaching numeracy: will we ever learn?' *Mathematics Teaching* 168, 3–5.

Bauersfeld, H. (1988) 'Interaction, construction and knowledge: alternative perspectives for mathematics education', in D. Grouws, T. Cooney and D. Jones (eds), *Perspectives on Research on Effective Mathematics Teaching*, pp. 27–46, Reston, VA: National Council of Teachers of Mathematics.

Beaton, A., Mullis, I., Martin, M., Gonzales, E., Kelly, D. and Smith, T. (1996) *Mathematics Achievement in the Middle School Years: IEA's Third International Mathematics and Science Study*, Chestnut Hill, MA: Boston College.

Bell, A. (1993a) 'Principles for the design of teaching', *Educational Studies in Mathematics* 24(1), 5–34.

Bell, A. (1993b) 'Some experiments in diagnostic teaching', *Educational Studies in Mathematics* 24(1), 115–37.

Berry, J. and Graham, T. (1991) 'Using concept questions in teaching mathematics', *International Journal of Mathematics Education, Science & Technology* 22(5), 749–57.

Bierhoff, H. (1996) *Laying the Foundations of Numeracy*, London: Institute of Social and Economic Research.

Black, P. J. and Wiliam, D. (1998) 'Assessment and classroom learning', *Assessment in Education: Principles, Policy and Practice* 5(1), 7–73.

Bliss, J., Askew, M. and Macrae, S. (1996) 'Effective teaching and learning: scaffolding revisited', *Oxford Review of Education* 22(1), 37–61.

Brophy, J. (1981) 'Teacher praise: a functional analysis', *Review of Educational Research* 51(1), 5–32.

Brown, A. (1987) 'Metacognition, executive control, self-regulation and other more mysterious mechanisms', in F. H. Weinhart and R. H. Kluwe (eds), *Metacognition, Motivation and Understanding*, pp. 65–116, Hillsdale, NJ: Lawrence Erlbaum.

Brown, M. (1996) 'FIMS and SIMS: the first two IEA International Mathematics Surveys', *Assessment in Education* 3(2), 181–200.

Brown, M. (1999a) 'Comparing standards internationally', in B. Jaworski and D. Phillips (eds), *Problems of Interpreting International Comparative Data*, Oxford: Symposium Books, pp. 183–205.

Brown, M. (1999b) 'Is more whole-class teaching the answer?', *Mathematics Teaching* 169, 5–7.

Brown, M., Askew, M., Baker, Dave, Denvir, H. and Millett, A. (1998) 'Is the National Numeracy Strategy research-based?', *British Journal of Educational Studies* 46(4), 362–85.

Brown, M., Millett, A., Bibby, T. and Johnson, D. C. (2000) 'Turning our attention from the what to the how: the National Numeracy Strategy', *British Educational Research Journal* 26(4), 457–71.

Butler R. (1987) 'Task-involving and ego-involving properties of evaluation: effects of different feedback conditions on motivational perceptions, interest and performance', *British Journal of Educational Psychology* 79(4), 474–82.

Butler, R. (1988) 'Enhancing and undermining intrinsic motivation: the effects of task-involving and ego-involving evaluation on interest and performance', *British Journal of Educational Psychology* 58, 1–14.

Cardelle-Elawar, M. (1992) 'Effects of teaching metacognitive skill to students with low mathematics ability', *Teaching and Teacher Education* 8(2), 109–21.

Cardelle-Elawar, M. (1995) 'Effects of metacognitive instruction on low achievers in mathematics problems', *Teaching and Teacher Education* 11(1), 81–95.

Centre for Innovation in Mathematics Teaching (CIMT) (1997) *Mathematics Enhancement Project (MEP)*, Exeter: University of Exeter.

Cobb, P. and Bauersfeld, H. (eds) (1995) *The Emergence of Mathematical Meaning: Interacting in Classroom Culture*, Hillsdale, NJ: Lawrence Erlbaum.

Cobb, P., Boufi, A., McClain, K. and Whitenack, J. (1997) 'Reflective discourse and collective reflection', *Journal for Research in Mathematics Education* 28(3), 258–77.

Cockcroft, W. H. (1982) *Mathematics Counts*, London: HMSO.

Crowther, G. (1959) *15 to 18: A Report of the Central Advisory Council for Education*, London: HMSO.

DES (1985) *Mathematics from 5–16: Curriculum Matters*, London: HMSO.

DfEE (1998) *Teaching: High Status, High Standards*, London: Department for Education and Employment.

DfEE (1999a) *The National Numeracy Strategy: Framework for Teaching Mathematics*, Cambridge: Cambridge University Press.

DfEE (1999b) *The National Numeracy Strategy: Mathematical Vocabulary*, Watford: BEAM.

DfEE (2000) *The National Numeracy Strategy: Framework for Teaching Mathematics Year 7*, Cambridge: Cambridge University Press.

DfEE (2001a) *Key Stage 3 National Strategy: Framework for Teaching Mathematics: Years 7, 8 and 9*, London: Department for Education and Employment.

DfEE (2001b) *Key Stage 3 National Strategy: Management Guide: Lessons from the Pilot*, London: Department for Education and Employment.

DfEE/QCA (1999) *The National Curriculum for England: Mathematics*, London: HMSO.

Flavell, J. H. (1976) 'Metacognitive aspects of problem solving', in L. B. Resnick (ed.), *The Nature of Intelligence*, pp.231–5, Hillsdale, NJ: Lawrence Erlbaum.

Foxman, D. (1985) *Mathematical Development: Review of the First Phase of Monitoring: Report on the Series of Annual Surveys of the Mathematical Performance of 11 and 15 year olds Held from 1978–1982 Inclusive*, London: HMSO.

Gardiner, T. (1995) 'Mathematics hamstrung by long divisions', *The Sunday Times*, 22 January 1995.

Gipps, C. (1990) *Assessment: A Teacher's Guide to the Issues*, London: Hodder & Stoughton.

Gipps, C. (1994) *Beyond Testing: Towards a Theory of Educational Assessment*, London: Falmer Press.

Girling, M. (1977) 'Towards a definition of basic numeracy', *Mathematics Teaching* 81(5), 4–5.

Glaser, R. (1995) 'Expert knowledge and the process of thinking', in P. Murphy, M. Selinger, J. Bourne and M. Bridges (eds), *Subject Learning in the Primary Curriculum*, pp. 274–88, London: Routledge/Oxford University Press.

Good, T. L. and Grouws, D.A. (1975) 'Process–product relationships in 4th grade mathematics classrooms', Report for National Institute of Education, Columbia, MO: University of Missouri (Report number: NE-G-00-0-0123).

Graham, T., Rowlands, S., Jennings, S. and English, J. (1999) 'Towards whole class interactive teaching', *Teaching Mathematics and its Applications* 18(2), 50–60.

Gray, S. (1991) 'Ideas in practice: metacognition and mathematical problem solving', *Journal of Developmental Education* 14(3), 24–8.

Greer, B. and Mulhern, G. (1989) *New Directions in Mathematics*, London: Routledge.

Groves, S. (1994) 'Calculators: a learning environment to promote number sense', *Proceedings of the American Research Association*, New Orleans, USA.

Harris, S., Keys, W. and Fernandes, C. (1998) *Third International Mathematics and Science Study: Third National Report: Performance Assessment*, London: NFER.

Hart, K. (1981) *Children's Understanding of Mathematics: 11–16*, London: John Murray.

Hart, K. (1988) 'Fractions', in K. M. Hart (ed.), *Mathematics 11–16: Some Research Findings*, pp. 19–21. Leicester: The Mathematical Association.

Hembree, R. and Dessart, D. (1992) 'Research on calculators in mathematics education', in J. Fey and C. Hirsch (eds), *Calculators in Mathematics Education*, pp. 23–32, Reston, VA: National Council for Teachers of Mathematics.

Hoyles, C., Morgan, C. and Woodhouse, G. (1999) *Rethinking the Mathematics Curriculum*, London: Falmer Press.

Jaworski, B. and Phillips, D. (eds) (1999) *Comparing Standards Internationally*, Oxford: Symposium Books.

Jones, S. (1992) 'The Assessment of Mathematical Modelling', unpublished M.Ed. dissertation, University of Wales, Swansea.

Jones, S. and Tanner, H. (1997) 'Do calculators count?' *Micromath* 13(3), 31–5.

Kennewell, S., Parkinson, J. and Tanner, H. (2000) *Developing the ICT Capable School*, London: Routledge/Falmer.

Keys, W., Harris, S. and Fernandes, C. (1996) *Third International Mathematics and Science Study: First National Report: Part 1: Achievement in Mathematics and Science at Age 13 in England*, London: NFER.

Keys, W., Harris, S. and Fernandes, C. (1997) *Third International Mathematics and Science Study: First National Report: Part 2: Patterns of Mathematics and Science Teaching in Lower Secondary Schools in England and Ten Other Countries*, London: NFER.

Küchemann, D. (1981) 'Algebra', in K. M. Hart (ed.), *Children's Understanding of Mathematics: 11–16*, pp. 102–19, London: John Murray.

Lave, J. (1988) *Cognition in Practice*, Cambridge: Cambridge University Press.

Lew, H. (1999) 'New goals and directions for mathematics education in Korea', in C. Hoyles, C. Morgan and G. Woodhouse, *Rethinking the Mathematics Curriculum*, London: Falmer Press.

Love, E. and Mason, J. (1992) *Teaching Mathematics: Action and Awareness*, Milton Keynes: Open University Press.

Love, E. and Mason, J. (1995) 'Telling and asking' in P. Murphy, M. Selinger, J. Bourne and M. Briggs (eds), *Subject Learning in the Primary Curriculum*, pp. 252–67, London: Routledge/Oxford University Press.

Mathematical Association (1992) *Mental Methods in Mathematics: A First Resort*, Leicester: Mathematical Association.

Mullis, I., Martin, M., Gonzalez, E., O'Connor, K., Chrostowski, S., Gregory, K., Garden, R. and Smith, T. (2001) *Mathematics Benchmarking Report: TIMSS 1999 – Eighth Grade*, Boston, MA, IEA, Boston College.

NCC (1989) *Mathematics in the National Curriculum: Non-Statutory Guidance for Teachers*, York: HMSO.

Nunes, T., Schliemann, A. D. and Carraher, D.W. (eds) (1993) *Street Mathematics and School Mathematics*, New York: Cambridge University Press.

OECD (2000) *Measuring Student Knowledge and Skills: The PISA 2000 Assessment of Reading, Mathematical and Scientific Literacy*, OECD, Paris.

Perks, P. and Prestage, S. (2001) *Teaching the National Numeracy Strategy at Key Stage 3: A Practical Guide*, London: David Fulton.

Polya, G. (1948) *How to Solve it* (5th edn), Princeton, NJ: Princeton University Press.

Prawat, R. (1989a) 'Promoting access to knowledge, strategy and disposition in students: a research synthesis', *Review of Educational Research* 59(1), 1–41.

Prawat, R. (1989b) 'Teaching for understanding: three key attributes', *Teaching and Teacher Education* 5(4), 315–28.

QCA (2000) *Bridging Units in Mathematics: Algebra – Introducing Symbols*, Sudbury: Qualifications and Assessment Authority.

QCA (2001a) Assessment for learning, http://www.qca.org.uk/ca/5-14/afl/ (Accessed: 1.12.01).

QCA (2001b) Using assessment to raise achievement in mathematics, http://www.qca.org.uk/ca/5-14/afl/afl_maths.pdf (Accessed: 1.12.01).

Reynolds, D. and Farrell, S. (1996) *Worlds Apart? A Review of International Surveys of Educational Achievement Involving England*, London: HMSO.

Reynolds, D. (1998a) *Numeracy Matters: The Preliminary Report of the Numeracy Task Force*, London: Department for Education and Employment.

Reynolds, D. (1998b) *The Implementation of the National Numeracy Strategy: The Final Report of the Numeracy Task Force*, Sudbury: Department for Education and Employment.

Ruddock, G. (2000) *Third International Mathematics and Science Study Repeat (TIMSS-R): First National Report*. Nottingham: DfEE.

Ryan, J. and Williams, J. (2000) *Mathematical Discussions with Children: Exploring methods and misconceptions as a teaching strategy*, University of Manchester.

Schliemann, A. (1994) 'School children versus street sellers' use of the commutative law for solving multiplication problems', *Proceedings of the Eighteenth International Conference for the Psychology of Mathematics Education, Lisbon, Portugal*, 4, 209–16.

Schmidt, W. H., Jorde, D., Cogan, Leland S., Barrier, E., Gonzalo, I., Moser, U., Shimizu, K., Sawada, T., Valverde, G. A., McKnight, C., Prawat, R. S., Wiley, D. E., Raizen, A., Britton, E. D. and Wolfe, R. G. (1996) *Characterizing Pedagogical Flow: An Investigation of Mathematics and Science Teaching in Six Countries*, Dordrecht: Kluwer Academic Publishers.

Schoenfeld, A. H. (1985) *Mathematical Problem Solving*, New York: Academic Press.

Schoenfeld, A. H. (ed.) (1987) *Cognitive Science and Mathematical Education*, Hillsdale, NJ: Lawrence Erlbaum.

Schön, D. (1987) *Educating the Reflective Practitioner*, Oxford: Jossey-Bass.

Shuard, H., Walsh, A., Goodwin, J. and Worcester, V. (1991) *Calculators, Children and Mathematics*, London: Simon & Schuster, 1991.

Skemp, R. R. (1976) 'Relational understanding and instrumental understanding',

Mathematics Teaching 77, 20–6.

Stigler, P. G., Gonzales, P., Takako, K., Knoll, S. and Serrano, A. (1999) *The TIMSS Videotape Classroom Study: Methods and Findings from an Exploratory Research Project on Eighth Grade Mathematics Instruction in Germany, Japan and the United States*, NCES99-074, Washington, DC: US Government Printing Office.

Straker, A. (1997) *National Numeracy Project*, Reading: National Centre for Literacy and Numeracy.

Tanner, H. (1992) 'Teacher assessment of mathematics in the National Curriculum at Key Stage 3', *Welsh Journal of Education* 3(2) 27–34.

Tanner, H. (1997) 'Using and applying mathematics: developing mathematical thinking through practical problem solving and modelling', unpublished Ph.D. thesis, University of Wales, Swansea.

Tanner, H. and Jones, S. (1993) 'Developing metacognition through peer and self assessment', in T. Breiteig, I. Huntley and G. Keiser-Messmer (eds), *Teaching and Learning Mathematics in Context*, London: Ellis Horwood, pp. 228–41.

Tanner, H. and Jones, S. (1994) 'Using peer and self-assessment to develop modelling skills with students aged 11 to 16: a socio-constructive view', *Educational Studies in Mathematics* 27(4), 413–31.

Tanner, H. and Jones, S. (1995a) *Better Thinking, Better Mathematics*, University of Wales, Swansea.

Tanner, H. and Jones, S. (1995b) 'Teaching mathematical thinking skills to accelerate cognitive development', in *Proceedings of the 19th Conference of the International Group for the Psychology of Mathematics Education* (PME19), Recife, Brazil (3), 121–8.

Tanner, H. and Jones, S. (1997) 'Teaching children to think mathematically', in E. Pehkonen (ed.), *Solving Open-ended Problems*, pp. 106–20, Helsinki: University of Helsinki.

Tanner, H. and Jones, S. (1999a) 'Dynamic scaffolding and reflective discourse: the impact of teaching style on the development of mathematical thinking', in *Proceedings of the 23rd Conference of the International Group for the Psychology of Mathematics Education* (PME23), Haifa (4), 257–64.

Tanner, H. and Jones, S. (1999b) 'Scaffolding metacognition: reflective discourse and the development of mathematical thinking', in *Proceedings of the British Educational Research Association* (BERA-99), Brighton, online: http://www.leeds.ac.uk/educol/bera99.htm (Accessed: 1 April 2000).

Tanner, H. and Jones, S. (2000a) 'Scaffolding for success: reflective discourse and the effective teaching of mathematical thinking skills', in T. Rowland and C. Morgan (eds), *Research in Mathematics Education Volume 2: Papers of the British Society for Research into Learning Mathematics*, pp. 19–32, London: British Society for Research into Learning Mathematics.

Tanner, H. and Jones, S. (2000b) *Becoming a Successful Teacher of Mathematics*, London: Routledge/Falmer.

Tanner, H., Jones, S. and Treadaway, M. (1999) 'Schools that add value: raising standards in mathematics', in *Proceedings of the British Educational Research Association* (BERA-99), Brighton, online: http://www.leeds.ac.uk/educol/bera99.htm (Accessed: 1 April 2000).

Vygotsky, L. S. (1962) *Thought and Language*, Cambridge, MA MIT Press.

Vygotsky, L. S. (1978) translated by M.Cole, V. John-Steiner, S. Scribner and E. Souberman, *Mind and Society: The Development of Higher Psychological Processes*, Cambridge, MA: Harvard University Press.

Wheatley, G. N. (1991) 'Constructivist perspectives on science and mathematics learning', *Science Education* 75(1), 9–21.

Wiliam, D. (1999a) 'Formative assessment in mathematics, part 1: close questioning', *Equals: Mathematics and Special Educational Needs* 5(2), 15–8.

Wiliam, D. (1999b) 'Formative assessment in mathematics, part 2: feedback', *Equals: Mathematics and Special Educational Needs* 5(3), 8–15.

Wiliam, D. (2000a) 'Formative assessment in mathematics, part 3: the learner's role', *Equals: Mathematics and Special Educational Needs* 6(1), 19–22.

Wiliam, D. (2000b) *Integrating Formative and Summative Functions of Assessment*, paper presented to Working Group 10 of the International Congress on Mathematics Education, Makuhari, Tokyo, August 2000 (Accessed 1.3.02 at http://www.kcl.ac.uk.//depsta/education/hpages/ICME9%3DWGA10.pdf).

Wiliam, D., Askew, M., Rhodes, V., Brown, M. and Johnson, D. (1997) *Approaches to Teaching Numeracy in Primary Schools: Discover, Transmit or Connect?* London: King's College.

Williams, J. and Ryan, J. (2000) 'National testing and the improvement of classroom teaching: can they coexist?', *British Educational Research Journal* 26(1), 49–73.

Wood, T. (1994) 'Patterns of interaction and the culture of mathematics classrooms', in S. Lerman (ed.), *Cultural Perspectives on the Mathematics Classroom*, pp. 148–68, Dordrecht: Kluwer Academic.

Young, R. (1992) *Critical Theory and Classroom Talk*. The Language and Education Library 2: Multilingual Matters Ltd, Adelaide.

Index